# Report Regarding the Actions of the Pennsylvania State University Related to the Child Sex Abuse Committed by Gerald Sandusky

## The Penn State Report

### July 12, 2012

### Freeh Sporkin & Sullivan, LLP

Published by OccupyBawlStreet.com Press

ISBN-13: 978-0615709697

ISBN-10: 0615709699

Subject Headings:

1. Sandusky, Jerry
2. Paterno, Joe
3. Child sexual abuse -- Pennsylvania -- State College
4. Liability for child sexual abuse -- Pennsylvania
5. Pennsylvania State University -- Administration
6. Pennsylvania State University. Athletic Dept.
7. Pennsylvania State University. Board of Trustees

## Copyright Notice

**Cover, Title & Copyright Page© 2012 OccupyBawlStreet.com Press**

**The document following this notice is a work of the Commonwealth of Pennsylvania, an "open record" in the public domain under the Pennsylvania Right-to-Know Law, and is not subject to copyright protection in the United States. Foreign copyrights may apply.**

# Report of the Special Investigative Counsel Regarding the Actions of The Pennsylvania State University Related to the Child Sexual Abuse Committed by Gerald A. Sandusky

Freeh Sporkin & Sullivan, LLP
July 12, 2012

# TABLE OF CONTENTS

Scope of Review and Methodology..................................................................8

Independence of the Investigation................................................................11

Executive Summary..........................................................................................13

- Findings
- Recommendations for University Governance, Administration, and the Protection of Children in University Facilities and Programs

Timeline of Significant Events.......................................................................19

Chapter 1: The Pennsylvania State University – Governance and Administration....................................................................................................31

    I.    Key Leadership Positions
        A.    President
        B.    Executive Vice President and Provost ("EVP-Provost")
        C.    Senior Vice President - Finance and Business ("SVP-FB")
        D.    General Counsel
    II.    Principal Administrative Areas
        A.    University Police and Public Safety ("University Police Department")
        B.    Office of Human Resources ("OHR")
        C.    Department of Intercollegiate Athletics ("Athletic Department")
        D.    Outreach
    III.    Administrative Controls
        A.    Policies and Procedures
        B.    Oversight and Internal Controls

**Chapter 2: Response of University Officials to the Allegation of Child Sexual Abuse Against Sandusky – 1998** ..................................................39

    I.    Sandusky's Association with Penn State
        A.    Sandusky's Criminal Activity 1995-1998
    II.    Events of May 3, 1998 at the Lasch Building
    III.    Investigation of Sandusky - 1998
        A.    May 4 – 6, 1998: Police Report, Initial Investigation and Psychological Evaluation of the Victim
        B.    May 7 – 9, 1998: A Second Evaluation of the Victim
        C.    May 12 - 19, 1998: Police Overhear Sandusky Admit to Showering with the Victim
        D.    Late May 1998: District Attorney's Decision to Not Prosecute Sandusky
        E.    June 1, 1998: University Police Speak with Sandusky
    IV.    Involvement of University Officials in the Sandusky Investigation
        A.    May 4 – 30, 1998: Notifications and Updates to Spanier, Schultz, Paterno and Curley
        B.    June 1 – 10, 1998: Report to University Officials on Sandusky Interview and Case Closure
        C.    2011 Grand Jury Testimony of Spanier, Schultz, Paterno and Curley
        D.    University Officials Do Not Notify the Board of the Sandusky Investigation
        E.    Sandusky's Criminal Activity 1998 – 2001

**Chapter 3: Sandusky's Retirement from the University – 1999** ..................................................55

    I.    Sandusky's Decision to Retire
    II.    Negotiating the Agreement
    III.    Sandusky's Retirement Agreement

**Chapter 4: Response of University Officials to the Allegation of Child Sexual Abuse Against Sandusky – 2001** ..................................................62

- I. Janitors' Observations of Sandusky – 2000
- II. McQueary's Observations of Sandusky – 2001
- III. University Leaders' Response to McQueary's Observations
    - A. February 11, 2001: Paterno Reports Sandusky Incident to Schultz and Curley
    - B. February 11, 2001: Schultz Discusses "Reporting of Suspected Child Abuse" with University's Outside Legal Counsel
    - C. February 12, 2001: Initial Response of Spanier, Schultz and Curley to Sandusky Incident
    - D. Schultz and Curley Meet with McQueary – February 2001
    - E. February 25, 2001: Spanier, Schultz and Curley Meet Again to Discuss Sandusky Incident
    - F. February 27, 2001: Curley Proposes Revised Response to the Sandusky Incident
- IV. **Curley Meets with Sandusky – March 1998**
- V. **March 19, 2001: Curley Meets with Second Mile Leadership**
- VI. **University Officials Do Not Notify the Board of the Sandusky Incident**
- VII. **Sandusky's Criminal Activity After 2001**

## Chapter 5: Response of University Officials to the Grand Jury Investigation – 2010, 2011 .................80

- I. **Subpoenas Issued for the Grand Jury Testimony of Senior University Officials**
    - A. Law Enforcement Interviews of University Personnel
- II. *Patriot-News* Article Reveals Sandusky Investigation – March 2011
- III. Board of Trustees Meeting – May 2011

IV. University Response to the Presentment and Criminal Charges Against Sandusky, Schultz and Curley – October and November 2011
- A. Baldwin, Spanier and Garban Learn of Presentment and Criminal Charges – October and November 2011
- B. Board of Trustees Conference Call – November 5, 2011
- C. Board of Trustees Meeting – November 6, 2011
- D. Board of Trustees Conference Call – November 8, 2011
- E. Board of Trustees Meeting – November 9, 2011

## Chapter 6: Board of Trustees ..............97

- I. Board Structure and Responsibilities
- II. The Board's Duty of Oversight and Reasonable Inquiry
    - A. The Board's Failure of Oversight and Reasonable Inquiry in 1998 and 2001
    - B. The Board's Failure of Reasonable Inquiry in 2011

## Chapter 7: Sandusky's Post-Retirement Interactions with the University ..............103

- I. Sandusky's Ongoing Contacts with the University
    - A. Sandusky's Continued Access to University Facilities
    - B. Sandusky's Continued Access to the Nittany Lion Club at Beaver Stadium
    - C. Sandusky's Football Camps at University Campuses
    - D. Sandusky's Continued Business Dealings with the University
    - E. Failure to Prohibit Sandusky's Access to University Facilities
- II. Sandusky's Post-Retirement Involvement in Second Mile Activities
    - A. Penn State and the Second Mile Organization
    - B. "Collaborative Relationship" between Penn State and Second Mile

　　　　　C.　　Second Mile Camps on Penn State Campuses

**Chapter 8:　Federal and State Child Sexual Abuse Reporting Requirements** ..................................................................................................110

　　　　I.　　The Federal "Clery Act"
　　　　　　A.　　Campus Security Authorities ("CSAs")
　　　　　　B.　　Collecting Crime Statistics
　　　　　　C.　　Issuance of Timely Warnings
　　　　　　D.　　Preparation of an Annual Safety Report
　　　　II.　　The University's Failure to Implement the Clery Act
　　　　III.　　Pennsylvania Child Sexual Abuse Reporting Requirements
　　　　IV.　　Implications of the University's Failure to Report Allegations of Child Sexual Abuse
　　　　V.　　Improvements in Clery Act Compliance Since November 2011

**Chapter 9:　The Protection of Children in University Facilities and Programs** ............................................................................................................120

　　　　I.　　University Policies for the Protection of Non-Student Minors
　　　　　　A.　　AD 39, *Minors Involved in University-Sponsored Programs or Programs held at the University and/or Housed in University Facilities*
　　　　　　B.　　HR 99, *Background Check Process*
　　　　II.　　Implementation of the University's Child Protection Policies
　　　　III.　　Use of University Facilities by Third Parties for Youth Programs

**Chapter 10:　Recommendations for University Governance, Administration, and the Protection of Children in University Facilities and Programs** ........................................................................................................127

　　　　　1.0　　Penn State Culture

2.0  Administration and General Counsel: Structure, Policies and Procedures

3.0  Board of Trustees: Responsibilities and Operations

4.0  Compliance: Risk and Reporting Misconduct

5.0  Athletic Department: Integration and Compliance

6.0  University Police Department: Oversight, Policies and Procedures

7.0  Management of University Programs for Children and Access to University Facilities

8.0  Monitoring Change and Measuring Improvement

## Appendices

- Appendix A – Exhibits
- Appendix B – Pennsylvania State University Policies: AD 67, AD 72, HR 99

# SCOPE OF REVIEW AND METHODOLOGY

Freeh Sporkin & Sullivan LLP, ("FSS"), was engaged by the Special Investigations Task Force ("Task Force") on behalf of The Pennsylvania State University's Board of Trustees ("Board" or "Trustees")[a] as Special Investigative Counsel on November 21, 2011. As Special Investigative Counsel, FSS was asked to perform an independent, full and complete investigation of:

- The alleged failure of Pennsylvania State University personnel to respond to, and report to the appropriate authorities, the sexual abuse of children by former University football coach Gerald A. Sandusky ("Sandusky");
- The circumstances under which such abuse could occur in University facilities or under the auspices of University programs for youth.

In addition, the Special Investigative Counsel was asked to provide recommendations regarding University governance, oversight, and administrative policies and procedures that will better enable the University to prevent and more effectively respond to incidents of sexual abuse of minors in the future.

To achieve these objectives the Special Investigative Counsel developed and implemented an investigative plan to:

- Identify individuals associated with the University at any level or in any office, who knew, or should have known, of the incidents of sexual abuse of children committed by Sandusky, the substance of their knowledge, and the point at which they obtained that knowledge;
- Examine how these incidents became known to, and were handled by, University Trustees, staff, faculty, administrators, coaches or others, with

---

[a] The members of the Special Investigations Task Force are: Chairman, Kenneth C. Frazier, Chief Executive Officer and President, Merck & Co., Inc.; Vice Chairman, Ronald J. Tomalis, Secretary of the Pennsylvania Department of Education; H. Jesse Arnelle, Attorney; Guion S. Bluford, Jr., Ph.D., Colonel, United States Air Force (retired); Mark H. Dambly, President, Pennrose Properties, LLC; Keith W. Eckel, Sole Proprietor and President, Fred W. Eckel & Sons Farms, Inc.; Daniel R. Hagen, Ph.D., Immediate Past-Chair, The Pennsylvania State University Faculty Senate, Professor, College of Agricultural Sciences; Rodney P. Hughes, Doctoral Student, The Pennsylvania State University; Karen B. Peetz, Chairman, Board of Trustees, The Pennsylvania State University, Vice Chairman and Chief Executive Officer, Financial Markets and Treasury Services, Bank of New York Mellon.

particular regard to institutional governance, decision making, oversight and culture.
- Identify any failures and their causes on the part of individuals associated with the University at any level or in any office, or gaps in administrative processes that precluded the timely and accurate reporting of, or response to, reports of these incidents.

The Special Investigative Counsel implemented the investigative plan by:

- Conducting over 430 interviews of key University personnel and other knowledgeable individuals to include: current and former University Trustees and Emeritus Trustees; current and former University administrators, faculty, and staff, including coaches; former University student-athletes; law enforcement officials; and members of the State College community at the University Park, Behrend, Altoona, Harrisburg and Wilkes-Barre campuses, and at other locations in Delaware, Pennsylvania, New York, Maryland and the District of Columbia, and by telephone;
- Analyzing over 3.5 million pieces of pertinent electronic data and documents;
- Reviewing applicable University policies, guidelines, practices and procedures;
- Establishing a toll-free hotline and dedicated email address to receive information relevant to the investigation, and reviewing the information provided from telephone calls and emails received between November 21, 2011 and July 1, 2012;
- Cooperating with law enforcement, government and non-profit agencies, including the National Center for Missing and Exploited Children (NCMEC), and athletic program governing bodies;
- Benchmarking applicable University policies, practices and procedures against those of other large, public and private universities and youth-serving organizations; and
- Providing interim recommendations to the Board in January 2012 for the immediate protection of children.

The information in this report was gathered under the applicable attorney-client privilege and attorney work product doctrine, and with due regard for the privacy of the interviewees and the documents reviewed. All materials were handled and maintained in a secure and confidential manner. This report sets forth the essential findings of the investigation, pursuant to the appropriate waiver of the attorney-client privilege by the Board.

Citations in this report have been redacted to protect the identity of people who spoke with the Special Investigative Council. Citations also include references to the internal database maintained by the Special Investigative Council to collect and analyze documents and emails. The references include citation to a unique identifying number assigned to each individual piece of information and are located in the endnotes and footnotes of this report.

# INDEPENDENCE OF THE INVESTIGATION

The Special Investigative Counsel's mandate was made clear in the public statement of Trustee Kenneth C. Frazier announcing this investigation. "No one is above scrutiny," Frazier said. "[Freeh] has complete rein to follow any lead, to look into every corner of the University to get to the bottom of what happened and then to make recommendations that ensure that it never happens again." Frazier assured the Special Investigative Counsel that the investigation would be expected to operate with complete independence and would be empowered to investigate University staff, senior administrators, and the Board of Trustees.

The Special Investigative Counsel operated with total independence as it conducted this investigation. Its diverse membership included men and women with extensive legal, law enforcement and child protection backgrounds who were experienced in conducting independent, complex and unbiased investigations. None of the Special Investigative Counsel's attorneys or investigators attended The Pennsylvania State University or had any past or present professional relationship with the University. The Special Investigative Counsel maintained a secure workspace that was separate from all other University offices and classrooms. The workspace was accessible to the public only when accompanied by a member of the Special Investigative Counsel team. The Special Investigative Counsel's computer systems were not connected to the University's network.

The Special Investigative Counsel had unfettered access to University staff, as well as to data and documents maintained throughout the University. The University staff provided a large volume of raw data from computer systems, individual computers and communications devices. The Special Investigative Counsel performed the forensic analysis and review of this raw data independent of the University staff. From this review and analysis, the Special Investigative Counsel discovered the most important documents in this investigation – emails among former President Graham B. Spanier, former Senior Vice President-Finance and Business Gary C. Schultz and Athletic Director Timothy M. Curley from 1998 and 2001 - relating to Sandusky's crimes. The Special Investigative Counsel immediately provided these documents to law enforcement when they were discovered.

The Special Investigative Counsel interviewed a cross-section of individuals including current and former University faculty and staff members, Trustees, and student-athletes. The interviews covered a wide range of academic, administrative and athletic topics relating to Sandusky's crimes and the allegations against Schultz and Curley; as well as the governance and oversight function of the University's administrators and Board of Trustees. The temporal scope of the interviews ranged from the late 1960s, when Sandusky first attended the University, to the present.

The witnesses interviewed in this investigation, with few exceptions, were cooperative and forthright. Very few individuals declined to be interviewed, including some who declined on the advice of counsel (i.e., Sandusky, Schultz, Curley and former University outside legal counsel Wendell Courtney). At the request of the Pennsylvania Attorney General, the Special Investigative Counsel did not interview former Pennsylvania State University Director of Public Safety Thomas Harmon or former coach Michael McQueary, among others. Although the information these individuals could have provided would have been pertinent to the investigation, the findings contained in this report represent a fair, objective and comprehensive analysis of facts. Moreover, the extensive contemporaneous documentation that the Special Investigative Counsel collected provided important insights, even into the actions of those who declined to be interviewed.

No party interfered with, or attempted to influence, the findings in this report. The Special Investigative Counsel revealed this report and the findings herein to the Board of Trustees and the general public at the same time. No advance copy was provided to the Board or to any other person outside of the Special Investigative Counsel's team, and the work product was not shared with anyone who was not part of the Special Investigative Counsel's team.

# EXECUTIVE SUMMARY

On November 4, 2011 the Attorney General of the Commonwealth of Pennsylvania ("Attorney General") filed criminal charges against Gerald A. Sandusky ("Sandusky") that included multiple counts of involuntary deviate sexual intercourse, aggravated indecent assault, corruption of minors, unlawful contact with minors and endangering the welfare of minors. Several of the offenses occurred between 1998 and 2002, during which time Sandusky was either the Defensive Coordinator for The Pennsylvania State University ("Penn State" or "University") football team or a Penn State professor Emeritus with unrestricted access to the University's football facilities. On November 4, 2011, the Attorney General filed criminal charges against the University's Athletic Director ("AD") Timothy M. Curley ("Curley") and Senior Vice President Finance and Business ("SVP-FB"), Gary C. Schultz ("Schultz") for failing to report allegations of child abuse against Sandusky to law enforcement or child protection authorities in 2002[b] and for committing perjury during their testimony about the allegations to the Grand Jury in Dauphin County, Pennsylvania, in January 2011.

On June 22, 2012, a Centre County jury in Bellefonte, Pennsylvania found Sandusky guilty of 45 counts of the criminal charges against him. As of the date of this report, the charges against Curley and Schultz have not been heard by the court.

The criminal charges filed against these highly respected University and community leaders are unprecedented in the history of the University. Several senior University leaders who had knowledge of the allegations did not prepare for the possibility that these criminal charges would be filed. In the days and weeks surrounding the announcement of the charges, University leaders (referred to on campus as "Old Main") and the University's Board of Trustees ("Board" or "Trustees"), struggled to decide what actions the University should take and how to be appropriately transparent about their actions. The high degree of interest exhibited by members of the University community, alumni, the public and the national media put additional pressure on these leaders to act quickly.

On November 11, 2011, the Trustees formed the "Special Investigations Task Force ("Task Force") of the Board of Trustees of The Pennsylvania State University" and

---

[b] This date was later determined by the Special Investigative Counsel to be 2001.

selected Trustees Kenneth C. Frazier and Ronald J. Tomalis to lead its efforts. On November 21, 2011 the Task Force engaged the law firm of Freeh Sporkin & Sullivan, LLP ("FSS") as Special Investigative Counsel, to conduct an investigation into the circumstances surrounding the criminal charges of sexual abuse of minors in or on Penn State facilities by Sandusky; the circumstances leading to the criminal charges of failure to report possible incidents of sexual abuse of minors; and the response of University administrators and staff to the allegations and subsequent Grand Jury investigations of Sandusky. In addition, the Special Investigative Counsel was asked to provide recommendations regarding University governance, oversight and administrative procedures that will better enable the University to effectively prevent and respond to incidents of sexual abuse of minors in the future.

The Pennsylvania State University is an outstanding institution nationally renowned for its excellence in academics and research. There is a strong spirit of community support and loyalty among its students, faculty and staff. Therefore it is easy to understand how the University community was devastated by the events that occurred.

## FINDINGS

The most saddening finding by the Special Investigative Counsel is the total and consistent disregard by the most senior leaders at Penn State for the safety and welfare of Sandusky's child victims. As the Grand Jury similarly noted in its presentment,[1] there was no "attempt to investigate, to identify Victim 2, or to protect that child or any others from similar conduct except as related to preventing its re-occurrence on University property."

Four of the most powerful people at The Pennsylvania State University – President Graham B. Spanier, Senior Vice President-Finance and Business Gary C. Schultz, Athletic Director Timothy M. Curley and Head Football Coach Joseph V. Paterno – failed to protect against a child sexual predator harming children for over a decade. These men concealed Sandusky's activities from the Board of Trustees, the University community and authorities. They exhibited a striking lack of empathy for Sandusky's victims by failing to inquire as to their safety and well-being, especially by not attempting to determine the identity of the child who Sandusky assaulted in the Lasch Building in 2001. Further, they exposed this child to additional harm by alerting

Sandusky, who was the only one who knew the child's identity, of what McQueary saw in the shower on the night of February 9, 2001.

These individuals, unchecked by the Board of Trustees that did not perform its oversight duties, empowered Sandusky to attract potential victims to the campus and football events by allowing him to have continued, unrestricted and unsupervised access to the University's facilities and affiliation with the University's prominent football program. Indeed, that continued access provided Sandusky with the very currency that enabled him to attract his victims. Some coaches, administrators and football program staff members ignored the red flags of Sandusky's behaviors and no one warned the public about him.

By not promptly and fully advising the Board of Trustees about the 1998 and 2001 child sexual abuse allegations against Sandusky and the subsequent Grand Jury investigation of him, Spanier failed in his duties as President. The Board also failed in its duties to oversee the President and senior University officials in 1998 and 2001 by not inquiring about important University matters and by not creating an environment where senior University officials felt accountable.

Once the Board was made aware of the investigations of Sandusky and the fact that senior University officials had testified before the Grand Jury in the investigations, it should have recognized the potential risk to the University community and to the University's reputation. Instead, the Board, as a governing body, failed to inquire reasonably and to demand detailed information from Spanier. The Board's overconfidence in Spanier's abilities to deal with the crisis, and its complacent attitude left them unprepared to respond to the November 2011 criminal charges filed against two senior Penn State leaders and a former prominent coach. Finally, the Board's subsequent removal of Paterno as head football coach was poorly handled, as were the Board's communications with the public.

Spanier, Schultz, Paterno and Curley gave the following reasons for taking no action to identify the February 9, 2001 child victim and for not reporting Sandusky to the authorities:

- Through counsel, Curley and Schultz stated that the "humane" thing to do in 2001 was to carefully and responsibly assess the best way to handle vague but troubling allegations. According to their counsel, these men were good people trying to do their best to make the right decisions.[2]

- Paterno told a reporter that "I didn't know exactly how to handle it and I was afraid to do something that might jeopardize what the university procedure was. So I backed away and turned it over to some other people, people I thought would have a little more expertise than I did. It didn't work out that way."[3]
- Spanier said, in his interview with the Special Investigative Counsel, that he never heard a report from anyone that Sandusky was engaged in any sexual abuse of children. He also said that if he had known or suspected that Sandusky was abusing children, he would have been the first to intervene.[4]

Taking into account the available witness statements and evidence, the Special Investigative Counsel finds that it is more reasonable to conclude that, in order to avoid the consequences of bad publicity, the most powerful leaders at the University – Spanier, Schultz, Paterno and Curley – repeatedly concealed critical facts relating to Sandusky's child abuse from the authorities, the University's Board of Trustees, the Penn State community, and the public at large.

The avoidance of the consequences of bad publicity is the most significant, but not the only, cause for this failure to protect child victims and report to authorities. The investigation also revealed:

- A striking lack of empathy for child abuse victims by the most senior leaders of the University.
- A failure by the Board to exercise its oversight functions in 1998 and 2001 by not having regular reporting procedures or committee structures in place to ensure disclosure to the Board of major risks to the University.
- A failure by the Board to make reasonable inquiry in 2011 by not demanding details from Spanier and the General Counsel about the nature and direction of the grand jury investigation and the University's response to the investigation.
- A President who discouraged discussion and dissent.
- A lack of awareness of child abuse issues, the Clery Act, and whistleblower policies and protections.

- A decision by Spanier, Schultz, Paterno and Curley to allow Sandusky to retire in 1999, not as a suspected child predator, but as a valued member of the Penn State football legacy, with future "visibility" at Penn State and ways "to continue to work with young people through Penn State," essentially granting him license to bring boys to campus facilities for "grooming" as targets for his assaults. Sandusky retained unlimited access to University facilities until November 2011.
- A football program that did not fully participate in, or opted out, of some University programs, including Clery Act compliance. Like the rest of the University, the football program staff had not been trained in their Clery Act responsibilities and most had never heard of the Clery Act.
- A culture of reverence for the football program that is ingrained at all levels of the campus community.

## RECOMMENDATIONS FOR UNIVERSITY GOVERNANCE, ADMINISTRATION, AND THE PROTECTION OF CHILDREN IN UNIVERSITY FACILITIES AND PROGRAMS

From the results of interviews with representatives of the University's Office of Human Resources, Office of Internal Audit, Office of Risk Management, Intercollegiate Athletics, Commonwealth Campuses, Outreach, the President's Council, Faculty Senate representatives and the Board of Trustees, and benchmarking similar practices at other large universities, the Special Investigative Counsel developed 120 recommendations for consideration by University administrators and the Board in the following eight areas:

- The Penn State Culture
- Administration and General Counsel: Structure, Policies and Procedures
- Board of Trustees: Responsibilities and Operations
- Compliance: Risk and Reporting Misconduct
- Athletic Department: Integration and Compliance
- University Police Department: Oversight, Policies and Procedures
- Programs for Non-Student Minors and Access to Facilities
- Monitoring Change and Measuring Improvement

These recommendations are detailed in Chapter 10 of this report, and include several that the Special Investigative Counsel recommended to the Board in January 2012. The recommendations made at that time were designed to assist the University in preparing for its upcoming summer programs for children.

These steps should assist the University in improving structures, policies and procedures that are related to the protection of children. Some of these recommendations will help the University more fully comply with federal and state laws and regulations dealing with the protection of children. Other recommendations support changes in the structure and operations of the Board, or promote enhancements to administrative processes and procedures. Most importantly, the recommendations should create a safer environment for young people who participate in its programs and use its facilities.

One of the most challenging of the tasks confronting the Penn State community is transforming the culture that permitted Sandusky's behavior, as illustrated throughout this report, and which directly contributed to the failure of Penn State's most powerful leaders to adequately report and respond to the actions of a serial sexual predator. It is up to the entire University community – students, faculty, staff, alumni, the Board, and the administration – to undertake a thorough and honest review of its culture. The current administration and Board of Trustees should task the University community, including students, faculty, staff, alumni, and peers from similar institutions and outside experts in ethics and communications, to conduct such a review. The findings from such a review may well demand further changes.

# TIMELINE OF SIGNIFICANT EVENTS

**1969**
- Sandusky joins the Penn State football coaching staff.

**February 1998**
- After learning that Paterno has told Sandusky that he would not become the next head football coach, Curley begins discussions with Sandusky about other positions at the University, including an Assistant AD position that Sandusky turns down. Curley keeps Spanier and Schultz informed by email.

**May 3, 1998**
- *Sandusky assaults Victim 6[c] in Lasch Building shower.*

---

[c] The young boys victimized by Sandusky are designated in this report in the same manner as the Grand Jury presentment.

**May 4-30, 1998**

- Victim 6's mother reports to the University Police Department that Sandusky showered with her 11-year old son in the Lasch Building on Penn State campus. The police promptly begin an investigation.

- Schultz is immediately informed of the investigation and notifies Spanier and Curley. Schultz's confidential May 4, 1998 notes about Sandusky state: "Behavior – at best inappropriate @ worst sexual improprieties" and "At min – Poor Judgment." Schultz also notes: "Is this opening of pandora's box?" and "Other children?"

- University Police Department Chief Harmon emails Schultz: "We're going to hold off on making any crime log entry. At this point in time I can justify that decision because of the lack of clear evidence of a crime."

- Curley notifies Schultz and Spanier that he has "touched base with" Paterno about the incident. Days later, Curley emails Schultz: "Anything new in this department? Coach is anxious to know where it stands."

- Board meeting on May 15: Spanier does not notify the Board of the ongoing investigation.

**June 1998**

- District Attorney declines to bring charges against Sandusky.

- University Police detective and Department of Public Welfare caseworker interview Sandusky in Lasch Building so as not to put Sandusky "on the defensive." Sandusky admits hugging Victim 6 in the shower but says there was nothing "sexual about it." The detective advised Sandusky not to shower with any child. Sandusky stated he "wouldn't."

- Harmon emails Schultz: officers "met discreetly" with Sandusky and "his account of the matter was essentially the same as the child's." Sandusky said "he had done this with other children in the past. Sandusky was advised that there was no criminal behavior established and that the matter was closed as an investigation."

- Schultz emails Curley and Spanier: "I think the matter has been appropriately investigated and I hope it is now behind us."

**January 1999**

- Curley emails Spanier and Schultz: Sandusky wants to coach one more year and then transition to an outreach program.

**May-August 1999**

- Sandusky writes a letter to Curley saying, because he will not be next head football coach, he is considering retirement. Sandusky also seeks "to maintain a long-term relationship with the University."

- Curley emails Spanier and Schultz, discussing Sandusky's retirement options: "Joe did give him the option to continue to coach as long as he was the coach." Suggests possibility of Sandusky "coaching three more seasons."

- Sandusky proposes continuing connection with Penn State, including running a middle school youth football camp and finding "ways for [Sandusky] to continue to work with young people through Penn State." Paterno handwriting on the note states: "Volunteer Position Director – Positive Action for Youth."

- A retirement agreement with Sandusky is reached in June 1999, including an unusual lump sum payment of $168,000, an agreement for the University to "work collaboratively" with Sandusky on Second Mile and other community activities, and free lifetime use of East Area Locker Room facilities.

- As the retirement package is being finalized, Curley requests the emergency re-hire of Sandusky for the 1999 football season, which is approved.

- In August 1999, Sandusky is granted "emeritus" rank, which carries several privileges, including access to University recreational facilities. Documents show the unusual request for emeritus rank originated from Schultz, was approved by Spanier, and granted by the Provost, who expressed some uneasiness about the decision given Sandusky's low academic rank and the precedent that would be set.

**December 1999**
- Sandusky brings Victim 4 to 1999 Alamo Bowl in Texas.
- *Sandusky assaults Victim 4 at team hotel.*

**November 2000**
- *Sandusky assaults Victim 8 in Lasch Building shower.*
- Janitor observes assault by Sandusky, but does not report the assault for fear that "they'll get rid of all of us." Another janitor concludes that the University will close ranks to protect the football program.

**February 9, 2001**
- *Sandusky assaults Victim 2 in Lasch Building Shower.*
- McQueary witnesses the assault by Sandusky.

**February 10-12, 2001**

- McQueary reports the assault to Paterno on Saturday, February 10; Paterno tells McQueary, "you did what you had to do. It's my job now to figure out what we want to do."

- Paterno reports the incident to Curley and Schultz on Sunday, February 11 as Paterno did not "want to interfere with their weekends."

- On Sunday, February 11, Schultz consults with University outside counsel Wendell Courtney "re reporting of suspected child abuse."

- On Monday, Spanier, Schultz and Curley meet to discuss a situation that Spanier describes as "unique", and a "heads-up" meeting; Schultz's confidential notes indicate he spoke to Curley, reviewed the history of the 1998 incident, and agreed that Curley would discuss the incident with Paterno and recommend that Curley meet with Sandusky. Schultz notes state: "Unless he confesses to having a problem, [Curley] will indicate we need to have DPW review the matter as an independent agency concerned w child welfare."

- Schultz asks University Police Department Chief Harmon if the report of the 1998 incident is in police files; Harmon responds that it is.

**February 25-26, 2001**

- Spanier, Schultz and Curley meet and devise an action plan, reflected in Schultz's notes: "3) Tell chair* of Board of Second Mile 2) Report to Dept of Welfare. 1) Tell JS [Sandusky] to avoid bringing children alone into Lasch Bldg *who's the chair??" The plan is confirmed in a subsequent email from Schultz to Curley.

**February 27-28, 2001**

- Curley emails Schultz and Spanier and says he [Curley] has changed his mind about the plan "after giving it more thought and talking it over with Joe [Paterno] yesterday." Curley now proposes to tell Sandusky "we feel there is a problem" and offer him "professional help." "If he is cooperative we would work with him to handle informing" the Second Mile; if Sandusky does not cooperate, "we don't have a choice and will inform" DPW and the Second Mile. "Additionally, I will let him know that his guests are not permitted to use our facilities."

- Spanier emails Curley and Schultz: "This approach is acceptable to me." He adds: "The only downside for us is if the message isn't 'heard' and acted upon, and we then become vulnerable for not having reported it. But that can be assessed down the road. The approach you outline is humane and a reasonable way to proceed."

- Schultz concurs with the plan in an email to Curley and Spanier: "this is a more humane and upfront way to handle this." Schultz adds, "we can play it by ear" about informing DPW of the assault.

**March 5, 2001**

- Scheduled date of meeting between Curley and Sandusky. In his 2011 Grand Jury testimony, Curley said he told Sandusky "we were uncomfortable" about the incident and would report it to the Second Mile. Curley says he also told Sandusky to stop bringing children to the athletic facilities. Sandusky's counsel later reports that no accusation of sexual abuse was made at this meeting and that Sandusky offered to provide the name of the boy to Curley, but Curley did not want the boy's name.

**March 16, 2001**

- Board of Trustees meeting: Spanier does not report the Sandusky incident to the Board.

**March 19, 2001**

- Curley meets with the executive director of the Second Mile and "shared the information we had with him." The Second Mile leadership concludes the matter is a "non-incident," and takes no further action.

**July 24, 2001**
- Schultz leads a transaction to sell a parcel of University property to The Second Mile for $168,500 – the same as the University's 1999 acquisition cost.

**August 2001**
- *Sandusky assaults Victim 5 in Lasch Building shower.*

**September 21, 2001**
- Board of Trustees meeting: Board approves land sale to The Second Mile; neither Spanier nor Schultz disclose any issue concerning Sandusky.

**January 7, 2010**
- The University receives subpoenas from the Pennsylvania Attorney General for personnel records and correspondence regarding Sandusky.

**September 16, 2010**
- *Patriot-News* reporter contacts Spanier; the two exchange emails as to Spanier's knowledge of an investigation of Sandusky for suspected criminal activity while he was a Penn State employee.

**December 28, 2010 - January 11, 2011**

- Then-Penn State General Counsel Cynthia Baldwin speaks to the Attorney General's Office staff about Grand Jury subpoenas for Schultz, Paterno and Curley; alerts Spanier of subpoenas; meets with Schultz, Paterno and Curley to discuss Sandusky; and calls former University outside counsel Wendell Courtney about his knowledge of Sandusky.

- Courtney emails Schultz: Baldwin "called me today to ask what I remembered about JS issue I spoke with you and Tim about circa eight years ago. I told her what I remembered. She did not offer why she was asking, nor did I ask her. Nor did I disclose that you and I chatted about this."

- Courtney emails Baldwin that "someone ... contacted Children and Youth Services to advise of the situation so that they could do whatever they thought was appropriate under the circumstances, while being apprised of what PSU actions were, i.e., advising JS to no longer bring kids to PSU's football locker rooms."

**January 12, 2011**

- Schultz, Paterno and Curley testify before the Grand Jury.

**March 31, 2011**

- *Patriot-News* publishes article on Sandusky investigation.

**April 1, 2011**

- A Trustee emails Spanier, asking if the Board will be briefed about the Sandusky investigation reported in the paper. Spanier tells the Trustee: "Grand Jury matters are by law secret, and I'm not sure what one is permitted to say, if anything. I'll need to ask Cynthia [Baldwin] if it would be permissible for her to brief the Board on the matter."

**April 13, 2011**

- The Trustee emails Spanier again: "despite grand jury secrecy, when high ranking people at the university are appearing before a grand jury, the university should communicate something about this to its Board of Trustees." Spanier responds, downplaying the significance of the investigation: "I'm not sure it is entirely our place to speak about this when we are only on the periphery of this." Spanier asks Baldwin to call the Trustee.

- Spanier appears before the Grand Jury.

- Spanier separately emails Baldwin, noting "[the Trustee] desires near total transparency. He will be uncomfortable and feel put off until he gets a report."

**April 17, 2011**

- Spanier, Baldwin and then Board Chair Garban have a conference call to discuss the Sandusky Grand Jury.

**May 12, 2011**

- Board of Trustees meeting: Spanier and Baldwin brief Board on status of Grand Jury investigation; Spanier and Baldwin downplay importance of the investigation to Penn State. The Board asks a few limited questions.

**July 15, 2011**

- Board of Trustees meeting: Spanier and Baldwin do not update the Board on the Sandusky investigation. The Board does not ask about the Sandusky investigation.

**September 9, 2011**

- Board of Trustees meeting: Spanier and Baldwin do not update the Board on the Sandusky investigation. The Board does not ask about the Sandusky investigation.

**October 27-28, 2011**
- Baldwin receives information on upcoming Grand Jury indictment.
- Baldwin, Spanier and Curley meet; Baldwin and Spanier also meet with Garban.
- Spanier, Baldwin, Garban and staff draft press statement expressing "unconditional support" for Schultz and Curley.

**October 29, 2011**
- Sandusky attends Penn State home football game and sits in Nittany Lion Club in Beaver Stadium.

**November 4, 2011**
- Courtney emails Schultz a newspaper story about the Sandusky charges. Schultz replies: "I was never aware that 'Penn State police investigated inappropriate touching in a shower' in 1998."
- Criminal charges filed against Sandusky in Centre County; Grand Jury presentment attached as Exhibit A to criminal complaint.
- Criminal charges are filed against Schultz and Curley in Dauphin County; Grand Jury presentment attached as Exhibit A to criminal complaint.

**November 5, 2011**

- Sandusky is arrested.

- Grand Jury presentment released, noting there was no "attempt to investigate, to identify Victim 2 or to protect that child or any others from similar conduct, except as related to preventing its re-occurrence on University property."

- A Trustee asks Spanier, "What is going on, and is there any plan to brief the Board before our meeting next week?" Baldwin advises Spanier to tell the Trustee, "you are briefing the chair and the Board will be briefed next week."

- Spanier issues a press release expressing "unconditional support" for Schultz and Curley; with regard to child victims, Spanier only states, "Protecting children requires the utmost vigilance."

- Spanier emails Baldwin: Spanier says that if the Board is briefed, "it will be nothing more than what we said publicly." The Board meets on a conference call that evening.

- A senior administrator suggests an independent review of Penn State's intercollegiate athletics. Baldwin replies, "If we do this, we will never get rid of this group in some shape or form. The Board will then think that they should have such a group." Spanier agrees.

**November 6, 2011**

- Board of Trustee meeting: Board places Curley on administrative leave; Schultz re-retires. Spanier issues a second press release stating that Curley and Schultz voluntarily changed their employment status. Board members disagree and express frustration at changed tone of press release. Spanier says he only made "grammatical" edits to the press release.

**November 7, 2011**

- Pennsylvania Attorney General and Pennsylvania State Police Commissioner announce charges against Sandusky, Schultz and Curley at a press conference.

- A Trustee writes to other Board members: "Unfortunately the statement that was issued last night, in my opinion, did not reflect the sense of the Board."

**November 8, 2011**

- Board of Trustees conference call: Third press release issued, expressing "outrage" at the "horrifying details" of the Grand Jury presentment, and announcing the formation of an investigative task force to review issues relating to the criminal charges.

**November 9, 2011**

- Board of Trustees meeting: Board removes Spanier as President; names Rodney Erickson as Interim President (becomes permanent President on November 17, 2011); removes Paterno as Head Football Coach.

- Board sends message to Paterno to phone the Board Vice Chair, who telephonically notifies Paterno that he is no longer Penn State's Head Football Coach.

- Board holds press conference announcing its actions.

- Students demonstrate in protest on Penn State campus.

# CHAPTER 1
# THE PENNSYLVANIA STATE UNIVERSITY – GOVERNANCE AND ADMINISTRATION

## KEY FINDINGS

- Although the University has a central Human Resources department headed by an Associate Vice President, each school and other large departments (such as Intercollegiate Athletics) has its own HR staff. Those individual departments sometimes relaxed or opt out of the standard rules or procedures in implementing University policies and rules.
- The University's administrative controls include over 350 policies and related procedures, however, oversight of compliance with these policies is decentralized and uneven.
- The University has no centralized office, officer or committee to oversee institutional compliance with laws, regulations, policies and procedures; certain departments monitored their own compliance issues with very limited resources.
- The Department of Intercollegiate Athletics ("Athletic Department"), involving approximately 800 student-athletes, has an Associate Athletic Director responsible for compliance and was significantly understaffed.
- Responsibility for Clery Act compliance previously resided with a sergeant in the University Police Department who was only able to devote minimal time to Clery Act compliance.

The Pennsylvania State University ("Penn State" or "University") is one of four public universities within the Commonwealth System of Higher Education and the only "land-grant" educational institution in Pennsylvania. In 1989, the Pennsylvania Legislature designated the University as a "state-related" institution that receives some state appropriated funding, yet remains autonomous from the state's direct control, maintaining its own Board of Trustees ("Board" or "Trustees").

University Park is the central administrative campus for the University located in State College, Pennsylvania. The University has 19 additional campuses located throughout the state, and offers degrees in 160 majors and 150 graduate disciplines. There are 76,460 undergraduate students and 9,745 graduate students that currently attend the University.[5] The University's annual operating budget is approximately $4.1 billion[6] and its endowment is valued at approximately $1.7 billion.[7]

The University's President is responsible for the academic and administrative functions of the institution, including the University's College of Medicine.[8] The academic program includes 17 colleges within the undergraduate and graduate programs, and six research institutes.[9] The President, along with other senior administrators and officials, is responsible for administering University policies and procedures; managing the endowment; handling legal matters; and overseeing the operation of the University's 10 business units, including those related to campus safety, internal audit, human resources, and facilities.

## I. KEY LEADERSHIP POSITIONS

### A. President

The Board delegates operations and control of the University to the President and his/her designees.[10] As the chief executive officer, the President establishes policies and procedures for operation of the University and reports to the Board on a regular basis.[11] The President also meets regularly with the President's Council, which consists of 17 direct reports including the General Counsel, the Director of the Board of Trustees, and the Senior Vice President - Finance and Business.[12] Graham B. Spanier was President from September 1, 1995 to November 9, 2011. Rodney A. Erickson, appointed on November 9, 2011,[13] is the current President.

## B. Executive Vice President and Provost ("EVP-Provost")

The Executive Vice President and Provost serves as chief executive officer in the President's absence and is involved in nearly all operations of the University. The Provost also is the University's chief academic officer, responsible for the academic administration of the University's academic units (colleges, schools and campuses) and research, as well as the general welfare of the faculty and students.[14] The EVP-Provost is a member of the President's Council. Rodney A. Erickson was EVP-Provost from July 1, 1999 until November 9, 2011.[15] Robert N. Pangborn was named the Interim EVP-Provost on November 15, 2011.[16]

## C. Senior Vice President – Finance and Business ("SVP-FB")

The Senior Vice President – Finance and Business sits on the President's Council and manages the University's endowment (with assistance from the University Investment Council). The SVP-FB also oversees 10 business units involved with the University's daily operations, including University Police and Public Safety, Office of Internal Audit, and Human Resources. Gary C. Schultz was the SVP–FB from January 1, 1995 to June 30, 2009, when he retired.[17] Albert Horvath replaced Schultz from July 1, 2009 until he resigned on September 14, 2011.[18] Spanier asked Schultz to temporarily return to the position in 2011 while a search was conducted for a successor to Horvath. Schultz held the temporary position from September 15, 2011 until November 6, 2011.[19]

## D. General Counsel

Until 2010, the University outsourced most of its legal work to McQuaide Blasko, a law firm in Centre County, Pennsylvania. The Board of Trustees reassessed this legal services model in 2009 based on a study conducted by the SVP-FB and approved the establishment of the Office of General Counsel for the University. The General Counsel is a member of the President's Council. In January 2010, Spanier appointed Cynthia Baldwin, a former Board member and Chair, as the first General Counsel and Vice President of the University. The Board approved Baldwin's appointment on January 22, 2010.[20] Baldwin retired on June 30, 2012 and has been succeeded by Stephen S. Dunham, pending final approval by the Board of Trustees.

# II. Principal Administrative Areas

The University has 22 principal administrative areas:[21]

| | |
|---|---|
| Office of the President | Government Affairs |
| Alumni Relations | Health Affairs and Medicine |
| Affirmative Action Office | Human Resources |
| Athletics | Outreach and Cooperative Extension |
| Commonwealth Campuses | Research and Graduate School |
| Development | Undergraduate Education |
| Diversity | University Relations |
| Educational Equity | Student Affairs |
| Executive Vice President and Provost | Physical Plant |
| Finance and Business | Planning, Institutional Assessment |
| General Counsel | Vice President for Administration |

Several components of these principal administrative areas are particularly important to this investigation: the University Police and Public Safety Department; the Office of Human Resources; the Office of Risk Management; the Office of Internal Audit; Outreach and Intercollegiate Athletics.[22]

## A. University Police and Public Safety ("University Police Department")

The University Police Department is part of the Finance and Business unit. It has jurisdiction over all crimes that occur on University grounds. Its officers have the same authority as municipal police officers and enforce both the laws of the Commonwealth of Pennsylvania and University regulations. As part of its responsibilities, the University Police Department collects campus crime statistics that the University must publish annually to comply with The Jeanne Clery Disclosure of Campus Security Policy and Campus Crime Statistics Act, 20 U.S.C. § 1092(f) ("Clery Act").[23]

The University Police Department is currently staffed with 46 full-time sworn officers. They are assisted by approximately 200 auxiliary officers and escorts who assist with crowd and traffic control at special events and security at residence halls.[24] The police officers provide 24-hour patrol services to the campus and University-owned properties. In addition to the police officers at University Park, approximately 73 full-time and 30 part-time sworn officers work at the various Commonwealth campuses. University Police work regularly with the Pennsylvania State Police, State College Borough Police and surrounding police agencies.[25]

The University Police Department is headed by a Director who reports to the Assistant Vice President of Police and Public Safety ("AVP-Police and Public Safety") who, in turn, reports to the SVP-FB.[26] David E. Stormer was the AVP-Police and Public Safety until April 1998,[27] after which the AVP-Police and Public Safety position was eliminated.[28] In 1998, Thomas R. Harmon was the Director. When Harmon retired in 2005, Stephen G. Shelow became Director. In April 2011, Shelow took over the re-created position of AVP-Police and Public Safety.[29] Tyrone Parham is the current Director and reports to Shelow.[30]

## B. Office of Human Resources ("OHR")

The University's OHR is responsible for employee recruitment and background checks, compensation and benefits, professional development and employee relations.[31] Its senior official, Associate Vice President Susan M. Basso, also reports to the SVP-FB.[32] Basso replaced Billie Sue Willits who was Associate Vice President from 1989 until 2010.[33] Although there is a central HR department headed by an Associate Vice President, each school and other large departments (such as Intercollegiate Athletics) has its own HR staff.[34] Those individual departments are charged with enforcing University rules and policies in their own groups but, in practice, they sometimes relaxed or opted out of the standard rules or procedures.[35]

## C. Department of Intercollegiate Athletics ("Athletic Department")

The Athletic Department is organized into 30 sports teams and oversees approximately 800 athletes.[36] The Athletic Department is headed by a Director who is not a Vice President, but who sits by invitation on the President's Council and reports to the President. Timothy M. Curley was the Director of Athletics from December 1993 until November 6, 2011.[37] On November 16, 2011, David M. Joyner was named the Acting AD.[38]

The largest sport in the Athletic Department is the football program, which is led by a Head Coach who reports to the AD. Joseph V. Paterno was Head Coach of the football program from 1966 until November 9, 2011.[39] Bill O'Brien was named the new Head Coach on January 6, 2012.[40]

The Athletic Department also conducts sports camps for children. Historically, the Associate Athletic Director for Football Operations and assistant football coaches have directed the football sports camps without the involvement of the Head Coach.[41] Richard J. Bartolomea has been the Sports Camp Coordinator since 1993.

### D. Outreach

The Penn State Outreach program conducts numerous activities, including running various youth camps on campus. The Outreach program is led by the Vice President of Outreach, who also sits on the President's Council. Dr. James H. Ryan was the Vice President of Outreach in 1998 and continued in that position until 2003, when Dr. Craig D. Weidemann took over the position, which he still holds.[42] Outreach oversaw the sports camps until November 2010, when the responsibility was transferred to the Athletic Department.[43]

## III. ADMINISTRATIVE CONTROLS

The University's administrative controls include over 350 policies and related procedures designed to ensure reasonable control over its operations.[44] However, as discussed further below, oversight of compliance with such policies is decentralized throughout various University departments and of uneven quality among the departments.

### A. Policies and Procedures

The University has had a fairly comprehensive set of policies and procedures in place to safeguard the campus community, promote ethical conduct and encourage crime reporting since 1986. Examples of relevant policies include the following:

- AD12 – Sexual Assault, Relationship and Domestic Violence, and Stalking (created in 1996)
- AD39 – Minors Involved in University-Sponsored Programs or Programs Held at the University and/or Housed in University Facilities (created in 1992)
- AD41 – Sexual Harassment (created in 1998)
- AD47 – General Standards of Professional Ethics (created in 1986)
- AD67 – Disclosure of Wrongful Conduct and Protection from Retaliation (created in 2010)
- AD99 – Background Check Process (created in 2012)
- RA20 – Individual Conflict of Interest (created in 2009)

- RA21 – Institutional Financial Conflict of Interest Involving Sponsored Projects, Dedicated Gifts, Research, Scholarship, and Technology Transfer (created in 2003)
- The Penn State Principles (created in 2001)[45]

**B. Oversight and Internal Controls**

**1. Compliance.** The University has no centralized office, officer or committee to oversee institutional compliance with laws, regulations, policies and procedures.[46] Rather, certain departments monitor their own compliance issues, some with very limited resources. As an example, the Athletic Department has an Associate Athletic Director responsible for National Collegiate Athletic Association ("NCAA") compliance, but that group is significantly understaffed.[47] The responsibility for Clery Act compliance previously resided with a sergeant in the University Police Department who was able to devote only minimal time to Clery Act compliance.[48] The University Police Department appointed a full-time Clery Compliance Officer on March 26, 2012.[49]

**2. Risk Management.** The University's Office of Risk Management ("ORM") identifies and manages potential risks throughout the University relating to financial, physical and reputational loss. The scope of the ORM's work includes managing risks involving physical, personnel and financial resources, privacy, and legal and regulatory compliance,[50] but in reality, most of its work centers on assessing contract-based risks.[51]

**3. Audit.** The University has internal and external auditing processes that focus on financial and business matters. The Office of Internal Audit ("OIA"), established in 2003, evaluates a range of operational risks throughout the University and oversees an "Ethics Hotline" for reporting financial fraud and human resources issues.[52] The OIA has full access to all University activities, records, property and personnel, including direct access to the President of the University and the Board of Trustees.[53] The OIA is led by an Internal Audit Director who reports to the SVP-FB, and to the Chairman of the Board of Trustees' Subcommittee on Audit[54] (recently renamed the Committee on Finance, Business and Capital Planning).

The OIA has conducted audits relating to compliance with various University policies and procedures, although it is not responsible for ensuring compliance with such policies.[55] The OIA has reviewed the University policies for screening summer camp counselors, but not the policies regarding background checks of University employees.[56] The OIA has not conducted any audits regarding Clery Act compliance or the safety of minors on campus or summer camps.[57]

The internal auditors issue annual reports on financial matters, which are shared with the Board at its annual meetings. They also perform annual audits on the University's compliance with certain NCAA rules.[58] In addition to the internal audits conducted by the OIA, independent accountants also audit the University.[59]

# CHAPTER 2
# RESPONSE OF UNIVERSITY OFFICIALS TO THE ALLEGATION OF CHILD SEXUAL ABUSE AGAINST SANDUSKY – 1998

## KEY FINDINGS

- Before May 1998, several staff members and football coaches regularly observed Sandusky showering with young boys in the Lasch Building (now the East Area Locker Building or "Old Lasch"). None of the individuals interviewed notified their superiors of this behavior.
- University Police and the Department of Public Welfare responded promptly to the report by a young boy's mother of a possible sexual assault by Sandusky in the Lasch Building on May 3, 1998.
- While no information indicates University leaders interfered with the investigation, Spanier, Schultz, Paterno and Curley were kept informed of the investigation.
- On May 5, 1998, Schultz's notes about the incident state: "Is this opening of pandora's box? Other children?"
- On June 9, 1998, Schultz emails Spanier and Curley: "I think the matter has been appropriately investigated and *I hope it is now behind us* [emphasis added]."
- Detective recalled interviewing Sandusky in the Lasch Building so as not to put him "on the defensive." The detective advised Sandusky not to shower with any child and Sandusky said he "wouldn't." At the conclusion of the investigation, no charges were filed against Sandusky.
- Spanier, Schultz, Paterno and Curley did not even speak to Sandusky about his conduct on May 3, 1998 in the Lasch Building.
- Despite their knowledge of the criminal investigation of Sandusky, Spanier, Schultz, Paterno and Curley took no action to limit Sandusky's access to Penn State facilities or took any measures to protect children on their campuses.
- Spanier and Schultz failed to report the 1998 investigation to the Board of Trustees.
- Sandusky was convicted of several assaults that occurred after the 1998 incident. Some of these sexual assaults against young boys might have been prevented had Sandusky been prohibited from bringing minors to University facilities and University football bowl games.

## I. Sandusky's Association with Penn State

Gerald A. Sandusky ("Sandusky") was a student at Penn State from 1962-1966. While an undergraduate he played on the football team, and after his graduation in 1966 he became a graduate assistant in the football program for one year. Sandusky was a physical education instructor and coach at Juniata College from 1967-1968 and at Boston University from 1968-1969. He returned to Penn State in 1969 as an assistant football coach and assistant professor of physical education. He held the positions for 30 years until his retirement in 1999. Sandusky reported to Head Football Coach Joseph Paterno ("Paterno") for his entire career at Penn State. Sandusky was granted tenure in 1980.

Sandusky gained a national reputation as a successful defensive coach. He was well-known in the community and highly thought of for his work with youth.

Sandusky authored or coauthored three books - two about coaching linebackers, and *Touched: The Jerry Sandusky Story*, an autobiography that focuses on his claimed passion for helping disadvantaged youth. According to Sandusky's autobiography, it was his interest in young people that motivated him to found the "Second Mile," a non-profit organization that provides various services and activities for disadvantaged boys and girls in Pennsylvania. Many Penn State officials and some members of the Board of Trustees ("Board" or "Trustees") or their families supported the Second Mile through volunteer service and donations. Over the years, the University has allowed the Second Mile to use its facilities for a variety of educational and support programs for youth.

### A. Sandusky's Criminal Activity 1995-1998

Before May 1998, several staff members and football coaches regularly observed Sandusky showering with young boys in the Lasch Building (now the East Area Locker Building or "Old Lasch"). None of the individuals interviewed by the Special Investigative Counsel notified their superiors of this behavior. Former Coach Richard Anderson testified at Sandusky's trial in June 2012 that he often saw Sandusky in the showers with children in the football facilities but he did not believe the practice to be improper.[60]

The Centre County jury convicted Sandusky in June 2012 of assaulting three different boys at Penn State's football facilities and other places on campus before May 1998. These assaults occurred against Victim 4 (assaults on various dates from October 1996 to December 2000 at, among other places, the East Area Locker Building ("Old Lasch") and Lasch Football Building ("Lasch Building"); Victim 7 (assaults on various dates from September 1995 to December 1996 at East Area Locker Building and elsewhere); and Victim 10 (assaults on various dates from September 1997 to July 1999 in an outdoor pool at University Park and elsewhere).[61]

Another adult male, not part of the June 2012 Sandusky trial, alleged that he was molested by Sandusky over 100 times as a child and that Sandusky took him to the Penn State Rose Bowl game in Pasadena, California in 1995.[62] He also said that Sandusky brought him to the Penn State football locker room showers where Sandusky fondled him and performed oral sex on him.

## II. Events of May 3, 1998 at the Lasch Building

According to Centre County court records and University Police Department records, on the afternoon of May 3, 1998, Sandusky called the home of an 11-year-old boy[63] and invited him to go to a Penn State athletic facility that evening to exercise.[64] The boy, who met Sandusky through the Second Mile youth organization about a month earlier, accepted the invitation.[65] Sandusky picked up the boy at about 7:00 p.m., and took him to the Lasch Building on the Penn State campus.[66] As the central facility for Penn State football, the Lasch Building contained a number of exercise machines as well as dressing rooms, showers and Sandusky's office, which for many years was the office closest to Paterno's.

Sandusky and the boy went to a coaches' locker room, where the two wrestled and Sandusky tried to "pin" the boy.[67] After wrestling, the boy changed into clothes that Sandusky provided and followed him to work out on exercise machines.[68] When they finished exercising, Sandusky kissed the boy's head and said, "I love you."[69] Sandusky and the boy then went to a coaches' locker room[70] where Sandusky turned on the showers and asked the boy if he wanted to shower.[71] The boy agreed and began to turn on a shower several feet from Sandusky.[72] Sandusky directed him to a shower head closer to Sandusky, saying it took some time for the water to warm up.[73]

While in the shower, Sandusky wrapped his hands around the boy's chest and said, "I'm gonna squeeze your guts out."[74] The boy then washed his body and hair.[75] Sandusky lifted the boy to "get the soap out of" the boy's hair, bringing the boy's feet "up pretty high" near Sandusky's waist.[76] The boy's back was touching Sandusky's chest and his feet touched Sandusky's thigh.[77] The boy felt "weird" and "uncomfortable" during the time in the shower.[78]

Sandusky brought the boy home around 9:00 p.m. and left. The boy's mother noticed that her son's hair was wet and he told her that he had showered with Sandusky. The mother also observed that her son was acting in a way that he did when he was upset about something,[79] that he did not sleep well and took another shower the next morning.[80]

## III. Investigation of Sandusky – 1998

### A. May 4–6, 1998: Police Report, Initial Investigation and Psychological Evaluation of the Victim

At 7:43 a.m. on May 4, 1998, the boy's mother called Alycia Chambers, a licensed State College psychologist[81] who had been working with her son, to see if she was "overreacting" to Sandusky's showering with her son.[82] The psychologist assured the mother that she was not overreacting and told her to make a report to the authorities.[83] The boy's mother called the University Police Department and reported the incident to Detective Ron Schreffler around 11:00 a.m.[84]

Around 11:30 a.m., Detective Schreffler interviewed the boy.[85] The boy told Schreffler what happened with Sandusky the previous evening,[86] and added that a 10-year-old friend of his had been in a shower with Sandusky on another occasion where Sandusky similarly squeezed the friend.[87]

Later that day, Chambers met with the boy[88] who told her about the prior day's events and that he felt "like the luckiest kid in the world" to get to sit on the sidelines at Penn State football games.[89] The boy said that he did not want to get Sandusky in "trouble," and that Sandusky must not have meant anything by his actions.[90] The boy did not want anyone to talk to Sandusky because he might not invite him to any more games.[91] Chambers made a report to the Pennsylvania child abuse line[92] and also consulted with colleagues. Her colleagues agreed that "the incidents meet all of our definitions, based on experience and education, of a likely pedophile's pattern of building trust and gradual introduction of physical touch, within a context of a 'loving,' 'special' relationship."[93]

That afternoon Schreffler contacted John Miller, a caseworker with the Centre County Children and Youth Services ("CYS") about the allegation.[94] However, there were several conflicts of interest with CYS's involvement in the case[95] (e.g., CYS had various contracts with Second Mile - including placement of children in a Second Mile residential program;[96] the Second Mile's executive director had a contract with CYS to conduct children's evaluations;[97] and the initial referral sheet from Chambers indicated the case might involve a foster child).[98] In light of these conflicts, the Department of Public Welfare ("DPW") took over the case from CYS on May 5, 1998. DPW officials in Harrisburg, Pennsylvania took the lead because of Sandusky's high profile and assigned it to caseworker Jerry Lauro.[99]

Schreffler also contacted Karen Arnold, Centre County prosecutor in the District Attorney's office, to discuss the case.[100] Schreffler had decided to call the prosecutor at the outset of the investigation so he did not "have to worry about Old Main sticking their nose in the investigation," which he knew from experience could occur.[101]

Around 8:00 p.m. on May 4, 1998, Schreffler and Miller spoke with the boy's friend about his contact with Sandusky.[102] The friend stated that he had gone to the Penn State campus on two occasions with Sandusky, whom he met through the Second Mile.[103] Sandusky took him to the Lasch Building, where they wrestled and then showered together.[104] While in the shower, Sandusky came from behind and lifted him in a bear hug.[105] Following this interview, Schreffler and Miller re-interviewed the first boy.

On May 6, 1998, Schreffler reviewed voicemail messages and caller identification information from the home of the victim. Sandusky had called the boy twice on May 3, 1998 and once on May 6, 1998. Sandusky left a voicemail on May 6, 1998, inviting the boy to work out. The boy did not return the call.[106]

### B. May 7–9, 1998: A Second Evaluation of the Victim

On May 7, 1998, Chambers provided a copy of her written report to Schreffler. Chambers said she was pleased with the response of the agencies involved, as the "gravity of the incidents seems to be well appreciated."[107]

Also on May 7, 1998, Lauro interviewed the boy's mother. According to Schreffler's notes, Lauro had received copies of the boy's recorded statement,[108] yet Lauro advised the Special Investigative Counsel that he did not have full access to the facts of the case and was unaware of psychologist Chambers' evaluation.[109] Lauro said that if he "had seen [Chambers'] report, I would not have stopped the investigation," which he thought at the time fell into a "gray" area and involved possible "boundary" issues.[110]

Schreffler had a discussion with Arnold that day as well. Arnold told Schreffler to postpone a second psychological evaluation of the boy until an additional investigation could be completed.[111] Nonetheless, a second evaluation of the boy occurred on May 8, 1998 as part of DPW's investigation. Counselor John Seasock, who had a contract to provide counseling services to CYS, conducted the evaluation.[112]

During the meeting with Seasock the boy described the incident with Sandusky.[113] Given that the boy did not feel forced to engage in any activity and did not voice discomfort to Sandusky, Seasock opined that "there seems to be no incident which could be termed as sexual abuse, nor did there appear to be any sequential pattern of logic and behavior which is usually consistent with adults who have difficulty with sexual abuse of children."[114] Seasock's report ruled out that the boy "had been placed in a situation where he was being 'groomed for future sexual victimization.'"[115] Seasock recommended that someone speak with Sandusky about what is acceptable with young children and explained, "The intent of the conversation with Mr. Sandusky is not to cast dispersion (sic) upon his actions but to help him stay out of such gray area situations in the future."[116]

On May 9, 1998, Schreffler discussed the outcome of Seasock's evaluation with Seasock.[117] While Seasock said he identified some "gray areas," he did not find evidence of abuse and had never heard of a 52-year-old man "becoming a pedophile."[118] When Schreffler questioned Seasock's awareness of details of the boy's experience, Seasock acknowledged he was not aware of many of the concerns Schreffler raised but stated Sandusky "didn't fit the profile of a pedophile,"[119] and that he couldn't find any indication of child abuse.

Seasock served as an independent contractor at Penn State from 2000 to 2006. His first payment from Penn State was made on April 20, 2000 for $1,236.86.[120] His total payments were $11,448.86.[121] The Special Investigative Counsel did not find any evidence to suggest that these payments had any relation to Seasock's work on the Sandusky case in 1998. According to the Second Mile's counsel, there was no business relationship between Seasock and the Second Mile.[122]

## C. May 12-19, 1998: Police Overhear Sandusky Admit to Showering with the Victim

On May 12, 1998, Sandusky called the boy again and arranged to pick him up at his house the next day. On May 13, 1998, Schreffler and a State College police officer went to the boy's house and hid inside. When Sandusky arrived they covertly listened in to his conversation with the boy's mother.[123] Schreffler overheard Sandusky say he had gone to the boy's baseball game the night before but found the game had been cancelled.[124] The boy's mother told Sandusky that her son had been acting "different" since they had been together on May 3, 1998 [125] and asked Sandusky if anything had happened that day. Sandusky replied, "[w]e worked out. Did [the boy] say something happened?"[126] Sandusky added that the boy had taken a shower, and said "[m]aybe I worked him too hard."[127] Sandusky also asked the boy's mother if he should leave him alone, and she said that would be best. Sandusky then apologized.[128]

On May 19, 1998, at the direction of the police, the boy's mother met with Sandusky again in her home. As they listened from another room,[129] the officers heard the mother ask Sandusky about the bear hug in the shower, and whether his "private parts" touched the boy while they hugged. Sandusky said, "I don't think so ... maybe."[130] He also said he had showered with other boys before, but denied having "sexual feelings" when he hugged her son.[131] He admitted telling the boy that he loved him. Sandusky asked to speak with her son and the mother replied that she did not feel that was a good idea as her son was confused and she did not want Sandusky to attend any of the boy's baseball games. Sandusky responded, "I understand. I was wrong. I wish I could get forgiveness. I know I won't get it from you. I wish I were dead."[132]

The law enforcement officers did not question Sandusky at this time. Had the officers been better trained in the investigation of child sexual abuse they would have interrogated Sandusky directly after his confrontation with the boy's mother. A timely interview with Sandusky may have elicited candid responses such as the identification of other victims.

### D. Late May 1998: District Attorney's Decision to Not Prosecute Sandusky

Sometime between May 27, 1998 and June 1, 1998, the local District Attorney declined to prosecute Sandusky for his actions with the boy in the shower in the Lasch Building on May 3, 1998. A senior administrator of a local victim resource center familiar with the 1998 incident said the case against Sandusky was "severely hampered" by Seasock's report.[133]

The District Attorney at the time of the 1998 incident has been missing for several years and has been declared dead. The prosecutor assigned to the Sandusky case declined to be interviewed by the Special Investigative Counsel.

### E. June 1, 1998: University Police Speak with Sandusky

On June 1, 1998, Schreffler and Lauro interviewed Sandusky. Lauro said he did not discuss an interview strategy with Schreffler before meeting with Sandusky. Lauro recalled that the interview took place in a small weight room in the Lasch Building while Sandusky was seated on a weight bench and [134] that Lauro asked most of the questions.[135] Schreffler recalled that the interview was conducted in an office in the Lasch Building so as not to put Sandusky on the defensive.[136]

According to the interview notes in the case file, Sandusky told the interviewers that he hugged the boy in the shower but said there "wasn't anything sexual about it." Sandusky also said that he had showered with other boys in the past. Lauro advised Sandusky that it was a mistake to shower with kids. Sandusky agreed and said, "honest to God nothing happened."[137] Schreffler advised Sandusky not to shower with any child and Sandusky replied that he "wouldn't."[138] Schreffler and Lauro also told Sandusky that the police[139] could not determine if a sexual assault occurred. No notes or records reflect that Schreffler or Lauro consulted with the District Attorney during or after the interview.

Lauro also told the Special Investigative Counsel that he never spoke to Schreffler about whether improper actions took place between Sandusky and the boy.[140] Lauro stated, "it wasn't until Schreffler told me that there wasn't anything to the case that I closed mine."[141] Schreffler's file notes state that Lauro agreed that no sexual assault occurred.[142]

## IV. Involvement of University Officials in The Sandusky Investigation

### A. May 4 - 30, 1998: Notifications and Updates to Spanier, Schultz, Paterno and Curley

On the advice of counsel, Schultz and Curley declined to meet with the Special Investigative Counsel to discuss their knowledge and actions pertaining to the 1998 Sandusky incident. However, the Special Investigative Counsel discovered and reviewed numerous emails between Spanier, Schultz and Curley concerning the incident, and reviewed some of Schultz's files and handwritten notes as well. These documents provide a contemporaneous record of the 1998 events.

It is not known how Schultz learned of the incident involving Sandusky, but it is clear that he knew of it by the time he attended a meeting about it at 5:00 p.m. on May 4, 1998. In documents Schultz held confidentially in his office and that had been concealed from the Special Investigative Counsel, Schultz had handwritten notes summarizing this meeting.[d] Other notes written by Schultz and contemporaneous records pertaining to the matter indicate that then-University Police Department Chief Thomas Harmon regularly informed Schultz of the investigation's progress. In fact, when the case began, Harmon told Schreffler that he wanted to be kept updated on the case so he could "send everything up the flag pole" and advise Schultz.[143]

Schultz's confidential notes dated May 4, 1998 state: a woman reported that her "11 1/2 yr old son" who had been involved with the Second Mile was taken by "Jerry" to the football locker rooms; that taped police interview reflected "Behavior - at best inappropriate @ worst sexual improprieties;" the conduct was "At min – Poor Judgment;" that Sandusky and the child were in the shower, and Sandusky "came up behind & gave him a bear hug - said he would squeeze guts out – all;" and that the boy's ten-year-old friend "claims same thing went on with him." The notes conclude with the words "Critical issue - contact w genitals? Assuming same experience w the second boy? Not criminal."[144]

---

[d]Exhibit 2-H. Schultz's notes do not indicate who was present at the meeting.

It is not clear if Schultz, or another person, determined the matter was "not criminal" on the first day of the investigation. Schultz's confidential notes also show that sometime before 9:00 a.m. on May 5, 1998, Harmon reported to Schultz that the victim had been re-interviewed and had provided additional details about the incident[145] and demonstrated "on chair how Jerry hugged from back hands around abdmin (sic) & down to thighs - picked him up and held him at shower head - rinse soap out of ears."[e] The notes also state that "the mother had spoken to a psychologist who had been seeing the boy, who would call child abuse hot line & will generate an incident no - with Dept of Public Welfare;" and that the police interviewed the second boy who reported "Similar acct. Locker room. Wrestling. Kissed on head. Hugging from behind in shower. No allegation beyond that."[146] Schultz's notes end with these questions: "Is this opening of pandora's box? Other children?"[147]

By May 5, 1998, Schultz had communicated with Curley about the Sandusky incident. In an email from Curley to Schultz and Spanier at 5:24 p.m. captioned "Joe Paterno," Curley reports, "I have touched base with the coach. Keep us posted. Thanks."[f] In an interview with the Special Investigative Counsel, Spanier said he did not recall this email, and pointed out that he received numerous emails everyday that provide him with updates on various issues.[148] In a written statement from Spanier, he characterized the May 5, 1998 email as a "vague reference with no individual named."[g]

On May 5, 1998, Schultz also learned from Harmon that the Penn State University Police were "going to hold off" making any crime log entry for the Sandusky allegations.[149] The crime log entry would have been a public record of the incident concerning Sandusky with the boy, yet Harmon reported to Schultz before noon on May 5 that "[w]e're going to hold off on making any crime log entry. At this point in time I can justify that decision because of the lack of clear evidence of a crime."[150]

Schreffler said he delayed pulling an incident number for the Sandusky investigation because it was his normal procedure for drug investigations and he was not initially sure of what type of investigation he had.[151] Schreffler did not know why the report ultimately was opened as an "Administrative Information" file but said he

---

[e] Exhibit 2-I.
[f] Exhibit 2-A (Control Number 00643730).
[g] Exhibit 2-J.

may have been the one who decided on the label.[152] All pages of the police report are labeled "Administrative Information."[153]

Schreffler also noted that no referral of the Sandusky incident was made to the Penn State Office of Human Resources ("OHR").[154] Schreffler said such referrals routinely were made in other cases.[155] A senior OHR official recalled no report of the Sandusky incident in 1998, and the OHR files contained no such report.[156] The official thought the Sandusky case was so "sensitive" that it was handled by Schultz alone.[157] The official said no written policy required OHR to be notified by the campus police of incidents involving employees, but it was "very rare" for OHR not to be notified.[158]

Harmon continued to provide Schultz with information about DPW's role in the investigation and their potential conflict of interest with the Second Mile.[159] Harmon provided an update to Schultz on May 8, 1998 reporting that Lauro "indicated that it was his intent to have a psychologist who specializes in child abuse interview the children. This is expected to occur in the next week to week and a half. I don't anticipate anything to be done until that happens."[160]

As the investigation progressed, Curley made several requests to Schultz for updates. On May 13, 1998 at 2:21 p.m., Curley emailed Schultz a message captioned "Jerry" and asked, "Anything new in this department? Coach is anxious to know where it stands."[h] Schultz forwarded Curley's note to Harmon,[161] who provided an email update that Schultz then forwarded to Curley.[162] The reference to Coach is believed to be Paterno.

On May 18, 1998, Curley requested another update by email.[i] Schultz responded that there was no news and that he did not expect to hear anything before the end of the week.

On May 30, 1998, Curley asked for another update by email.[163] Schultz was on vacation at the time, but responded on June 8, 1998, saying that he understood before he left for vacation that "DPW and Univ Police services were planning to meet with him. I'll see if this has happened and get back to you."[164]

---

[h] Exhibit 2-B (Control Number 00641616).
[i] Exhibit 2-C (Control Number 00644098).

## B. June 1 - 10, 1998: Report to University Officials on Sandusky Interview and Case Closure

Sometime between May 27 and June 1, 1998, when he learned Sandusky would not face criminal charges, Harmon called Schultz to advise him of the District Attorney's decision.[165] On June 1, 1998, the same day as Sandusky's interview, Harmon sent Schultz an email describing the interview. Harmon reported that the DPW caseworker and Schreffler "met discreetly" with Sandusky, and his "account of the matter was essential[ly] the same as the child's."[j] Sandusky said "he had done this with other children in the past." The investigators told Sandusky there "was no criminal behavior established [and] that the matter was closed as an investigation." Sandusky was "a little emotional" and concerned as to how this incident might affect the boy. Harmon's message to Schultz did not mention that Sandusky was told not to shower with children.

On June 9, 1998, after returning from a vacation, Schultz updated Curley and Spanier on the Sandusky interview by email. He wrote that the investigators:

> met with Jerry on Monday and concluded that there was no criminal behavior and the matter was closed as an investigation. He was a little emotional and expressed concern as to how this might have adversely affected the child. I think the matter has been appropriately investigated and *I hope it is now behind us.* [emphasis added].[k]

Schultz's message to Curley and Spanier also did not mention that Sandusky was advised not to shower with children.

Neither Harmon nor Schultz's emails set forth, or suggest, that they planned to discuss the incident with Sandusky, to review or monitor his use of University facilities, to discuss his role at the Second Mile and his involvement in Second Mile overnight programs operated in Penn State facilities, or to consider the propriety of a continuing

---

[j]Exhibit 2-D (Control Number 00645223).
[k]Exhibit 2-E (Control Number 00646346).

connection between Penn State and the Second Mile. There also is no mention of whether Sandusky should receive counseling.[l]

Further, the emails do not indicate that any officials attempted to determine whether Sandusky's conduct violated existing University policy or was reportable under The Jeanne Clery Disclosure of Campus Security Policy and Campus Crime Statistics Act, 20 U.S.C. § 1092(f) ("Clery Act"). The emails also do not indicate if any person responsible for Penn State's risk management examined Sandusky's conduct. A risk management review might have resulted in the University providing contractual notice to its insurers about the incident, imposition of a general ban on the presence of children in the Lasch Building, or other limitations on Sandusky's activities.[m]

After Curley's initial updates to Paterno, the available record is not clear as to how the conclusion of the Sandusky investigation was conveyed to Paterno.[166] Witnesses consistently told the Special Investigative Counsel that Paterno was in control of the football facilities and knew "everything that was going on."[167] As Head Coach, he had the authority to establish permissible uses of his football facilities. Nothing in the record indicates that Curley or Schultz discussed whether Paterno should restrict or terminate Sandusky's uses of the facilities or that Paterno conveyed any such expectations to Sandusky. Nothing in the record indicates that Spanier, Schultz, Paterno or Curley spoke directly with Sandusky about the allegation, monitored his activities, contacted the Office of Human Resources for guidance, or took, or documented, any personnel actions concerning this incident in any official University file.

Spanier told the Special Investigative Counsel that no effort was made to limit Sandusky's access to Penn State.[168] Spanier said he was unaware that Sandusky

---

[l] When Penn State officials considered meeting with Sandusky in 2001 in response to allegations that he brought children into the Lasch Building showers, Curley wrote "I would plan to tell him we are aware of the first situation. I would indicate we feel there is a problem and we want to assist the individual to get professional help." Exhibit 2-F (Control Number 00679428).

[m] Penn State officials were familiar with the issues of liability that could arise from Sandusky bringing minors to the Lasch Building. For example, notes maintained by Paterno reflect that Sandusky proposed several continuing connections with Penn State when he retired in 1999. Among these connections was that he would have continuing "[a]ccess to training and workout facilities." A handwritten note on this proposal reads: "Is this for personal use or 2nd Mile kids. No to 2nd Mile. Liability problems." Exhibit 2-G (Control Number JVP000027).

continued to run camps at Penn State and have access to children sleeping in Penn State dormitories.[169]

Spanier never declared Sandusky a "persona non grata" on Penn State campuses, as he did toward a sports agent who, before the 1997 Citrus Bowl, bought $400 worth of clothing for a Penn State football player. Spanier was very aggressive in that case[170] and banned the agent from campus. Spanier said the agent "fooled around with the integrity of the university, and I won't stand for that."[171] The University conducted its own investigation, and provided the results to law enforcement.[172] In an email dated May 13, 1998, Spanier said, "The idea is to keep [the sports agent] off campus permanently, to keep him away from current athletes, and to keep him away from current graduates or students whose eligibility has recently expired."[173]

Despite his initial concern about "Old Main sticking their nose in the investigation" Schreffler told the Special Investigative Counsel that no one from the University interfered with the Sandusky investigation.[174] The Special Investigative Counsel did not find any evidence of interference by University administrators with the 1998 Sandusky investigation.

## C. 2011 Grand Jury Testimony of Spanier, Schultz, Paterno and Curley

When he appeared before the Grand Jury in January 2011, to answer questions about the 1998 incident involving Sandusky, Schultz testified that he did not recall that he, "knew anything about the details of what the allegation was from the mother." He stated, "I do recall there was a mother with a young boy who reported some inappropriate behavior of Jerry Sandusky. But I don't recall it being reported in the Lasch Building or anything of that sort."[175] On November 4, 2011, Schultz emailed Wendell Courtney, Penn State's former outside legal counsel, stating, "I was never aware that 'Penn State police investigated inappropriate touching in a shower' in 1998."[176]

At the same Grand Jury hearing in January 2011, Curley was asked if an incident involving alleged criminal conduct by a coach on campus would be brought to his attention. Curley said he thought so, but did not know. Curley then was asked, "[b]ut the 1998 incident was never brought to your attention?" He replied, "[n]o, ma'am, not that I recall."[177]

52

Paterno also testified in January 2011 before the Grand Jury. Paterno was asked, "Other than the [2001] incident that Mike McQueary reported to you, do you know in any way, through rumor, direct knowledge or any other fashion, of any other inappropriate sexual conduct by Jerry Sandusky with young boys?" Paterno responded, "I do not know of anything else that Jerry would be involved in of that nature, no. I do not know of it. You did mention — I think you said something about a rumor. It may have been discussed in my presence, something else about somebody. I don't know. I don't remember, and I could not honestly say I heard a rumor."[178] The Special Investigative Counsel requested an interview with Paterno in December 2011. Through his counsel, Paterno expressed interest in participating but died before he could be interviewed. Paterno's family has publicly denied that Paterno had knowledge of the 1998 incident.[179]

Spanier told the Special Investigative Counsel that his first knowledge of the 1998 event came when he was before the Grand Jury on April 13, 2011.[180] Yet notes from Spanier's interview on March 22, 2011 with members of the Attorney General's Office reflect he was asked, "[d]id you have info @ the 1998 incident?"[181] Cynthia Baldwin, who was then General Counsel, confirmed to the Special Investigative Counsel that Spanier was asked about the 1998 event in the interview before the Grand Jury appearance.[182] According to Baldwin, after the interview, Spanier said the interview "was no big deal" and he was "quite comfortable" going before the Grand Jury.[183] Finally, on January 4, 2011, when State Police came to Penn State to obtain a copy of the 1998 police report concerning Sandusky, Albert Horvath, then Senior Vice President - Finance and Business said he would "let Graham and Tim know" that the police requested the 1998 report as part of a "Jerry Sandusky investigation which has been ongoing for the past year."[184]

### D. University Officials Do Not Notify the Board of the Sandusky Investigation

The Penn State Board of Trustees met on May 14 and 15, 1998. Nothing in the Board's records or from the Special Investigative Counsel's interviews of Trustees indicates that Spanier, or any University official, notified the Board of the Sandusky investigation, or that there were any contemporaneous discussions with Board members of the 1998 Sandusky investigation. In 1998, the Board of Trustees did not have a process or a committee structure for receiving regular reports from University officials on risk issues such as the Sandusky investigation.

## E. Sandusky's Criminal Activity 1998 - 2001

The Centre County jury convicted Sandusky in June 2012 of assaulting five different boys at Penn State's football facilities and other places on campus after May 1998. These assaults occurred against Victim 2 (assault in the Lasch Building in February 2001); Victim 3 (assaults on various dates from July 1999 to December 2001 in the Lasch Building and at other places); Victim 4 (assaults on various dates from 1999 to 2000 in Old Lasch and the Lasch Building and a Penn State football bowl trip to Texas in December 1999); Victim 5 (assault in August 2001 in the Lasch Building); and Victim 8 (assault in November 2000 in the Lasch Building).[185]

# CHAPTER 3
# SANDUSKY'S RETIREMENT FROM THE UNIVERSITY – 1999

## KEY FINDINGS

- Before the May 1998 incident, Sandusky knew that he was not going to be selected to succeed Joseph Paterno as Head Football Coach at Penn State.
- Curley talked with Sandusky about his future role with the football program and offered him the possibility of an Assistant Athletic Director position.
- Sandusky explored taking an early retirement and requested several benefits from Penn State (i.e., a $20,000 yearly annuity in addition to his pension; to run a middle school youth football camp; "active involvement in developing an outreach program featuring Penn State Athletics;" and finding "ways for [Sandusky] to continue to work with young people through Penn State."
- On June 29, 1999, Spanier approved a one-time lump sum payment to Sandusky of $168,000. A senior University Controller's office official and a retired Senior Vice President both stated that they had never known the University to provide this type of payment to a retiring employee.
- While Sandusky's retirement agreement was being finalized, Curley sought and received authorization for Sandusky to be re-employed as an "emergency hire" for the 1999 football season.
- Sandusky was also awarded "emeritus" rank, with special privileges including access to the University's East Area locker room complex. Sandusky's positions in the University did not meet the general eligibility requirements for this honor, yet University administrators found themselves in a "bind" because Spanier had promised the emeritus rank to Sandusky.
- The Special Investigative Counsel found no evidence to indicate that Sandusky's retirement was related to the police investigation of him in 1998.

## I. Sandusky's Decision to Retire

Before the May 3, 1998 incident in the Lasch Building, Curley had already spoken with Sandusky about his future role in the University's football program. On February 8, 1998, for example, Curley emailed Spanier and Schultz, stating that he had several conversations over the past week with Sandusky about taking an Assistant Athletic Director position.[n] Curley stated in the email that Paterno had also met with Sandusky about his future with Penn State football.[186]

On February 9, 1998, Curley emailed Schultz and Spanier reporting that Sandusky did not want the Assistant Athletic Director position, and would continue coaching for the next year.[o] Curley told them Sandusky "will have 30 years in the system next year, which will give him some options after next season."[187] He added, "Joe tells me he made it clear to Jerry he will not be the next head coach."[188]

Curley's reference to the "system" is the Pennsylvania State Employees' Retirement System ("SERS") to which Sandusky belonged. From July 1, 1998 to June 30, 1999, SERS provided a "30-and-out" retirement window, allowing members like Sandusky who had 30 years of service to retire at any age without the usual early retirement penalty, and receive all retirement benefits earned to that date.[189] Without the window, the SERS code required that members have 35 years of credited service at any age - or reach age 60 - before they could retire with full benefits.[190]

Sandusky and others explored the possibility of starting a Division III football program at the University's Altoona campus where Sandusky could coach. Sandusky even spoke with a businessman who was a supporter of Penn State athletics in March 1998 about financing for the plan.[191] Paterno's undated, handwritten notes, maintained in his home office and provided to the Special Investigative Counsel by his attorney, discussed the plan, and suggested that Sandusky work on making "FB at Altoona Happen" until the "window closes."[192] If Sandusky could not get the program established before the window closed, "he retires with a pension fully vested with a severance pkg. which could include deferred income or a supplemental payment for 20 year (sic)."[193]

---

[n]Exhibit 3-A (Control Number 00644655).
[o]Exhibit 3-B (Control Number 03008143).

On May 19, 1998, a senior administrator in University Development and Alumni Relations emailed Spanier, Curley, Schultz and others raising questions to consider while conducting "a limited feasibility study" of football at Altoona that Spanier had requested.[194] The administrator reported that the financial support needed for the program could not be raised.[195] The Special Investigative Counsel found no evidence that the decision regarding the establishment of a football program at Altoona was related to the incident in the Lasch Building on May 3, 1998.[196]

## II. Negotiating the Agreement

On January 19, 1999, Curley wrote to Spanier and Schultz to report on a meeting with Sandusky.[p] Curley told them that Sandusky "is interested in going one more year and then transition into a spot that handles our outreach program."[197] Curley noted as a postscript that "[Sandusky] is not pleased about the entire situation as you might expect."[198]

Several notes and documents provided by Paterno's attorney to the Special Investigative Counsel pertain to Sandusky's retirement.[199] One page of these notes, which appear to be in Paterno's handwriting, relate a conversation, or planned conversation, between Paterno and Sandusky concerning Sandusky's coaching future. The notes state:

> We know this isn't easy for you and it isn't easy for us or Penn State. Part of the reason it isn't easy is because I allowed and at times tried to help you with your developing the 2nd Mile. If there were no 2nd Mile then I believe you belief [sic] that you probably could be the next Penn State FB Coach. But you wanted the best of two worlds and I probably should have sat down with you six or seven years ago and said look Jerry if you want to be the Head Coach at Penn State, give up your association with the 2nd Mile and concentrate on nothing but your family and Penn State. Don't worry about the 2nd Mile – you don't have the luxury of doing both. One will always demand a decision of preference. You are too deeply involved in both.[q]

---

[p]Exhibit 3-C (Control Number 03013385).
[q]Exhibit 3-D (JVP000017).

One of the documents provided from Paterno's file is a letter signed by Sandusky, dated May 28, 1999. In the letter Sandusky acknowledged that he would not be the next Penn State football head coach, and outlined options for his future.[r] Sandusky wanted an on-going relationship between the Second Mile and Penn State, as well as continuing "visibility" at Penn State.[200] Sandusky also wanted "active involvement in developing an outreach program featuring Penn State Athletes"[201] and sought "ways for [him] to continue to work with young people through Penn State."[202]

Also in the file was a "Retirement Requests" list from Sandusky.[s] This list included a request for a $20,000 yearly annuity to cover the difference between Sandusky's retiring with 30 years of service and retiring with 35 years of service,[203] and a title reflecting his relationship with Penn State. Sandusky also asked to run a middle school youth football camp.[204] Handwriting on the note states: "Volunteer Position Director – Positive Action for Youth."[205] An employee who worked closely with Paterno for 10 years and knew his handwriting identified this note as written by Paterno.[206]

On June 13, 1999, Curley updated Spanier and Schultz by email advising that Sandusky was leaning toward retirement if Penn State would agree to the $20,000 yearly annuity. Curley noted, "Joe did give him the option to continue to coach as long as [Paterno] was the coach."[t] Curley suggested another option of Sandusky "coaching three more seasons and we get creative with his base salary or some other scheme that makes him whole and then some, but doesn't cost us an arm and a leg," and stated he was not comfortable with the annuity.[207] Curley noted that "[s]ince Joe is okay with [Sandusky] continuing to coach this might make more sense to all concerned."[208] The Special Investigative Counsel did not find evidence that Sandusky's retirement was caused by the May 3, 1998 incident at the Lasch Building.

On June 13, 1999, Curley emailed Spanier and Schultz that he "touched base with Joe and we are in agreement that we should not do anything more for Jerry."[209] Two days later, Curley emailed Spanier that Sandusky appeared headed for taking retirement.[210] The next day, Schultz and Sandusky met to talk "about the supplemental annuity."[211] Schultz's notes say that he told Sandusky "we wanted to help [Sandusky]

---

[r]Exhibit 3-E (JVP000025-26).
[s]Exhibit 3-F (JVP000027).
[t]Exhibit 3-G (Control Number 03014658).

though [sic] this important decision."[212] Undated notes from Paterno indicated: "Jerry Annuity: Take 138 Buy Insurance > amount his retirement fund is worth. Variable Annuity and take full retirement."[213]

On June 17, 1999, Wendell Courtney, the University's then outside legal counsel, provided Curley with a draft "retirement perquisites" agreement for Sandusky that included having the University pay Sandusky a lifetime annuity of $12,000 per year.[214] The draft also provided that Sandusky and Penn State would "work collaboratively in the future in community outreach programs, such as the Second Mile."[215] A June 21, 1999 revision of the agreement added free use for life of "University weight rooms and fitness facilities available to faculty and staff."[216] On June 22, 1999, Sandusky and Curley agreed to revise the permitted use to include "a locker, weight rooms, fitness facilities and training room in the East Area locker room complex."[217]

After an issue arose over the taxation of annual annuity payments, the parties amended the draft agreement to provide Sandusky with a one-time lump sum payment of $168,000. The parties agreed to these terms on June 29, 1999.[u]

### III. Sandusky's Retirement Agreement

Penn State's payroll records show that Sandusky received a $168,000 special payment on June 30, 1999. After tax withholding and other deductions, the net amount was $111,990.18.[218] A senior official in the University Controller's office advised the Special Investigative Counsel that in his many years at the University, he had never heard of a payment being made to a retiring employee like the one made to Sandusky.[219] A retired Senior Vice President who worked at Penn State for over 32 years similarly said he had never heard of this type of lump sum payment being made to a retiring employee.[220] While the $168,000 lump sum payment made to Sandusky at his retirement in 1999 was unusual, the Special Investigative Counsel did not find evidence to show that the payment was related to the 1998 incident at the Lasch Building.

At the same time Sandusky's retirement agreement was being finalized, Curley sought to have him re-employed as an "emergency hire," because Sandusky had been "integrally involved in the planning and instructional aspects of preparation for this coming [1999] football season and is essential to the continuity of the program's success

---

[u] Exhibit 3-H (Control Number 006_0000043).

during this time frame."[221] Curley submitted a request for Sandusky's re-hire on June 30, 1999.[222] Sandusky was re-hired for 95 days at his existing salary plus a six percent cost of living increase.[223]

On August 31, 1999, Sandusky also was awarded "emeritus" rank, which carries with it a number of special privileges including access to the University's recreational facilities.[224] According to Penn State policy, this rank is granted to those who leave and hold the title of professor, associate professor, librarian, associate librarian, senior scientist, or senior research associate, or to personnel classified as executive, associate dean, or director of an academic unit in recognition of their meritorious service to the University.[225] Age and service qualifications also exist.[226] The President may grant or deny emeritus rank on "an exception basis."[227]

When he retired, Sandusky held the positions of assistant football coach and assistant professor of physical education, neither of which are among the positions listed as eligible for emeritus rank. On August 13, 1999, the then Assistant Vice President of Human Resources sent a fax to the Dean of the College of Health and Human Development ("Dean").[228] The fax included a draft memo from Schultz to Spanier that contained handwritten edits that changed the name of the memo's originator from Schultz to the Dean.[229] The former Dean did not recall the request but advised the Special Investigative Counsel that the request did take an unusual path.[230] The former Assistant Vice President, after being shown the Sandusky emeritus paperwork by the Special Investigative Counsel, said it was clear the request had come from Schultz or at least Schultz's office and was forwarded by the former Assistant Vice President to the former Dean for submission.[231]

When the Provost's office received the emeritus request, the staff conducted research to see if similar situations existed.[232] While not able to find "specific precedent," the staff found itself in a "bind" as Spanier had promised the emeritus rank to Sandusky.[233] A contemporaneous email from a staff member to the Provost explained that:

> [Spanier] told [Sandusky] that we would do this – he was wholly within his rights here since the policy [HR 25] says "The President may grant (or deny) Emeritus Rank on an exception basis" – then informed [Curley], who suggested going through the college and went to [the Dean], who then made the request of

60

us. (I had wrongly assumed all along that the request originated with [the Dean].)[v]

On August 31, 1999, Rodney Erickson, who had been Provost since July 1, 1999, honored Spanier's promise to grant Sandusky emeritus rank given the President's broad discretion under the policy.[234] He told the staff member that he hoped that "not too many others take that careful notice."[235] In an interview with the Special Investigative Counsel, Erickson described feeling "uneasiness" about the decision on Sandusky because of Sandusky's low academic title and the prior history of who was granted emeritus rank.[236] While the decision to grant Sandusky emeritus rank was unusual, the Special Investigative Counsel found no evidence to show that the emeritus rank was related to the 1998 events at the Lasch Building.

---

[v] Exhibit 3-I (Control Number RAE_000001).

# CHAPTER 4
# RESPONSE OF UNIVERSITY OFFICIALS TO THE ALLEGATION OF CHILD SEXUAL ABUSE AGAINST SANDUSKY – 2001

## KEY FINDINGS

- In the Fall of 2000, a University janitor observed Sandusky sexually assault a young boy in the East Area Locker Building and advised co-workers of what he saw. Also that evening, another janitor saw two pairs of feet in the same shower, and then saw Sandusky and a young boy leaving the locker room holding hands. Fearing that they would be fired for disclosing what they saw, neither janitor reported the incidents to University officials, law enforcement or child protection authorities.
- On Friday, February 9, 2001, University graduate assistant Michael McQueary observed Sandusky involved in sexual activity with a boy in the coach's shower room in the University's Lasch Building. McQueary met with and reported the incident to Paterno on Saturday, February 10, 2001. Paterno did not immediately report what McQueary told him, explaining that he did not want to interfere with anyone's weekend.
- McQueary testified that he reported what he saw to Paterno because "he's the head coach and he needs to know if things happen inside that program and inside that building." He said that Paterno's response was that he [Paterno] needed to "tell some people about what you saw" and would let McQueary know what would happen next. After Sandusky's arrest, Paterno told a reporter that he told McQueary, "I said you did what you had to do. It's my job now to figure out what we want to do."
- On Sunday, February 11, 2001, Paterno met with and reported the incident to Curley and Schultz.
- On Sunday, February 11, 2001, Schultz reached out to then University outside legal counsel Wendell Courtney to discuss the "reporting of suspected child abuse." Courtney conducted legal research on this issue and had another conference with Schultz about it that day.
- On February 12, 2001, Schultz and Curley met with Spanier to give him a "heads up" about the report concerning Sandusky. Spanier said this meeting was "unique" and that the subject matter of a University employee in a shower with a child had never come up before

- A contemporaneous "confidential" note of a February 12, 2001 meeting between Schultz and Curley reflects that the men "[r]eviewed 1998 history." The note states that Schultz and Curley "[a]greed [Curley] will discuss w JVP [Paterno] & advise we think [Curley] should meet w JS [Sandusky] on Friday. Unless he confesses to having a problem, [Curley] will indicate we need to have DPW [Department of Public Welfare] review the matter as an independent agency concerned w child welfare." Without ever speaking to McQueary, Schultz and Curley had already decided that not reporting Sandusky's conduct to authorities may be an option.
- On February 12, 2001, Schultz asked University Police Chief Tom Harmon if a police report still existed of the 1998 incident. Harmon replied that it did.
- By February 12, 2001, Schultz and/or Curley had: met with Paterno who reported what McQueary had told him; had a "heads up" meeting with Spanier advising him about the incident; discussed the "reporting of suspected child abuse" with outside counsel; reviewed the history of the 1998 incident; checked to see if the incident was documented in police files; agreed that Curley would discuss with Paterno the idea of approaching Sandusky to see if he would "confess to having a problem;" and researched the Board membership of the Second Mile.
- There is no information indicating that Spanier, Schultz, Paterno or Curley made any effort to identify the child victim or determine if he had been harmed.
- At a February 25, 2001 meeting, Spanier, Schultz, and Curley discussed an action plan for addressing the Sandusky incident. Schultz's handwritten notes from this meeting indicate: "3) Tell chair* of Board of Second Mile 2) Report to Dept of Welfare. 1) Tell JS [Sandusky] to avoid bringing children alone into Lasch Bldg* who's the chair??"
- On February 26, 2001 Schultz emailed Curley, confirming the plan from the prior day's meeting. This email and several that follow are written in unusually cryptic tones, without the use of proper names or titles.
- On February 27, 2001, however, after discussing the matter with Paterno the day before, Curley recommended a different course of action to Spanier and Schultz: they would offer Sandusky "professional help;" assist him in informing "his organization" (the Second Mile) about the allegation; and, if Sandusky was "cooperative," not inform the Department of Public Welfare of the allegation.
- Advising Sandusky that the February 9, 2001 assault in the Lasch Building had been reported exposed the victim to additional harm because only Sandusky knew his identity.

- On March 5, 2001, Curley met with Sandusky and told him: we are "uncomfortable" with this information about the incident, that he was going to report the incident to the Executive Director of the Second Mile; and that Sandusky was not to be in athletic facilities with any young people. According to Sandusky's counsel, Curley never accused Sandusky of abusing children or used the words "sex" or "intercourse" during the discussion.
- Schultz and Spanier, having prior knowledge of the 1998 child sex abuse allegation against Sandusky, approved Curley's revised plan. Spanier noted in an email that the "only downside for us is if the message isn't 'heard' and acted upon, and we then become vulnerable for not having reported it. But that can be assessed down the road. The approach you outline is humane and a reasonable way to proceed."
- Curley met with the Second Mile executive director in March 2001, and reported that an unidentified person saw Sandusky in the locker room with a young boy, was "uncomfortable" with the situation, and that Curley had discussed the incident with Sandusky and determined nothing inappropriate had occurred.
- Curley told the Second Mile's executive director that Sandusky would not be permitted to bring children onto the Penn State campus in order to avoid publicity issues; Curley also asked the executive director to emphasize that to Sandusky.
- The Second Mile executive director informed two Second Mile Trustees about the incident involving Sandusky and they concluded it was a non-incident for Second Mile and there was no need for further action.
- The Second Mile executive director also met with Sandusky and passed on Curley's prohibition about bringing children on campus. Sandusky replied that the prohibition applied only to the locker rooms.
- Board meeting, March 15-16, 2001: There is no record that the President briefed the Board about the ongoing investigation of Sandusky.
- On September 21, 2001, Schultz obtained Board approval for the sale of a parcel of Penn State land to the Second Mile. The Board minutes do not reflect any contemporaneous discussion of the 2001 investigation, the propriety of a continuing relationship between Penn State and the Second Mile, or the risks involved by allowing Sandusky to be prominently associated with Penn State. Schultz even issued a press release about the transaction lauding Sandusky.
- After the February 2001 incident, Sandusky engaged in improper conduct with at least two children in the Lasch Building. Those assaults may well have been prevented if Spanier, Schultz, Paterno and Curley had taken additional actions to safeguard children on University facilities.

## I. Janitors' Observations of Sandusky – 2000

According to the testimony of witnesses in Gerald A. Sandusky's ("Sandusky") trial in Centre County in June 2012,[237] in the Fall of 2000, a temporary University janitor ("Janitor A")[238] observed a man, later identified to him as Sandusky, in the Assistant Coaches' locker room showers of the Lasch Building with a young boy in the Fall of 2000. Sandusky had the boy pinned against the wall and was performing oral sex on him. The janitor immediately told one of his fellow janitors ("Janitor B") what he had witnessed, stating that he had "fought in the [Korean] War...seen people with their guts blowed out, arms dismembered... . I just witnessed something in there I'll never forget."

On that same night, Janitor B observed two pairs of feet in this same shower at the Lasch Building but could not see the upper bodies of the two persons.[239] He waited for the two to finish their shower, and later saw Jerry Sandusky and a young boy, around the age of 12, exit the locker room holding hands.[240] Janitor B frequently saw Sandusky in the Lasch Building after hours, usually accompanied by one or more young boys.[241] Janitor B closely followed Penn State football, and knew Sandusky from watching football games.[242]

A senior janitorial employee ("Janitor C") on duty that night spoke with the staff, who had gathered with Janitor A to calm him down.[243] Janitor C advised Janitor A how he could report what he saw, if he wanted to do so. Janitor B said he would stand by Janitor A if he reported the incident to the police, but Janitor A said, "no, they'll get rid of all of us."[244]

Janitor B explained to the Special Investigative Counsel that reporting the incident "would have been like going against the President of the United States in my eyes."[245] "I know Paterno has so much power, if he wanted to get rid of someone, I would have been gone."[246] He explained "football runs this University," and said the University would have closed ranks to protect the football program at all costs.[247w]

---

w Some individuals interviewed identified the handling of a student disciplinary matter in 2007 as an example of Paterno's excessive influence at the University. The April 2007 incident involved a fight at an off-campus apartment in which several individuals were severely injured by Penn State football players. The former University official responsible for the student disciplinary process, who the Special Investigative Counsel interviewed, perceived pressure from the Athletics Department, and particularly

Later the same night, two of these janitors saw Sandusky in the parking lot, driving by slowly and looking into the windows of the Lasch building.[248] The first time was around 11:00 p.m., the second was around 2:00 a.m.[249] The young boy was not observed with Sandusky at these times. Janitor B thought that Sandusky had returned to determine whether anyone had called the police to report the incident.[250]

## II. McQueary's Observations of Sandusky – 2001

The November 2011 Grand Jury presentment described an incident, observed by Penn State assistant football coach Michael McQueary, of a "sexual nature" between Sandusky and a boy in the Lasch Building that allegedly took place in March 2002. During this investigation, the Special Investigative Counsel found evidence that this incident actually occurred on or about February 9, 2001 and promptly reported this information to the Pennsylvania Attorney General's Office.[251]

McQueary testified at a December 2011 Grand Jury hearing, and again on June 12, 2012 at Sandusky's criminal trial, about what he saw. At the time of the incident, McQueary was a graduate assistant with the football program and had gone to the support staff locker room in the Lasch Building around 9:00 or 9:30 p.m. on a Friday night.[252] Upon opening the locker room door, McQueary heard "rhythmic slapping sounds" from the shower.[253] McQueary looked into the shower through a mirror and saw Sandusky with a "prepubescent" 10- or 12-year-old boy.[254] McQueary saw Sandusky "directly behind" the boy with his arms around the boy's waist or midsection.[255] The boy had his hands against the wall, and the two were in "a very sexual position."[256] McQueary believed Sandusky was "sexually molesting" the boy and "having some type of intercourse with him" although he "did not see insertion nor was there any verbiage or protest, screaming or yelling."[257]

McQueary testified that he slammed his locker shut and moved toward the shower.[258] He said Sandusky and the boy separated and looked directly at McQueary

---

the football program, to treat players in ways that would maintain their ability to play sports, including during the 2007 incident.[-] Interview (3-9-12) When the Student Affairs Office ("SAO") sanctioned the players involved, the sanctions were subsequently reduced by Spanier to enable players to participate in football practice. [-] Interview (3-22-12) A senior staff member in the SAO advised that his office handles over 4,000 cases a year of off-campus student conduct violations. [-] Interview (12-12-11) In all of the cases he has managed over the years, this incident and one other involving a football player were the only incidents in which issued sanctions were reduced. [-] Interview (12-12-11); [-] Interview (3-22-12)

without saying a word.[259] Seeing the two had separated, McQueary said he "thought it was best to leave the locker room."[260] McQueary went to his office and called his father[x] for advice.[261] He then went to his father's house to discuss the matter further.[262] The two decided McQueary should tell Head Football Coach Joseph V. Paterno ("Paterno"), who was McQueary's immediate superior, about the incident.[263]

McQueary testified that he called Paterno at home around 7:30 or 8:00 a.m. the next morning and told him that he needed to meet with him.[264] McQueary recalled Paterno said he did not have a job for McQueary,[y] so "if that's what it's about, don't bother coming over."[265] McQueary told him the matter was "something much more serious"[266] and Paterno agreed to a meeting. McQueary went to Paterno's home to talk, and according to his Grand Jury and trial testimony, he told Paterno he saw Sandusky and "a young boy in the shower and that it was way over the lines."[267] Recalling the activity as "extremely sexual in nature," McQueary described the "rough positioning" of Sandusky and the boy "but not in very much detail" and without using the terms "sodomy" or "anal intercourse."[268]

Paterno told the Grand Jury in 2011 that he recalled having this discussion with McQueary on a Saturday morning[269] and that McQueary told him he saw Sandusky "fondling, whatever you might call it -- I'm not sure what the term would be -- a young boy" in the showers at the Lasch Building.[270] Paterno explained, "[o]bviously, he was doing something with the youngster. It was a sexual nature. I'm not sure exactly what it was. I didn't push Mike to describe exactly what it was because he was very upset."[271]

McQueary testified that he reported what he saw to Paterno because "he's the head coach and he needs to know if things happen inside that program and inside that

---

[x]John McQueary and his supervisor (a medical doctor) heard Mike McQueary's initial report of the Lasch Building events the evening it happened. Preliminary Hearing Trans. (12-16-11), 134. John McQueary advised his son to report the matter to Paterno, and neither John McQueary nor his boss advised him to immediately call the police. Id. John McQueary later had a conversation with Schultz about what his son saw, and how Schultz handled the situation. Id. The conversation may have come up in discussions John McQueary had with Schultz in mid-May 2001 about a past due amount on a lease for a medical business where John McQueary worked. See Control Number 00675188.

[y]McQueary was hired as a permanent assistant football coach in 2004. The Special Investigative Counsel found no information to suggest that McQueary's selection for that job was related to his witnessing Sandusky assault a boy in the shower room at the Lasch Building. Three witnesses stated that McQueary was very well-qualified for the position. [-] Interview (3-8-2012); [-] Interview (3-12-2012); [-] Interview (3-1-2012).

building."[272] He said that Paterno's response was that he [Paterno] needed to "tell some people about what you saw" and would let McQueary know what would happen next.[273] After Sandusky's arrest, Paterno told a reporter that he told McQueary, "I said you did what you had to do. It's my job now to figure out what we want to do."[274]

No record or communication indicates that McQueary or Paterno made any effort to determine the identity of the child in the shower or whether the child had been harmed.

### III. University Leaders' Response to McQueary's Observations

#### A. February 11, 2001: Paterno Reports Sandusky Incident to Schultz and Curley

Paterno also testified to the Grand Jury that he "ordinarily would have called people right away, [after hearing McQueary's report] but it was a Saturday morning and I didn't want to interfere with their weekends." Paterno thought he spoke to Curley "early the next week" or "within the week."[275] Paterno had a telephone call with Curley and said, "[h]ey, we got a problem, and I explained the problem to him."[276] When asked if the "information that [he] passed along was substantially the same information that [McQueary]" had given him, Paterno said "yes."[277]

Curley testified to the same Grand Jury that Paterno called him on a Sunday and asked him and Schultz to come to Paterno's home[278] where Paterno related that an assistant coach saw "two people" in the shower of the football building locker room.[279] Curley recalled that Paterno said the assistant saw the people through a mirror, "was uncomfortable with the activity in the shower area," and had reported the issue to Paterno.[280]

Schultz testified to the same Grand Jury in 2011 that he attended the meeting with Paterno and Curley and that it occurred in Schultz's office or "possibly" at Paterno's house.[281] Schultz told the Grand Jury that Paterno said "someone" had seen Sandusky and "some unnamed boy" engaging in "some behavior in the football locker room that was disturbing." He testified, "I believe the impression I got was it was inappropriate and he wanted to bring that to Tim Curley and my attention."[282] Schultz did not recall Paterno's precise words, and said Paterno described the events "in a very general way."[283] Schultz thought the conduct might involve "wrestling around activity" and Sandusky "might have grabbed the young boy's genitals or something of that sort."[284] Schultz said the "allegations came across as not that serious. It didn't appear at that time, based on what was reported, to be that serious, that a crime had occurred. We had no indication a crime had occurred."[285]

## B. February 11, 2001: Schultz Discusses "Reporting of Suspected Child Abuse" with University's Outside Legal Counsel

On Sunday, February 11, 2001, Schultz had a conference call about the "reporting of suspected child abuse" with Penn State's then outside legal counsel, Wendell Courtney.[z] Courtney conducted legal research on this issue and had another conference that day with Schultz about the matter.[286] Courtney charged 2.9 hours of time to Penn State for his legal work. Courtney's work on the 2001 matter is confirmed in an email Courtney sent to Schultz in 2011 when Penn State received subpoenas for testimony by Schultz and others concerning the criminal investigation of Sandusky.[aa]

Nearly 10 years later, on January 10, 2011, Courtney emailed Schultz and said, *"Gary - Cynthia Baldwin called me today to ask what I remembered about JS issue I spoke with you and Tim about circa eight years ago* [emphasis added]. I told her what I remembered. She did not offer why she was asking, nor did I ask her. Nor did I disclose that you and I chatted about this."[287] The initials "JS" in Courtney's 2011 email appear to indicate Jerry Sandusky.

Courtney served as Penn State's outside legal counsel for 28 years and was a partner at a law firm that performed legal work for the University for nearly 50 years. Based on the advice of counsel, Courtney declined to be interviewed by the Special Investigative Counsel. Thus, the Special Investigative Counsel was unable to learn Courtney's explanation about the legal work he performed on February 11, 2001.

## C. February 12, 2001: Initial Response of Spanier, Schultz and Curley to Sandusky Incident

After the Commonwealth brought criminal charges against Schultz in November 2011, Schultz's assistant removed some of the Sandusky files from Schultz's Penn State office and delivered them to Schultz. The assistant failed to disclose in two interviews with the Special Investigative Counsel that the Sandusky files had been removed.[288]

---

[z] Exhibit 5-A (McQuaide Blasko documents).
[aa] Exhibit 5-B (Control Number 11118161).

Only in May 2012 did the existence of these important files come to light so that the documents could be retrieved.[289]

Schultz's handwritten notes, which he marked as "confidential," reflect a Monday, February 12, 2001 meeting with Curley to discuss the Sandusky allegations. According to Schultz's notes, Curley and Schultz talked and first "[r]eviewed 1998 history."[bb] The notes state that Schultz and Curley "[a]greed [Curley] will discuss w JVP & advise we think [Curley] should meet w JS on Friday. Unless he 'confesses' to having a problem, TMC will indicate we need to have DPW review the matter as an independent agency concerned w child welfare."[290] The initials "JVP" in Schultz's notes appear to indicate Joseph V. Paterno. The initials "JS" in Schultz's notes appear to indicate Jerry Sandusky. The initials "TMC" appear to indicate Curley.

In an interview with the Special Investigative Counsel, Spanier said that he met with Schultz and Curley to discuss Sandusky around 2:30 p.m. on February 12, 2001.[291] Spanier said the men gave him a "heads up" that a member of the Athletic Department staff had reported to Paterno that Sandusky was in an athletic locker room facility showering with one of his Second Mile youth after a workout. Sandusky and the youth, according to Spanier, were "horsing around" or "engaged in horseplay."[292] Spanier said the staff member "was not sure what he saw because it was around a corner and indirect."[293] Spanier said this meeting was "unique" and that the subject matter of a University employee in a shower with a child had never come up before.[294] Spanier also said that he did not ask, nor did Schultz or Curley define, what was meant by "horsing around" or "horseplay."[295]

Spanier said he asked two questions: (i) "Are you sure that it was described to you as horsing around?" and (ii) "Are you sure that that is all that was reported?"[296] According to Spanier, both Schultz and Curley said "yes" to both questions. Spanier said the men agreed that they were "uncomfortable" with such a situation, that it was inappropriate, and that they did not want it to happen again.[297] Spanier says he asked Curley to meet with Sandusky and tell him that he must never again bring youth into the showers. Spanier said the men also agreed to inform the Second Mile that this direction was given to Sandusky and "we did not wish Second Mile youth to be in our showers."[298] Spanier said there was no mention of anything abusive or sexual, and he

---

[bb]Exhibit 5-C (Schultz documents).

was not aware of the hour of day, the specific building involved, the age of the child, or any other prior shower incident.[299] Spanier also said he did not ask for such details.

When then-Penn State General Counsel Cynthia Baldwin first heard that the Attorney General's office planned to subpoena Schultz, Paterno, and Curley to appear before the Grand Jury, she called Spanier to inform him of the news.[300] Baldwin's notes from this call on December 28, 2010 reflect that Baldwin informed Spanier of the situation.[301] Baldwin's notes of the call reflect that Spanier said he "[m]ay have consulted w/Wendell when Tim, Gary & Graham spoke" when he first heard of the 2001 incident.[302]

On February 12, 2001, at about 11:10 a.m., Schultz researched the internet about the Board members of the Second Mile, the charitable organization Sandusky founded.[303] On February 12, 2001, Schultz also asked Penn State University Police Chief Tom Harmon if a police file still existed for the 1998 event.[304] At 9:56 p.m., Harmon emailed Schultz to report, "[r]egarding the incident in 1998 involving the former coach, I checked and the incident is documented in our imaged a[r]chives."[cc]

By February 12, 2001, Schultz and/or Curley had: (i) given Spanier a "heads up" concerning a "unique" situation involving Sandusky in the showers with a child;[305] (ii) met with Paterno, who reported to them the "same information" McQueary had given to Paterno; (iii) discussed the "reporting of suspected child abuse" with Penn State's then outside legal counsel and also with Spanier,[306] (iv) reviewed the history of the 1998 Sandusky incident;[307] (v) checked to see if the 1998 police report on Sandusky was documented in University police files;[308] (vi) agreed that Curley would discuss with Paterno the idea about approaching Sandusky to see if he "confesses to having a problem;"[309] and, (vii) researched the Board membership of the Second Mile.[310] There is no indication that Spanier, Schultz, Paterno, Curley or any other leader at Penn State made any effort to determine the identity of the child in the shower or whether the child had been harmed.

### D. Schultz and Curley Meet with McQueary – February 2001

Schultz and Curley did not meet with McQueary to hear directly from him as to what he observed in the Lasch Building shower before taking these actions. McQueary

---

[cc] Exhibit 5-D (Control Number 00675162).

testified at the Grand Jury that he first heard from Curley when Curley called to arrange a meeting to discuss what McQueary had reported to Paterno on a Saturday morning, about "nine or 10" days earlier.[311] Curley could not recall how many days it was after hearing from Paterno that he met with McQueary to get the information directly from him, but he thought it was within a week.[312]

McQueary also testified to the Grand Jury that he met with Schultz and Curley either the same day he received Curley's call or the next day. McQueary said he told the men he saw Sandusky in the shower with a young boy, with Sandusky's arms wrapped around the boy.[313] McQueary said he told the men that the situation was "extremely sexual" and that McQueary "thought that some kind of intercourse was going on."[314] Curley testified to the Grand Jury that McQueary told him he had heard people in the shower who were "horsing around, that they were playful, and that it just did not feel appropriate."[315]

Schultz told the same Grand Jury that he did not recall specifically what McQueary reported, but his impression was that there was some physical conduct, some horsing around, some wrestling that resulted in contact with a boy's genitals in the context of wrestling.[316] Schultz testified that he did not understand the incident to have involved sexual conduct or intercourse.[317]

### E. February 25, 2001: Spanier, Schultz and Curley Meet Again to Discuss Sandusky Incident

On Thursday, February 22, 2001, Schultz sent an email to Spanier and Curley, stating, "Graham, Tim and I will meet at 2:00 p.m. on Sunday in Tim's office."[318] Spanier acknowledged the 2:00 p.m. meeting in an email to Schultz and Curley on February 23, 2001.[319] The February 25 meeting was arranged 12 days after McQueary notified Paterno about seeing Sandusky in the Lasch Building sexually abusing a young boy. McQueary testified before the Grand Jury that he met with Curley and Schultz about "nine or 10" days after the Saturday morning discussion with Paterno.[320]

Among documents that Schultz held confidentially in his office and that had been withheld from the Special Investigative Counsel, were handwritten notes for a meeting on "2/25/01." The notes do not identify who was present for the meeting, but indicate: "3) Tell chair* of Board of Second Mile 2) Report to Dept of Welfare. 1) Tell JS to avoid bringing children alone into Lasch Bldg * who's the chair??"[dd]

Spanier's hardcopy calendar of February 25, 2001 indicates a 2:00 p.m. appointment in "TMC office."[321] Spanier told the Special Investigative Counsel that the February 25 meeting was with only Curley.[322] He denied that Schultz was present.[323] He also denied that any mention was made of the Department of Public Welfare.[324] He stated that Curley was worried about how to handle things if he informed Sandusky that he was forbidden to bring Second Mile youth to Penn State facilities and Sandusky disagreed.[325] Spanier explained that he was concerned with Sandusky because the situation "doesn't look good, I was concerned with what people will think, the visibility and the public relations aspects of it. I was not concerned with criminality. There was no suggestion of anything about abuse or sexual contact."[326]

The next day, on February 26, 2001, Schultz sent an email to Curley confirming the plan from the prior day's meeting. Schultz wrote: "Tim, I'm assuming that you've got the ball to 1) talk with the subject ASAP regarding the future appropriate use of the University facility; 2) contacting the chair of the Charitable Organization; and 3) contacting the Dept of Welfare. As you know I'm out of the office for the next two weeks, but if you need anything from me, please let me know."[ee]

The February 26, 2001 email and related emails that follow among Curley, Schultz and Spanier over the next two days are unique from the hundreds of thousands of other emails reviewed by the Special Investigative Counsel. These messages are the rare documents where proper names and identifying information are replaced with generic references. Spanier told the Special Investigative Counsel that Curley communicated in "code" in sensitive emails because the Athletic Department was notorious for leaks.[327] When Curley communicated about other sensitive issues involving Sandusky, however, he did not use "code" words. For example, emails written between February 25 and February 28, 2001, refer to Sandusky as the "subject,"[328] the "person involved,"[329] or "the person."[330] The emails refer to the Second Mile as "his organization;" and to the Department of Public Welfare as "the other organization"[331] and the "other one."[332] This contrasts with emails written in 1998, concerning the police investigation, in which Curley and Schultz frequently referred to

---

[dd] Exhibit 5-E (Schultz documents).
[ee] Exhibit 5-F (Control Number 00677433).

Sandusky as "Jerry."[333] This also contrasts with emails written in 1999, concerning Sandusky's retirement, where Curley, Schultz and Spanier frequently referred to Sandusky as "Jerry."[334]

On March 22, 2011, Spanier met with members of the Pennsylvania Attorney General's Office accompanied by Baldwin.[335] The General Counsel's notes of that meeting reflect Spanier's statement that Schultz and Curley met with Spanier to explain that an employee had seen Sandusky "horsing around" in a shower with a child and thought they should bring the issue to Spanier's attention.[336] The notes also indicate that Spanier said to Schultz and Curley that if "nothing more detailed was reported, Tim should tell JS that we request that he not bring children into shower again. Since JS no longer employed that we advise chair of Board of Second Mile of what we heard."[337]

**F. February 27-28, 2001: Curley Proposes Revised Response to the Sandusky Incident**

On Tuesday, February 27, 2001, Curley emailed Schultz and Spanier:

I had scheduled a meeting with you this afternoon about the subject we discussed on Sunday. After giving it more thought and talking it over with Joe yesterday-- I am uncomfortable with what we agreed were the next steps. I am having trouble with going to everyone, but the person involved. I think I would be more comfortable meeting with the person and tell him about the information we received. I would plan to tell him we are aware of the first situation. I would indicate we feel there is a problem and we want to assist the individual to get professional help. Also, we feel a responsibility at some point soon to inform his organization and [sic] maybe the other one about the situation. If he is cooperative we would work with him to handle informing the organization. If not, we do not have a choice and will inform the two groups. Additionally, I will let him know that his guests are not permitted to use our facilities. I need some help on this one. What do you think about this approach?[ff][gg]

---

[ff] Exhibit 5-G (Control Number 00679428).
[gg] The Special Investigative Counsel discovered these emails after Joe Paterno died. When the Special Investigative Counsel questioned Paterno's representatives about the emails, they stated that because they did not have the benefit of the emails before Paterno's death, they were unable to inquire with Paterno about the emails.

Several people told the Special Investigative Counsel that Curley is a State College native with a long family history at Penn State, including his father and brothers who worked at Penn State.[338] A senior Penn State official referred to Curley as Paterno's "errand boy."[339] Athletic Department staff said Paterno's words carried a lot of weight with Curley, who would run big decisions by Paterno.[340] Others interviewed described Curley as "loyal to a fault" to University management and the chain of command, someone who followed instructions regardless of the consequences, and someone who avoided confrontation.[341]

Also on Tuesday, February 27, 2001, at 10:18 p.m., Spanier responded to Curley's proposal for dealing with Sandusky. Spanier emailed Curley and Schultz:

> Tim: This approach is acceptable to me. It requires you to go a step further and means that your conversation will be all the more difficult, but I admire your willingness to do that and I am supportive. The only downside for us is if the message isn't "heard" and acted upon, and we then become vulnerable for not having reported it. But that can be assessed down the road. The approach you outline is humane and a reasonable way to proceed.[342]

A reasonable conclusion from Spanier's email statement that "[t]he only downside for us is if the message isn't 'heard' and acted upon, and we then become vulnerable for not having reported it" is that Spanier, Schultz and Curley were agreeing not to report Sandusky's activity.

It also is reasonable to conclude from this email statement that the men decided not to report to a law enforcement or child protection authority because they already had agreed to "report" the incident to Second Mile. Spanier's oral and written statements to the Special Investigative Counsel do not address this "reported it" reference. Spanier told the Special Investigative Counsel that the comment related "specifically and only to [Curley's] concern about the possibility that [Sandusky] would not accept our directive and repeat the practice. Were that the outcome of his discussion I would have worried that we did not enlist more help in enforcing such a directive."[343]

Spanier said that his use of the word "humane" refers "specifically and only to my thought that it was humane of [Curley] to wish to inform Sandusky first and allow him to accompany [Curley] to the meeting with the president of the Second Mile.

Moreover, it would be humane to offer counseling to Sandusky if he didn't understand why this was inappropriate and unacceptable to us."[344]

On Wednesday, February 28, 2001, at 7:12 p.m., Schultz responded to Curley's proposal for dealing with Sandusky. Schultz wrote to Curley and Spanier:

> Tim and Graham, this is a more humane and upfront way to handle this. I can support this approach, with the understanding that we will inform his organization, with or without his cooperation (I think that's what Tim proposed). We can play it by ear to decide about the other organization.[hh]

The "other organization" mentioned by Schultz appears to be a reference to the Department of Public Welfare. Again, at no time did Spanier, Schultz, Paterno or Curley try to identify the child in the shower or whether the child had suffered harm. By advising Sandusky, rather than the authorities, that they knew about the February 9, 2001 assault, they exposed this victim to additional harm because only Sandusky knew the child victim's identity at the time.

On February 28, 2001, Curley emailed Schultz and Spanier, explaining in part that he was "planning to meet with the person next Monday on the other subject."[ii] Spanier replied the same day, telling Curley, "[i]f you need to start in one direction without me, do so. I think we are on the same wavelength and I will support you."[345]

## IV. Curley Meets with Sandusky – March 1998

Curley testified to the Grand Jury that he met twice with Sandusky, as Sandusky did not "initially" admit to being in the shower with a boy.[346] According to Curley's testimony, Sandusky later returned to admit he had been present.[347] Curley said he told Sandusky:

> [a]bout the information that we received, that we were uncomfortable with the information and that I was going to take the information and report it to the executive director of the Second Mile and that I did not want him in the future to be in our athletic facilities with any young people.[348]

---

[hh] Exhibit 5-G (Control Number 00679428).
[ii] Exhibit 5-H (Control Number 00676529).

While Sandusky declined an interview with the Special Investigative Counsel, Sandusky's counsel stated in a telephone call with the Special Investigative Counsel that Sandusky generally agreed with Curley's version of the 2002 incident, which Sandusky thought took place in 2001.[349] Sandusky's counsel said Curley told Sandusky that they had heard Sandusky had been in the shower with a young child, and someone felt this was inappropriate.[350] According to Sandusky's counsel, Curley never used the word sex or intercourse in the discussion.[351] Counsel said Sandusky offered to give the child's name to Curley, but Curley did not accept this invitation.[352] Counsel also said Curley told Sandusky he did not want Sandusky to bring children to the shower any more.[353] Sandusky's counsel said no one accused Sandusky of abusing kids.[354]

On March 7, 2001, Schultz's assistant wrote to Curley, asking if he had updated Schultz on the actions set out in Schultz's February 26, 2001 email.[jj] Before he left for vacation, Schultz had left directions for his assistant to check on this issue.[355] Curley reported to the assistant that he had updated Schultz.[356]

Schultz testified before the Grand Jury that he had the "impression that Tim did follow through and make sure Jerry understood that he was no longer permitted to bring Second Mile children into the football facility."[357] Penn State's General Counsel's notes from a March 2011 conversation with Spanier, reflect that Spanier said he "[b]umped into Tim Curley and Tim advised" that he had a conversation with Sandusky not to bring children into the shower again.[358]

Spanier told the Special Investigative Counsel that a "few days after the brief Sunday interaction, [he] saw [Curley] and he reported that both of the discussions had taken place, that those discussions had gone well and our directive accepted, and that the matter was closed."[359] Spanier did not know whether Sandusky ever received counseling.[360]

Paterno gave the following explanation to a reporter for the *Washington Post* as to why he did not more aggressively pursue the information that McQueary provided. "I didn't know exactly how to handle it and I was afraid to do something that might jeopardize what the University procedure was. So I backed away and turned it over to some other people, people I thought would have a little more expertise than I did. It

---

[jj]Exhibit 5-I (Control Number 00674655).

didn't work out that way." Paterno added, "In hindsight, I wish I had done more" and regretted that he had not.[361]

## V. March 19, 2001: Curley Meets with Second Mile Leadership

Curley testified at the Grand Jury that he met "the executive director of the Second Mile. I shared the information that we had with him." The Special Investigative Counsel found no written records concerning this meeting.

The Second Mile executive director declined to be interviewed. Counsel for the Second Mile told the Special Investigative Counsel, however, that the executive director told him that the executive director had a calendar entry for a meeting with Curley on March 19, 2001.[362] He also told counsel that during the executive director's meeting with Curley that Curley related that an unidentified person saw Sandusky in the locker room shower on campus with a boy and felt uncomfortable with the situation;[363] and that Curley had discussed the issue with Sandusky and concluded that nothing inappropriate occurred.[364] According to Counsel for the Second Mile, Curley told the executive director, that "to avoid publicity issues," the University would not permit Sandusky to bring kids on campus.[365] Curley also told the executive director that he was telling Second Mile so that the executive director could emphasize the issue to Sandusky.[366]

The executive director later advised two Second Mile Trustees of the meeting, and they concluded the matter was a "non-incident for the Second Mile and there was no need to do anything further."[367] He also talked to Sandusky, who admitted showering with boys but nothing more.[368] The executive director passed on Curley's advice on the prohibition against bringing kids on campus, and Sandusky responded that it applied only to the locker rooms.[369] The executive director urged him to get the issue clarified.[370]

## VI. University Officials Do Not Notify the Board of the Sandusky Incident

The Penn State Board of Trustees ("Board" or "Trustees") met on March 15 and 16, 2001. Nothing in the Board records or interviews of Trustees indicate any contemporaneous discussions of the 2001 Sandusky incident and investigation during the meeting. The Board did not have a process or committee structure at that time for receiving regular reports from University officials about matters of potential risk to the University, such as the allegation against Sandusky.

On July 24, 2001, Schultz met with leaders of the Second Mile and agreed to sell a parcel to the Second Mile for $168,500.[371] The University had bought the property in 1999 for $168,500.[372] On September 21, 2001, less than eight months after the Sandusky incident, the Board approved the sale of a parcel of land to the Second Mile.[373] Nothing in the Board's records or interviews of Trustees indicate any contemporaneous discussions of the 2001 Sandusky incident and investigation, the propriety of a continuing relationship between Penn State and the Second Mile, or the risks created by a public association with Sandusky when the land transaction was discussed. Schultz, who oversaw the transaction, did not make any disclosure of the Sandusky incident during the Board's review of the land deal. In fact, Schultz approved a press release, issued September 21, 2001 announcing the land sale in which he praised Sandusky for his work with Second Mile. [374]

## VII. Sandusky's Criminal Activity After 2001

The Centre County jury convicted Sandusky in June 2012 of assaulting two boys at Penn State's football facilities and other places on campus after February 2001. These assaults occurred against Victim 3 (assaults on various dates from July 1999 to December 2001 in the Lasch Building and at other places) and Victim 5 (assault in August 2001 in the Lasch Building).

At the preliminary hearing, Curley agreed that there was no "practical way to enforce [Sandusky] not bringing children onto the campus" after he was warned not to do so.[375] There is no indication that Spanier, Schultz, Paterno, or Curley had discussions about any other enforceable actions that could have been taken to safeguard children. Spanier told the Special Investigative Counsel that he did not do anything to prohibit Sandusky from using Penn State facilities, nor did he instruct anyone else to do so.[376]

# CHAPTER 5
# RESPONSE OF UNIVERSITY OFFICIALS TO THE GRAND JURY INVESTIGATION - 2010, 2011

## KEY FINDINGS

- In early 2010 the Pennsylvania Attorney General, in connection with a Grand Jury investigation of Sandusky, issued subpoenas to the University for certain documents; in late 2010 the Grand Jury issued subpoenas for Spanier, Schultz, Paterno, Curley and various members of the Athletic Department in relation to a Grand Jury investigation of Sandusky for child sexual abuse.
- In 2011, Spanier, Schultz, Paterno, Curley and various members of the Athletic Department testified before the Grand Jury. The Grand Jury appearances and the Sandusky investigation were reported in a news story on March 31, 2011.
- Neither Spanier nor the University's General Counsel, Cynthia Baldwin, briefed the Board of Trustees about the Grand Jury investigation of Sandusky or the potential risk to the University until the Board's meeting on May 11, 2011 and, then, only at the request of a Trustee who had read the March 31, 2011 article.
- After receiving a Trustee's request for more information about the Grand Jury investigation, Spanier emailed Baldwin noting that "[the Trustee] desires near total transparency. He will be uncomfortable and feel put off until he gets a report."
- At the May 2011 Board meeting, Spanier and Baldwin briefed the Board about the investigation, but minimized its seriousness by not fully describing the nature of the allegations or raising the issue of possible negative impact to the University.
- From March 31 – November 4, 2011, the Board did not make reasonable inquiry of Spanier or Baldwin about the Sandusky investigation or potential risks to the University.
- The Board did not take steps that might have protected the University, such as conducting an internal investigation, engaging experienced criminal counsel, or preparing for the possibility that the results of the Grand Jury investigation could have a negative impact on the University.
- Spanier and Baldwin opposed an independent investigation of the Sandusky issue, with Baldwin stating that "[i]f we do this, we will never get rid of this [outside investigative] group in some shape or form. The Board will then think that they should have such a group." Spanier agreed.

- Even after criminal charges were announced against Schultz and Curley in November 2011, Spanier continued to downplay the serious harm that could result to Penn State's reputation from the criminal charges, and issued a statement of "unconditional support" for Schultz and Curley.
- Within a few hours of the criminal charges becoming public, staff members advised Spanier that the Board needed to be updated. Spanier said that any briefing "will be nothing more than what we said publicly."
- Only after the presentment of criminal charges in November 2011 did the Board call for a Special Investigations Task Force to perform an independent investigation into the allegations, and to challenge Spanier's and Paterno's actions and failures.
- Until Sandusky's arrest in November 2011, Curley continued to invite him to numerous high-profile athletic events at the University, many of which he attended. During the Spring of 2011, Baldwin advised some University personnel that Sandusky's access to the Lasch Building could not be terminated because of his emeritus status and the fact that he had not been convicted of a crime.
- The Board was unprepared to handle the crisis that occurred when Sandusky, Curley and Schultz were charged. This contributed significantly to its poor handling of the firing of Paterno, and the subsequent severe reaction by the Penn State community and the public to the Board's oversight of the University and Paterno's firing.

## I. Subpoenas Issued for the Grand Jury Testimony of Senior University Officials

On January 7, 2010, the Grand Jury issued a subpoena seeking production of all the University employment and personnel records for Gerald A. Sandusky ("Sandusky").[377] The Penn State employee handling the subpoena consulted with a lawyer at McQuaide Blasko, the State College law firm that served at the time as outside legal counsel for Penn State, about how to respond to the subpoena.[378] This lawyer, who had no grand jury experience, then spoke with colleague Wendell Courtney, although this lawyer told the Special Investigative Counsel that they did not discuss any potential reason for the subpoena or any prior incidents involving Sandusky.[379] The lawyer also did not discuss the nature of the investigation with anyone from the Attorney General's Office.[380]

Through McQuaide Blasko, Penn State agreed with the Attorney General's Office on a non-disclosure order concerning the subpoena.[381] At the time, Penn State staff compiled a list of all persons who knew of the subpoena, which included Spanier, Paterno and Curley.[382]

On September 16, 2010, a *Patriot-News* reporter contacted Spanier. The two exchanged emails as to Spanier's knowledge of an investigation of Sandusky for suspected criminal activity while he was a Penn State employee.

On December 22, 2010, the McQuaide Blasko lawyer called then-University General Counsel Baldwin to inform her that a prosecutor from the Attorney General's Office had called McQuaide Blasko to say that the Grand Jury would like to hear testimony from "some very important people" at Penn State.[383] The lawyer also provided Baldwin with background information about the January 2010 subpoena.[384]

On December 28, 2010, at 9:30 a.m., Baldwin spoke with two prosecutors from the Attorney General's office, who explained that the office would be issuing subpoenas for Schultz, Paterno and Curley to appear before the Grand Jury.[385] Baldwin explained in an interview with the Special Investigative Counsel that she asked if the University or its staff were targets of the investigation.[386] According to Baldwin, the prosecutors said that they were looking at Sandusky, although Baldwin's notes of the conversation do not reflect discussion of this issue.[387] Baldwin did not seek the assistance of an attorney experienced in addressing criminal investigations or conducting internal investigations at that time.

At 9:45 a.m. on December 28, 2010, Baldwin informed Spanier of the situation.[388] Baldwin's notes of the call reflect: "[m]ay have consulted w/Wendell when Tim, Gary & Graham spoke."[389] At 10:01 a.m., Baldwin[390] met with Spanier and Schultz.[391]

On December 28, 2010, after Schultz spoke to Baldwin, he contacted Courtney.[392] On December 30, 2010, Courtney emailed Schultz, "[t]he attached is the last thing in my Penn State file re Sandusky. There is nothing regarding the issues we discussed."[393] The attachment to the email was a 1999 letter concerning Sandusky's retirement.[394]

On Monday, January 3, 2011, Baldwin met with Paterno.[395] Baldwin's notes indicate that Paterno recalled McQueary coming to see him on a Saturday morning.[396] According to the notes, Paterno said McQueary "[s]aw Jerry horsing around w the kid a young man in shower inappropriate behavior. Turned it over to Tim Curley. Notified Tim Curley didn't talk to Gary. No conv. since then."[397] Baldwin told the Special Investigative Counsel that she did not investigate the Sandusky matter or look for Schultz, Paterno or Curley emails in the University system that might relate to the Grand Jury's investigation.[398] Baldwin also met with Curley on January 3, 2011.

On January 3, 2011, a Pennsylvania State Police commander visited the University Police Department and reported that an investigation of "sexual allegations against a small child" involving Sandusky had been ongoing for the past year.[399] The commander said they were "wrapping everything up but were also collecting any and all reports of similar situations."[400] The University Police Department provided the commander with a copy of the 1998 police report.[401]

The next day, January 4, 2011, when Baldwin learned that the State Police had received a copy of the 1998 police report,[402] she asked the University Police Department for a copy of the report.[403] Baldwin told the Special Investigative Counsel that she reviewed the 1998 report to find out what happened and if there had been a full investigation.[404]

On January 9, 2011, Baldwin reached out to Courtney about the Grand Jury investigation. Courtney responded by email to Baldwin stating:

We don't have any file on the matter you and I discussed yesterday, and my recollection of events is as I stated yesterday. However, I also recall that someone (I don't think this was me, since if it was I would have written documentation of contact) contacted Children and Youth Services to advise of the situation so that they could do whatever they thought was appropriate under the circumstances, while being apprised of what PSU actions were, i.e., advising JS to no longer bring kids to PSU's football locker rooms.[405]

Baldwin advised the Special Investigative Counsel that, unknown to her at the time, Courtney emailed Schultz on January 10, 2011. In Courtney's email to Schultz he reported that: Baldwin "called me today to ask what I remembered about JS issue I spoke with you and Tim about circa eight years ago."[406] In the email Courtney said he told her what he remembered, and added that Baldwin "did not offer why she was asking, nor did I ask her. Nor did I disclose that you and I chatted about this."[407]

On January 11, 2011, Baldwin provided an update to Spanier on the Grand Jury investigation.[408] Baldwin told the Special Investigative Counsel that Spanier was surprised to hear of the subpoenas but was not excited over the matter.[409] Spanier told her that things would be fine.[410]

The next day, on January 12, 2011, Schultz, Paterno and Curley appeared before the Grand Jury. Baldwin told the Special Investigative Counsel that she went to the Grand Jury appearances as the attorney for Penn State,[411] and that she told both Curley and Schultz that she represented the University and that they could hire their own counsel, if they wished.[412]

## A. Law Enforcement Interviews of University Personnel

On February 15, 2011, Baldwin met with several assistant football coaches to interview them about Sandusky, his interactions with young boys, rumors about him in the community and his decision to retire from Penn State.[413] The next day, investigators from the Pennsylvania Attorney General's Office and the Pennsylvania State Police interviewed approximately eight coaches, with Baldwin present.[414] Between interviews, the investigators told Baldwin that they also wanted to interview Spanier so she scheduled that interview for them.[415]

On March 22, 2011, Spanier met with the Attorney General's investigators to answer questions about Sandusky. Baldwin attended the meeting and, according to her notes, the investigators asked Spanier about the 2002[416] incident and how Penn State handled the incident, why Sandusky retired in 1999, and the relationship between Penn State and the Second Mile.[417] On March 24, 2011, the Attorney General's Office issued a subpoena for Spanier to testify before the Grand Jury.[418]

## II. *Patriot-News* Article Reveals Sandusky Investigation – March 2011

On March 28, 2011, Curley received an email from a Harrisburg *Patriot-News* reporter asking about his testimony before the Grand Jury.[419] The reporter told Curley that the paper would be running a story soon about the investigation of Sandusky. Curley advised Baldwin, the Athletic Department and Penn State's communications staffs about the call and impending article.[420] On March 28, 2011, another *Patriot-News* reporter approached Spanier at a budget hearing in Harrisburg to obtain his comments about the story.[421] On March 30, 2011, Spanier received word that the *Patriot-News* would be running a story about a "former football coach" the next day.[422]

On March 31, 2011, the *Patriot-News* ran an article under the headline, "Jerry Sandusky, Former Penn State Football Staffer, Subject of Grand Jury Investigation."[423] The article reported that Sandusky was "the subject of a grand jury investigation into allegations that he indecently assaulted a teenage boy."[424] The article referred to a 2009 incident with a boy at Central Mountain High School and the 1998 incident at Penn State involving Sandusky showering with a 12-year-old-boy in the football building on Penn State's campus.[425] The article also noted that Schultz, Paterno and Curley were among those appearing before the Grand Jury.[426]

The day after the article was published, a Trustee emailed Spanier, asking "[w]hat is the story on allegations against Jerry Sandusky that required testimony by Joe Paterno and Tim Curley, and I heard, also Garry [sic] Schultz? Is this something the Board should know a [sic] be briefed on or what?"[427] Spanier replied by email to the Trustee and copied Baldwin and then Board Chairman Steve Garban. He stated, "I believe that Grand Jury matters are by law secret, and I'm not sure what one is permitted to say, if anything." Spanier told the Trustee he would check with Baldwin on whether it was "permissible" to brief the Board.[428] The next day, Baldwin emailed

Spanier to explain that those who "testify before the Grand Jury are not held to secrecy and can disclose if they so desire."[429] Baldwin offered to put together something for Spanier to provide to the Board.

On April 13, 2011, the Trustee emailed Spanier again and asked, "[w]hat is the outcome on this? I frankly think that, despite grand jury secrecy, when high ranking people at the university are appearing before a grand jury, the university should communicate something about this to its Board of Trustees."[430]

Spanier replied to the Trustee on the same day that he had recently learned "through media reports that the Grand Jury has been investigating for two years and has not yet brought charges. They continue their investigation. I'm not sure it is entirely our place to speak about this when we are only on the periphery of this."[431] Spanier went on to say that Baldwin would report on the issue at the next Board meeting.[432] Spanier separately emailed Baldwin, noting, "[the Trustee] desires near total transparency. He will be uncomfortable and feel put off until he gets a report."[433]

Spanier told the Special Investigative Counsel in July 2012 that the Grand Jury investigation "struck me as a Second Mile issue. This did not strike me as a Penn State issue."[434]

The same day that Spanier responded to the Trustee, he testified before the Grand Jury.[435] Baldwin joined Spanier for his appearance, explaining to the court and Spanier that she represented the University.

In response to the Trustee's emails concerning the Grand Jury investigation, Garban asked for a meeting with Baldwin and Spanier.[436] Garban told the Special Investigative Counsel that he met with Baldwin and Spanier in April 2011.[kk] Baldwin recalled that Spanier provided Garban with an update on the investigation and [437] that Spanier downplayed the Sandusky investigation.[438] Garban recalled Spanier saying "it was the third or fourth Grand Jury and nothing would come of it."[439] Baldwin told the Special Investigative Counsel that she believed that Spanier, as a member of the Board, and Garban, as its then Chair, would have relayed this information to the other Board members.[440]

---

[kk] Emails confirm the meeting was April 17, 2011.

Beyond one Trustee's request that Spanier brief the Board on the Grand Jury investigation of Sandusky, the March 31, 2011 *Patriot News* article went virtually unnoticed by the Board. The article was not disseminated to the full Board and many Board members did not read the article. The Board members who were aware of the article should have inquired further about Sandusky and the possible risks of litigation or public relations issues, and, most importantly, whether the University has effective policies in place to protect children on its campuses.

## III. Board of Trustees Meeting – May 2011

In his interview with the Special Investigative Counsel, Spanier said that at a dinner the evening before the May 12, 2011 Board meeting, he told four Board members about the status of the Sandusky investigation.[441] Spanier stated he told these Trustees at the dinner that he had testified before the Grand Jury.[442] The Special Investigative Counsel re-interviewed the four Trustees present for the dinner. None of the Trustees recalled Spanier mentioning anything at the dinner about the Sandusky Grand Jury or his testimony.[443]

In her interview with the Special Investigative Counsel, Baldwin stated that she provided a briefing on the Sandusky investigation to the Board at its regular meeting on May 12, 2011. Fifty minutes were set aside for the briefing but Baldwin recalled that her report lasted 20 minutes before Spanier directed her to leave. Several Trustees described the briefing as a three to five minute, "oh by the way" presentation, at the end of the day.[444]

In an affidavit Baldwin prepared for the Board in January 2012 to provide her recollection of the May 2011 briefing, she stated that she told the Board that the University did not appear to be a focus of the investigation.[445] Furthermore, she affirmed that she had also explained to the Board: (i) what a grand jury is; (ii) how it works; (iii) the fact that the grand jury process is confidential - although those who testify are free to divulge their testimony; (iv) that Schultz, Paterno, and Curley "had been interviewed" in January 2011 and Spanier "had been interviewed" in April 2011;[446] and (v) that those who testified had been asked about a 2002 incident in the football building.[II] She also stated that she told the Board that the University Police Department,

---

[II]Exhibit 6-A (Baldwin affidavit).

the District Attorney's Office, and Children and Youth Services had investigated an incident involving Sandusky in 1998 and that no charges had been filed.[447]

Baldwin told the Special Investigative Counsel that her affidavit had not been intended to list everything she told the Board.[448] She said that she also explained to the Board that a grand jury could return a "presentment" that, even if not alleging a crime, can nonetheless contain negative information about an institution.[449]

Board members had differing recollections of Baldwin's May 2011 report. Several Trustees had the impression that the Sandusky investigation involved issues at the Second Mile and did not involve Penn State.[450] Several Trustees recalled hearing that this was the third or fourth time a grand jury had investigated Sandusky and took that as an indication that criminal charges were not likely.[451] Some Trustees understood that some Penn State senior administrators had testified,[452] while others did not.[453] A common perception was that this was not an "important" issue for the University and the investigation was not a cause for concern.[454]

Some Trustees faulted Spanier and Baldwin for not informing the Board about the Sandusky investigation in a more useful manner.[455] The common complaint was that Spanier's and Baldwin's May 2011 report to the Board did not address the core question of why four senior Penn State officials needed to appear before the Grand Jury if the investigation did not "involve" Penn State. Their report also did not indicate that the Attorney General's investigators had spent two days interviewing the University's football coaching staff;[456] that the investigators had subpoenaed all emails dating back to 1997 for Spanier, Schultz, Paterno and Curley;[457] that investigators subpoenaed the names of all Penn State Physical Plant employees from 1990;[458] and that more football program staff[mm] were to testify before the Grand Jury.[459]

One Trustee said that Spanier may have been "left to float too freely by himself"[460] because he felt he could fix anything.[461] Other Trustees expressed that Spanier "filtered"[462] issues in the best light of a desired outcome;[463] showed Trustees "rainbows" but not "rusty nails;"[464] and "scripted" or "baked" issues leaving no room to debate issues or confront Spanier even when disagreement arose.[465] One Trustee

---

[mm] On May 12, 2011, the same day as the Board meeting, Baldwin interviewed a football equipment manager who had been approached that day by Attorney General investigators. According to Baldwin's notes, the manager advised her that McQueary had told him "that [McQueary] saw something that changed his life. [McQueary] had to tell Coach Paterno." Control Number 09325388.

called Spanier's "managing of messages" and the Board's reactive nature a "recipe for disaster."[466]

Trustees generally recalled that members asked Baldwin or Spanier few questions about the investigation.[467] The Trustees did not discuss whether the University should conduct an internal investigation to understand the facts and any potential liability issues, engage experienced criminal counsel, or prepare for the possibility that the Grand Jury investigation might result in some criticism of the University or its staff. One Trustee recalled that the Board did not ask for any investigation into the Sandusky issues because, from the way it was presented, the issue did not seem like a matter of concern.[468] In their report to the Board, Spanier and Baldwin significantly downplayed the nature of the Sandusky investigation and the potential damage it could cause the University. Given the information that was presented to them, the Board members did not reasonably inquire if the University had taken any measures to limit Sandusky's access to its facilities.

## IV. University Response to the Presentment and Criminal Charges Against Sandusky, Schultz and Curley - October and November 2011

### A. Baldwin, Spanier and Garban Learn of Presentment and Criminal Charges – October and November 2011

In late October 2011, Baldwin learned from an employee at the Attorney General's Office that "Curley and Schultz will be in our presentment," meaning that Curley and Schultz, two prominent Penn State officials, were about to be indicted.[469] Baldwin advised the Special Investigative Counsel that she understood the charges concerned the "duty to protect" and "reporting abuse." There was no mention of perjury.[470] On October 27, 2011, at 3:43 p.m., Baldwin sent Curley an urgent message to meet her and Spanier that evening.[471] They met at 8:00 p.m. and Baldwin told Curley and Schultz that they may be indicted by the Grand Jury.[472]

On October 28, 2011, Spanier and Baldwin had a series of meetings concerning the charges, including one with the Penn State Communications Office staff.[473] A staff member told the Special Investigative Counsel that during that meeting, Spanier said that he knew Curley and Schultz had done nothing wrong.[474] By 1:00 p.m. on October

28, 2011, Spanier had distributed a draft statement to Garban and the Communications staff that read:

> The allegations about a former coach are troubling, and it is appropriate that they be investigated thoroughly. Protecting children requires the utmost vigilance. With regard to the other indictments, I wish to say that Tim Curley and Gary Schultz have my unconditional support. I have known and worked daily with Tim and Gary for more than 16 years. I have complete confidence in how they have handled the allegations about a former University employee. Tim Curley and Gary Schultz operate at the highest levels of honesty, integrity and compassion. I am confident the record will show that these charges are groundless and that they conducted themselves professionally and appropriately.[475]

Spanier requested input from Baldwin and the Communications staff on the draft.[476] One of the communications staff members stated to the Special Investigative Counsel that the Communications staff member thought the phrase "unconditional support" was "horrendous" but others at the meeting were "sheep" and went along with Spanier's idea.[477] This officer remembered that Spanier said he should back up Curley and Schultz because he had asked them to take care of something, they did it, and something bad happened, and that he should not abandon them merely because things did not turn out well.[478]

In his interview with the Special Investigative Counsel, Spanier stated that the media did not focus on the part of his statement that was empathetic to the victims. When asked if the six words "[p]rotecting children requires the utmost vigilance" sufficiently reflected the harm suffered by children who had been abused on the Penn State campus, Spanier said it was not his "place to jump to any conclusions or declare someone guilty before there was any due process."[479] Spanier said he had not made an effort to investigate the facts concerning Sandusky, and did not want to appear to interfere with the police work.[480]

Spanier and Baldwin met with Garban at noon on October 28, 2011.[481] Baldwin told the Special Investigative Counsel that Garban was the "conduit" to the Board, and Baldwin intended that he pass the information about the charges to the Board members.[482] Garban had a different understanding, however, telling the Special

Investigative Counsel that, in his meeting with Spanier and Baldwin, Spanier said that he still thought nothing would come of the investigation because other grand juries had reviewed the matter without bringing charges.[483]

Over the weekend of October 28-30, 2011, Garban had conversations with Trustees John Surma and Jim Broadhurst and told them what he learned from Spanier and Baldwin.[484] Garban also spoke again with Spanier who told him Baldwin was going to try to convince the Attorney General's Office that they did not have a case.[485] Garban told the Special Investigative Counsel that he was "astounded" to see Sandusky in the Nittany Lion Club at the football game on October 29, 2011, given what he had learned.[486] Neither Garban, Spanier, Broadhurst, Surma nor Baldwin spoke to the remaining Board members about the impending charges until after the charges were filed against Sandusky, Curley and Schultz on November 4, 2011.

Spanier told the Special Investigative Counsel that Baldwin originally had been told that charges would not be brought until November 12, 2011.[487] Spanier said he planned to "scrap" the Board agenda for November 10 and devote the meeting to discussing Sandusky.[488] Spanier said that he took a senior Board staff person into his confidence on November 2 and told that person "we know charges are being brought. We will scrap the Trustee seminar agenda, and devote the day to this matter. It will be good timing, we will get ready."[489] After Spanier's interview, the Special Investigative Counsel re-interviewed the senior Board staff person. The staff person did not recall any conversation with Spanier about scrapping the Board agenda, or about charges that would be filed against Sandusky.[490]

On Friday, November 4, 2011, at 2:26 p.m., newspapers reported that Sandusky had been indicted on charges of indecent assault of minors, among others.[491] The initial stories, however, did not mention charges against Schultz or Curley.[492] The presentment, which was attached to the charging documents, had been inadvertently released on November 4, 2011. On Saturday, November 5, 2011, law enforcement officers arrested Sandusky on the criminal charges, and released a press statement detailing the allegations against Sandusky, Curley, Schultz and others at Penn State.[493]

In his interview with the Special Investigative Counsel, Spanier said that it was his idea to bring the Board together when the presentment was released so the Board could be properly informed.

On November 5, 2011, at 1:41 p.m., a Trustee emailed Spanier and Garban, asking when the Board would be briefed.[494] Ten minutes later, Baldwin advised Spanier that "[i]t may be best to tell [the Trustee] that you are briefing the chair and the Board will be briefed next week."[495] At 2:09 p.m., Spanier wrote to Baldwin, "Steve already said we should alert the Board, but at this point it will be nothing more than what we are saying publicly." Shortly thereafter on that day, Spanier released the statement expressing his "unconditional support" for Curley and Schultz.[496] Spanier remained "confident the record will show that these charges are groundless and that they conducted themselves professionally and appropriately."[497]

**B. Board of Trustees Conference Call - November 5, 2011**

Senior administration staff suggested to Spanier that he brief the Board,[498] and schedule a conference call for 5:00 p.m. on November 5, 2011. According to the Board's notes, Spanier began the call by stating that the charges against Curley and Schultz were erroneous, unfair and unfortunate, and he expected "exoneration."[499] Some Trustees questioned the quality of the University's investigation of the 2002 incident, but Spanier denied that the charges had anything to do with the University's investigative process.[500] One Trustee suggested an "independent investigation" by outside counsel and retention of a crisis management firm.[501] Another Trustee mentioned the employment status of Curley and Schultz.[502] A meeting was called for the next day in which crisis management and legal advisors would make presentations to the Board on how to approach the crisis.[503]

Spanier and Baldwin opposed an independent investigation of the Sandusky issue. Baldwin emailed Spanier that, "[i]f we do this, we will never get rid of this group in some shape or form. The Board will then think that they should have such a group."[504] Spanier agreed.[505]

In meetings with the Special Investigative Counsel, some Trustees recalled that Spanier wanted to wait for the regular Board meeting later in the week to discuss the matter.[506] A Trustee recalled that Spanier said he managed crises every day at Penn State and he could handle this issue.[507]

**C. Board of Trustees Meeting - November 6, 2011**

Garban called another Board meeting for Sunday, November 6, 2011, at 7:00 p.m. According to the Board notes, several members advocated for the formation of a task force to work with outside counsel on crisis management.[508] Other members questioned whether the Board had received the relevant information about the investigation.[509] One Board member suggested that Curley, Schultz and Spanier should be suspended from their duties, but Garban said Spanier should not be suspended.[510] Some Board members also observed that Spanier's public statements did not sufficiently address harm to the victims of Sandusky's crimes.[511]

Later in the evening of November 6, 2011, the University issued another press release stating that Curley asked to be placed on administrative leave and Schultz would re-retire so that both men could devote time to defending themselves.[512] The release also announced that a "task force" would review the University's policies and procedures on the protection of children.[513] The press release on November 7, 2011 reflected that Curley and Schultz had requested and been granted administrative leave. Some Board members were upset with the wording of the release, as they recalled that it was their decision to place Curley and Schultz on administrative leave.[514]

In meetings with the Special Investigative Counsel, several Trustees described the second press release as a "turning point" for Spanier.[515] Changes that Spanier made to the statement after the Board had agreed on its points angered several members.[516] This led some Trustees to grow concerned with Spanier's ability to lead.[517] In an interview with the Special Investigative Counsel, Spanier denied making anything other than minor grammatical changes to the Board's statement.[518]

Some Trustees thought Garban's history of being previously employed at Penn State, where as SVP-FB he reported directly to Spanier, hampered his ability to lead the Board.[519] Garban told the Trustees that he had not advised them about the presentment when he learned of it because he was not sure it would come to fruition.[520]

On November 7, 2011, a Board member questioned whether the prior day's statement reflected the "sense of the Board," and urged the Board to have another meeting.[521]

## D. Board of Trustees Conference Call - November 8, 2011

On November 8, 2011, the Board met again by conference call. Garban announced that he would turn the position of Board Chair over to Vice Chair John Surma. Surma then told the Board that he intended that they discuss forming a special investigative group of the Board, and deliberate on Paterno's and Spanier's leadership.[522]

The Board established the Special Investigations Task Force ("Task Force"). The Board also discussed University leadership,[523] but the members quickly decided that this type of discussion should be held in person.[524] Other members thought that no personnel action should occur until the investigation was completed.[525] The Board reached a consensus to delay decisions until the next day, and to issue a more thorough press release to express the Board's concerns.[526]

During the evening of November 8, 2011, the Board issued its own statement, expressing its outrage over "the horrifying details" of the Sandusky case.[527] The Board stated that it would appoint a special group to examine the circumstances of the charges, including "what failures occurred and who is responsible and what measures are necessary to ensure that this never happens at our University again and that those responsible are held fully accountable."[528] The Board's statement concluded: "We are committed to restoring public trust in the university."[529]

### E. Board of Trustees Meeting - November 9, 2011

The Board met again in person on the evening of November 9, 2011. Surma chaired the meeting.[530] The Board discussed Spanier first, and the consensus was that he would be terminated without cause.[531] Executive Vice President and Provost Rodney Erickson was named interim President.[532]

In interviews with the Special Investigative Counsel, all of the Trustees who participated in the deliberations regarding the personnel actions said the decision concerning Spanier was their clear consensus.[533] The decision to terminate Paterno was more difficult because Board members had different viewpoints about his role. Nevertheless, one Board member stated that each of the Trustees reached the same decision in a different way.[534]

Some Board members felt that Paterno could have done more after learning about Sandusky's activities.[535] Some Board members recall former athletes stating that

Paterno had tremendous control over what happened in his program.[536] Several Board members were disturbed by Paterno's attempt to usurp the Board's role by discussing his retirement plans for the end of the season and holding his own press conference.[537] Others said Paterno could not continue to function as coach in the current environment and had become a distraction.[538]

The Trustees have differing recollections of Governor Thomas Corbett's role in the Board discussion. Some Trustees recall people asking if the Governor was still on the phone line, as he was quiet during parts of the call.[539] Some Trustees, including Corbett himself, said Corbett did not assert himself more than other Trustees. At least one said Surma gave Corbett the opportunity to do so.[540] Some Trustees recall Corbett saying something right before the vote on Paterno along the lines of "I hope you'll remember the children."[541] Others described him as being vocal and playing a leadership role in the meeting.[542] One Trustee recalled Corbett saying that the Board needed to take decisive action or there might be a loss of support for Penn State. Corbett told the Special Investigative Counsel that he did not attend the May briefing on Sandusky and his representatives did not report about the meeting to him. Corbett further told the Special Investigative Counsel that, if he had attended the briefing, he would have asked more questions or prompted other Trustees to ask further questions.

Some Trustees felt that the discussion on Paterno's future with the football program was rushed and not sufficient for the situation.[543] One Trustee said the Board was seeking to act quickly when it instead should have acted in a more deliberate way, with all of the facts.[544] The same Trustee feared "getting in front of the facts."[545] Another Trustee argued for placing Paterno on administrative leave and for balancing the tremendous good Paterno did for Penn State against the "worst mistake of his life."[546] A Trustee commented that it was a sad, but necessary, action the Board had to take.[547] The Board did not explore the range of personnel actions available to them regarding Paterno's role in the football program before the Board concluded that Paterno should be removed as Head Football Coach."[548]

The Board did not have a plan in place to notify Paterno of its decision. None of the Board members seem to have considered alternative times or locations for meeting with Paterno and no one appears to have communicated with him in advance of the Board meeting that evening. In hindsight, some Trustees felt that they should have found a way to go to Paterno's home to notify him in person but at the time they did not feel it was feasible.

Some Trustees were concerned that the crowds and media around Paterno's home precluded having Paterno come to their meeting place or having Trustees go to his home so that they could tell him of its decision. Neither University officials nor the Board contacted local law enforcement about the possible public reaction to its decision, despite the growing crowds on campus and in State College.[549]

Some Trustees also were concerned that the media would report their decision about Paterno before he could be notified. Therefore, in order to inform Paterno of its decision to remove him from his position, the Board directed a staff member from the Athletic Department to deliver a note to Paterno at his home. The note directed Paterno to call a phone number that belonged to Surma. When Paterno called, Surma advised him that the Board was removing him from his position as Head Football Coach. Paterno ended the call without speaking further to Surma. Shortly thereafter, Paterno's wife called Surma to complain about the Board's treatment of her husband. The consequences of this awkward termination resulted in an outpouring of criticism against the Trustees by students, alumni and other Penn State supporters. Students demonstrated on the campus in protest and the media coverage was extraordinary and generally unfavorable.

Most of the Trustees agreed that the Board did not properly handle the termination of Paterno.[550] Some Trustees agreed that the Board was ill-prepared to address the situation.[551]

# CHAPTER 6
# BOARD OF TRUSTEES

## KEY FINDINGS

- The charter, by-laws and standing orders of the Penn State Board state that the Board "shall receive and consider thorough and forthright reports on the affairs of the University by the President or those designated by the President. It has a continuing obligation to require information or answers on any University matter with which it is concerned."
- In 1998 and 2001, the Board of Trustees failed to exercise its oversight and reasonable inquiry responsibilities. In that time, the Board did not have regular reporting procedures or committee structures in place to ensure disclosure to the Board of major risks to the University.
- Because the Board did not demand regular reporting of such risks, the President and senior University officials in this period did not bring major risks facing the University to the Board.
- The Board did not create a 'Tone at the Top' environment wherein Sandusky and other senior University officials believed they were accountable to it.
- Spanier and senior University officials did not make thorough and forthright reports to the Board, which itself equally failed in its continuing obligation to require information or answers on any University matter with which it is concerned.
- Some Trustees reported that their meetings felt "scripted" or that they were "rubber stamping" major decisions already made by Spanier and a smaller group of Trustees.
- After the Sandusky investigation became publicly known in late March 2011, the Board did not independently assess this information or further inquire, up to and including the May 12, 2011 Board meeting.
- After the May 2011 Board briefing on the Sandusky investigation, the Board did not reasonably inquire about this serious matter at Board meetings in July or September 2011.

## I. Board Structure and Responsibilities

Established by Charter, the Board of Trustees ("Board" or "Trustees") of The Pennsylvania State University ("Penn State" or "University") is the corporate body that has complete responsibility for the government and welfare of the University and all the interests pertaining thereto, including students, faculty, staff and alumni.[552]

The Board is composed of 32 members. Five are ex officio members: the University President; Governor of Pennsylvania; and secretaries of the departments of Agriculture, Education, and Conservation and Natural Resources. The Governor appoints six Trustees, the alumni elect nine Trustees, the Commonwealth's agricultural societies elect six Trustees, and the Board elects six members from business and industry groups. Elected terms and appointments begin on July 1 and Trustees serve three-year terms and can be reappointed. The six gubernatorial appointments are staggered with two appointed each year for three-year terms or "until their successors are appointed and confirmed." These appointments are subject to confirmation by the State Senate.[553] On May 16, 2003, the Board adopted term limits of 15 years applicable to alumni, agricultural, and business and industry Trustees.[554] Recently, President Erickson invited five additional representatives of several University constituencies, including alumni, faculty, staff and students, to participate in the University's Board committees and meetings, effective July 2012.

The Board also can confer "Trustee Emeritus" status on any living former member of the Board who served for 12 or more years with distinction. Trustees who served 20 years as of May 13, 2011, are entitled to automatic Emeritus status. Referred to as "Emeritus Trustees" or "Trustees Emeriti," these individuals are entitled to all Trustee privileges except those of making motions, voting and holding office.[555] There are currently 16 Emeritus Trustees.[556]

The Board operates under a Charter, Corporate By-Laws and Standing Orders. In the exercise of its responsibilities, the Board is guided by the following policies:

1. The authority for day-to-day management and control of the University, and the establishment of policies and procedures for the educational program and other operations of the University shall be delegated to the President, and by him/her, either by delegation to, or consultation with, the faculty and the student body in accordance with a general directive of

the Board. This delegation of authority requires that the Board rely on the judgment and decisions of those who operate under its authority. However, this reliance of the Board must be based upon its continuing awareness of the operations of the University. *Therefore, the Board shall receive and consider thorough and forthright reports on the affairs of the University by the President or those designated by the President. It has a continuing obligation to require information or answers on any University matter with which it is concerned.* Finally, upon request the Board shall advise the President on any University matter of concern to him/her. [emphasis added].

2. The Board of Trustees shall carry out certain responsibilities as a Board, without delegation. These responsibilities are:

   a. The selection of the President of the University;

   b. The determination of the major goals of the University and the approval of the policies and procedures for implementation of such goals;

   c. The review and approval of the operating and capital budget of the University;

   d. Such other responsibilities as law, governmental directives, or custom require the Board to act upon.

3. The Board of Trustees shall inform the citizens of the Commonwealth of Pennsylvania of the University's performance of its role in the education of the youth of Pennsylvania.

4. The Board of Trustees shall assist the President in the development of effective relationships between the University and the various agencies of the Commonwealth of Pennsylvania and the United States of America which provide to the University assistance and direction.[557]

The Board provides oversight to the University through its standing committees. As of 1998 the Board had three standing committees: (1) Committee on Educational Policy; (2) Committee on Finance and Physical Plant; and (3) Committee on Campus

Environment.[558] The Board established by Standing Order a Subcommittee for Audit on March 19, 2004, and a Subcommittee for Finance on September 19, 2008.[559]

At its meeting of March 16, 2012, the Board replaced the three standing committees with five new committees: (1) Committee on Academic Affairs and Student Life; (2) Committee on Finance, Business and Capital Planning; (3) Committee on Governance and Long-Range Planning; (4) Committee on Audit, Risk, Legal and Compliance; and (5) Committee on Outreach, Development and Community Relations. Each committee oversees its designated area(s) of responsibility and makes recommendations to the full Board for actions that enhance the functionality of the University.[nn] The Board meets six times each year.[560]

## II. The Board's Duty of Oversight and Reasonable Inquiry

An effective board exercises objective and independent judgment while overseeing systems to ensure that the institution operates according to the law and its governing framework. Under Pennsylvania law concerning non-profit boards, board members have not only a duty of loyalty, but also a duty of care, including "reasonable inquiry, skill and diligence, as a person of ordinary prudence would use under similar circumstances."[561] Indeed, the standing orders of the Penn State Board reflect this duty of inquiry, directing that the Board "shall receive and consider thorough and forthright reports on the affairs of the University by the President or those designates by the President. It has a continuing obligation to require information or answers on any University matter with which it is concerned."[562]

A board can breach its duty when it "utterly fails to implement any reporting or information system or controls" or having implemented such system or controls "consciously fails to monitor or oversee its operations thus disabling themselves from being informed of risks or problems requiring their attention."[563] The board breaches its duty not because a mistake occurs, but because the board fails to provide reasonable oversight in a "sustained or systematic" fashion.[564]

---

[nn] During the course of this investigation, the Special Investigative Counsel interviewed all current members of the Board, the majority of emeriti members and several former members. The Trustee interviews yielded a number of pertinent recommendations that are included in Chapter 10 of this report.

## A. The Board's Failure of Oversight and Reasonable Inquiry in 1998 and 2001

In 1998 and 2001, the Penn State Board failed to exercise its oversight functions. In that time, the Board did not have regular reporting procedures or committee structures in place to ensure disclosure to the Board of major risks. Because the Board did not demand regular reporting of these risks, Spanier and other senior University officials in this period did not bring up the Sandusky investigations. For example, the Board met in May 1998 and March 2001, but was not advised by Spanier regarding the Sandusky incidents. While Spanier failed to disclose these facts, the Board has a continuing obligation to require information about such an important matter. Similarly, in September 2001, the Board approved a favorable land deal to Sandusky's Second Mile, just six months after Sandusky was investigated for assaulting a young boy in the Lasch Building showers. The Board should have elicited such important information from senior University officials before the sale.

Some Trustees reported that their meetings felt "scripted" or that they were "rubber stamping" major decisions already made by Spanier and a smaller group of Trustees."[565] Sometimes Trustees learned of the President's decisions in public meetings where there were no questions or discussions.[566]

## B. The Board's Failure of Reasonable Inquiry in 2011

In 2011, the Board failed to perform its duty of inquiry, especially when it was on notice that the University was facing a major risk involving the Grand Jury investigation. While Spanier and Baldwin's May 2011 briefing to the Board downplayed the nature of the Grand Jury investigation of Sandusky, the Board members did not independently assess the information or demand detailed reporting from Spanier and Baldwin on this serious matter.[567] For example, Spanier and Baldwin indicated that the investigation did not involve the University, yet they did not explain why the Grand Jury called four senior Penn State officials to testify.[568] The Board did not inquire about the details of the Attorney General's investigation, including the request for subpoenas seeking historic email information for Spanier, Schultz, Paterno and Curley. When a Board member asked for more information, Spanier complained about this member, noting to Baldwin that "[the Trustee] desires near total transparency. He will be uncomfortable and feel put off until he gets a report."[569]

After the May 2011 briefing, Board members did not ask for further updates on the investigation at Board meetings in July and September 2011. The Board therefore did not meet its "continuing obligation to require information or answers on any University matter with which it is concerned."[570]

Further, because the Board did not push Spanier and other senior officials on such an important matter, Spanier did not feel accountable for keeping the Board immediately informed on serious developments, such as advance notice that Sandusky, Schultz and Curley faced criminal charges. The Board allowed itself to be marginalized by not demanding "thorough and forthright reports on the affairs of the University."[571]

Spanier's communications reflected his attitude toward keeping the Board informed of major developments. For example, hours after Spanier appeared before the Grand Jury, he communicated with a Trustee who asked about the status of the investigation. Spanier avoided the Trustee's question and asserted that he was "not sure it is entirely our place to speak about this when we are only on the periphery of this."[572] However, Spanier did not disclose that he had just been before the Grand Jury. Within a few hours of the criminal charges becoming public, staff members advised Spanier that the Board needed to be updated. Spanier said that any briefing "will be nothing more than what we said publicly."[573] He considered advising the Board that he was "briefing the Chair and the Board will be briefed next week."[574] When he finally briefed the Board, he focused on issues of alleged bias in the government's investigation, calling the charges "erroneous unfair and unfortunate."[575]

It was only on November 5, 2011, that members of the Board first began to press Spanier about the criminal charges. Noting that the charges presented a picture of a "sexual predator" and "perjury," one Trustee asserted that the Board had a duty of oversight and reporting.

# CHAPTER 7
# SANDUSKY'S POST-RETIREMENT INTERACTIONS WITH THE UNIVERSITY

## KEY FINDINGS

- Despite Spanier's, Schultz's, Paterno's and Curley's knowledge of criminal investigations of Sandusky regarding child abuse as early as 1998, they failed to control Sandusky's access to the University's facilities and campuses. In fact, Sandusky was allowed to have a key for, and continued to work out in, the Lasch Building until November 2011, and had keys to other Penn State facilities.
- Even after the Attorney General's investigation became public in March 2011, former Penn State General Counsel Baldwin said that because of Sandusky's "emeritus" status and because he had yet to be convicted, his access to University facilities could not be terminated.
- Between 2002 and 2008 the University also allowed Sandusky to use the University facilities at the Altoona and Behrend (Erie) campuses to run "Jerry Sandusky" summer football camps for youth. Although University policy required a Memorandum of Agreement (MOA) with all third parties using University facilities, Sandusky, who some admired "like a god" because he was a former football coach, was allowed to operate the camps without any MOA.
- The University continued to support the Second Mile throughout this time by providing facilities and services for the organization's day camps and fund-raisers. Sandusky was a corporate officer, volunteer and public "face" of the Second Mile throughout this time.
- The University's visible support of the Second Mile provided Sandusky with numerous opportunities to bring young boys to campus and to interact with them through various camps and activities.
- After his retirement, Sandusky retained access to the Nittany Lion Club, an exclusive seating area at Beaver Stadium. Sandusky continued to be invited by senior University officials and attend Nittany Lion Club events until his November 2011 arrest.
- If University leaders had not granted Sandusky full use of Penn State's football facilities and supported his ways to "work with young people through Penn State," sexual assaults of several young boys on the Penn State campus might have been prevented.

## I. Sandusky's Ongoing Contacts with The University

After his retirement from Penn State on June 30, 1999, Gerald A. Sandusky ("Sandusky") continued to maintain a prominent relationship with Penn State. Sandusky was able to use that relationship and the privileges he received in his retirement agreement to continue to bring young boys to University facilities and events.

Spanier, Schultz, Paterno and Curley were aware of the allegations against Sandusky in 1998 and 2001. Nonetheless, they put children in danger by permitting Sandusky to participate in these activities and by providing continued support to Second Mile activities.

### A. Sandusky's Continued Access to University Facilities

Sandusky had access to Penn State's exclusive football fitness facilities (i.e., the Lasch Football Building and the East Area Locker Room Building ("Old Lasch")) as part of his retirement agreement,[576] whereas emeritus rank provided him with access only to "University recreational facilities" (among other benefits).[577] Until October 31, 2011, Penn State football staff regularly saw Sandusky working out in the Lasch Building weight room.[578] Sandusky still had keys to the Lasch Building when he was arrested in November 2011.[579] As recently as 2010, Sandusky had a "sub-master" key to the press box at Beaver Stadium, as well as a key for the stadium gates.[580]

The University also provided Sandusky with an office in Old Lasch as a term of his 1999 retirement agreement and emeritus status.[581] Between 2007 and 2008, Sandusky relinquished his office for other sports teams due to a space shortage.[582] Sandusky was able to use this office to store personal notes and documents.[583] University officials were unaware that there were numerous boxes of Sandusky's documents and belongings in Old Lasch until the Attorney General's Office investigators and the Special Investigative Counsel found these documents in April 2012. The documents contained communications between Sandusky and Victim 4, as well as between Sandusky and other victims.

One of Sandusky's documents was a "contract" between Sandusky and Victim 4 that proposed various rewards, including a "possible bowl trip," for personal and school achievements.[584] Victim 4 testified at Sandusky's trial in June 2012 as to the existence of this contract. A former Second Mile counselor who worked with Sandusky at the Penn State camps recalled that Sandusky kept notes about campers during the camps. Campers were given written goals and benchmarks to achieve during the upcoming school year so the camper could return the following summer.[585]

## B. Sandusky's Continued Access to the Nittany Lion Club at Beaver Stadium

After his retirement, Sandusky had regular access to premium season seats for Penn State home football games in the Nittany Lion Club, an exclusive seating area accessible by invitation only.[586] In July 2011, for the first time, Curley deleted Sandusky's name from the annual invitation list for the 2011 football season.[587] In early September 2011, Sandusky's wife called the Nittany Lion Club staff to inquire about his season tickets.[588] The staff brought the issue to Curley, who reversed his previous decision and approved season tickets for Sandusky.[589] On October 7 and 8, 2011, Sandusky participated in the 25th anniversary celebration of the 1986 Penn State national championship team.[590] Sandusky attended six home games in the 2011 season, including the game played the week before criminal charges were filed against him.[591] After his arrest, Sandusky called the Nittany Lion Club and said that he would not attend the last game of the 2011 season.[592]

Several individuals advised the Special Investigative Counsel that, because of his continued attendance at the Nittany Lion Club, they were under the impression that Sandusky was cleared of the allegations in the newspaper reports and was no longer under investigation.[593]

## C. Sandusky's Football Camps at University Campuses

After Sandusky retired, the University allowed him to operate summer youth football camps at University facilities through his company, Sandusky and Associates. Sandusky used two University campuses for his camps, Behrend (in Erie) and Harrisburg. The Behrend campus hosted Sandusky's football camps from 2000 to 2008[594] and the Harrisburg campus hosted the Sandusky Football Camp in 2007 and 2008. Both of these campuses provided athletic and recreational facilities, food and lodging for the camps.

It was standard practice and procedure for the University to enter into a Memorandum of Agreement ("MOA")[595] with all external parties that utilized

University facilities. However, the Sandusky Football Camp repeatedly was allowed access to the Behrend campus for its overnight youth football camps without an MOA. The Behrend campus did obtain an insurance certificate from Sandusky and Associates but required only "a handshake" with him to permit him to run his youth football camps each year from 2000 to 2008.[596] Individuals interviewed by the Special Investigative Counsel stated that, during these years, Sandusky was treated as a celebrity and some University employees admired him "like a god."[597] He did not have to go through the usual administrative procedures because he was a former football coach at Penn State and a well-respected employee for over 30 years.[598]

### D. Sandusky's Continued Business Dealings with the University

The University continued to conduct business with Sandusky after his retirement. According to University accounting records, Penn State made 71 separate payments to Sandusky for travel, meals, lodging, speaking engagements, camps and other activities from January 5, 2000 through July 22, 2008.[599] Some of these activities included a speech at the American Football Coaches Association meeting in 2000,[600] a speech at the 2007 Penn State Leadership Conference for Student Organization leaders,[601] attendance at a 2000 Football Coaches Clinic held at the Behrend campus,[602] presentations at the 2002 Penn State Spring Conference[603] and the 2002 National Association of College and University Food Services Region II Conference.[604] On May 14, 2010, Curley wrote a letter of recommendation for Sandusky for the American Football Coaches Association Outstanding Achievement Award.

### E. Failure to Prohibit Sandusky's Access to University Facilities

Despite Spanier's, Schultz's, Paterno's and Curley's knowledge of criminal investigations of Sandusky regarding child abuse as early as 1998, they failed to control Sandusky's access to the University's facilities and campuses.

After news of the Sandusky investigation appeared in newspapers in March 2011, some members of the Athletic Department staff questioned Sandusky's continued access to athletic facilities.[605] Some members of the Athletics Department staff asked Penn State General Counsel Cynthia Baldwin if Sandusky could be restricted from the athletic facilities.[606][607] She told them that the University could not take his keys.[608]

Baldwin advised the Special Investigative Counsel that because of Sandusky's emeritus status and the fact that he had not been charged with a crime, his access could not be eliminated without the University being sued.[609] However, Baldwin said that she believed that either Curley or another Athletic Department staff member was going to ask Sandusky to return his keys voluntarily. Baldwin did not recall any further discussion of the topic until Sandusky was charged.[610] At that time, Baldwin requested a human resources supervisor in the Athletic Department to ask Sandusky's lawyer for Sandusky's keys.[611] Before that was done, however, the University changed the locks on the building so that Sandusky would no longer have access.[612][613] The supervisor told the Special Investigative Counsel that the supervisor did not know if Sandusky ever returned his keys.

## II. Sandusky's Post-Retirement Involvement In Second Mile Activities

### A. Penn State and the Second Mile Organization

The Second Mile is a non-profit organization for underprivileged youth founded by Sandusky in 1977, when he was the Defensive Coordinator for the Penn State football team. Second Mile began as a group foster home for the purpose of helping troubled boys. Over the years, it evolved into a statewide, three-region charity dedicated to the welfare of children. Since its founding, Second Mile has been closely intertwined with the University. In 2011, more than three-quarters of the Second Mile Board were University alumni. University students served as interns and volunteers at Second Mile events and solicited donations from local businesses for these charitable events.

Wendell Courtney was the outside legal counsel at Penn State from 1980 until 2010. From 2008 to 2011, he was also legal counsel for the Second Mile and sat on its Board.

Sandusky acted as a corporate officer, key fundraiser, and the "face"[614] of the organization while continuing to coach football at the University. When he retired from the University in 1999 he became a paid consultant for the Second Mile until August 2010, when he retired[615] from that role. Sandusky remained a part of Second Mile through his presence and contacts even after his retirement.

## B. "Collaborative Relationship" Between Penn State and Second Mile

An article posted on the University's website on July 1, 1999 announced Sandusky's retirement. In this article, Curley stated that Sandusky is "the founder of Second Mile ... [and] will continue to offer his services on a volunteer basis to the athletic department's Lifeskills and Outreach programs."[616] In the same announcement, Paterno praised Sandusky for his contributions to the University's football program and stated that Sandusky was "... a person of great character and integrity."[617] In a memorandum dated August 23, 1999 from Second Mile Chairman Robert Poole to the Second Mile Board, Poole wrote that beginning in January 2000, Sandusky would become a paid consultant for the organization and earn $57,000 per year plus travel expenses.[618]

In Sandusky's retirement agreement with the University, both parties agreed to "work collaboratively" in community outreach programs such as the Second Mile.[619] The collaboration took several forms. Penn State football staff and players helped Sandusky with annual Second Mile Golf Tournaments held at the Penn State golf course(s) from 2003 to 2011.[620] Each year the Second Mile distributed playing cards that displayed both Penn State and Second Mile logos and contained images of Penn State football players, coaches and other student-athletes. A number of the University's football players and other student-athletes routinely volunteered for Second Mile youth programs.

In addition, in February 2009, Schultz contacted a bank on behalf of Sandusky and the Second Mile. Schultz advised the bank "the Second Mile is raising funds to support an expansion of their facilities here in State College.... Would you be agreeable to meet with Jerry Sandusky ... and me? They are really good people and this is a great cause related to kids."[621] Bank officials agreed to meet with Sandusky.[622]

The University's visible support of the Second Mile provided Sandusky with numerous opportunities to bring young boys to campus and to interact with them through various camps and activities.

## C. Second Mile Camps on Penn State Campuses

Between 1999 and 2008, the Second Mile operated six one-week long summer youth camps at the University Park campus as well as at other non-University locations.

Sandusky operated numerous summer youth camps at various Commonwealth campuses through Second Mile and his own corporation, Sandusky and Associates.[623]

At the University Park campus, camp activities were held at various locations including classrooms, an outdoor swimming pool, athletic fields and football facilities.[624] Sandusky frequently visited the boys' camps during the swimming pool activity in the afternoon, and the night sessions, which were usually held in one of the football meeting rooms.[625]

Second Mile also offered a "Friend Program," a mentorship program that matched a college volunteer with an at-risk elementary student.[626] The Friend Program events took place in Blair, Centre, Clinton and Lancaster counties as well as in the Lehigh Valley and other locations in Pennsylvania. The Friend Program events included picnics, holiday parties, swimming and bowling.[627] Sandusky sometimes participated in the Friend Program at the Altoona campus. When he did, Sandusky often arrived accompanied by a boy from Second Mile who was not part of the invited group.[628] According to a Director of Programs for Second Mile, the last time he saw Sandusky participate in any Second Mile activities was in 2008.[629]

# CHAPTER 8
# FEDERAL AND STATE CHILD SEXUAL ABUSE REPORTING REQUIREMENTS

## KEY FINDINGS

- The Clery Act requires the University to collect crime statistics relating to designated crimes, including sexual offenses, occurring on University property, make timely warnings of certain crimes that pose an ongoing threat to the community, and prepare an annual safety report and distribute it to the campus community. The Clery Act requires "Campus Security Authorities," including coaches and athletic directors, to report crimes to police. From approximately 1991 until 2007, University officials delegated Clery Act compliance to the University Police Department's Crime Prevention Officer ("CPO"). The delegated CPO was not provided any formal training before taking over the position nor does he recall receiving any Clery Act training until 2007.

- In 2007, the Director of the University Police Department transferred the Clery Act compliance responsibility from the CPO to a departmental sergeant and instituted some Clery Act training programs. The sergeant could only devote minimal time to these duties. Despite the efforts of the University Police Department, awareness and interest in Clery Act compliance throughout the University remained significantly lacking.

- As of November 2011, the University's Clery Act policy was still in draft form and had not been implemented. Many employees interviewed were unaware that they were required to report incidents and had been provided with little, if any, training. Although University administrators identified compliance with laws and regulations as one of the top 10 risks to the University in 2009, Clery Act compliance had never been audited by the University's internal auditors or received attention from any other University department, including the Office of General Counsel.

- The University Police Department instituted an electronic report format in 2007 for easier reporting, but it received only one completed form between 2007 and 2011.

- Paterno, Curley and McQueary were obligated to report the 2001 Sandusky incident to the University Police Department for inclusion in Clery Act statistics and for determining whether a timely warning should be issued to the University community. No record exists of such a report. While Schultz and Spanier were arguably not Campus Security Authorities under the Clery Act, given the leadership positions they held within the University, they should have ensured that the University was compliant with the Clery Act with regard to this incident.

- Spanier advised the Special Investigative Counsel that although the University was "big" on compliance, he was not aware that the Clery Act policy had not been implemented; that anyone had ever advised him that the University was not in compliance with the Clery Act; or whether there had ever been an internal or external audit of the University's Clery Act compliance.

# I. The Federal "Clery Act"

The Jeanne Clery Disclosure of Campus Security Policy and Campus Crime Statistics Act, 20 U.S.C. § 1092(f) ("Clery Act"), is a federal law applicable to any institution ("Institution") of higher learning that participates in federal student financial aid programs. The Pennsylvania State University ("Penn State" or "University") participates in such programs and, therefore, must comply with the requirements of the Clery Act. The Clery Act is enforced by the United States Department of Education ("Department of Education"), which has the authority to issue fines for violations of the Clery Act or, in extreme cases, to end federal funding to the Institution.

The purpose of the Clery Act is to provide an Institution's students, parents and employees with information about campus safety so that members of the campus community can make informed decisions to protect themselves from crime. Among other things, the Clery Act requires Institutions to: (1) collect crime statistics relating to designated crimes ("Clery Crimes") occurring on designated locations associated with the Institution; (2) make timely warnings of certain Clery Crimes that pose an ongoing threat to the community; and, (3) prepare and distribute to the campus community an annual safety report that contains the crime statistics described above, as well as other information about the Institution's safety policies and procedures.[oo] Institutions are required to collect crime data from all "Campus Security Authorities."[pp]

## A. Campus Security Authorities ("CSAs")

The Department of Education establishes the regulations for implementing the Clery Act and broadly defines the term "Campus Security Authority" to include the following entities or individuals:

1. A campus police department or a campus security department of an Institution.

2. Any individual or individuals who have responsibility for campus security but who do not constitute a campus police department or a

---

[oo] 20 U.S.C. § 1092(f)(1), (3), (5). The Clery Act was originally passed in 1990, and Congress amended the law several times over the years.
[pp] 20 U.S.C. § 1092(f)(1)(F); 34 C.F.R. § 668.46(a).

campus security department . . . such as an individual who is responsible for monitoring entrance into Institutional property.

3. Any individual or organization specified in an institution's statement of campus security policy as an individual or organization to which students and employees should report criminal offenses.

4. *An official of an institution who has significant responsibility for student and campus activities* including, but not limited to, student housing, student discipline, and campus judicial proceedings. [emphasis added][qq]

The Department of Education has defined the last group of CSAs to include, among others, the following individuals:

- A dean of students who oversees student housing, a student center or student extracurricular activities.
- *A director of athletics, a team coach* or a faculty advisor to a student group. [emphasis added]
- A student resident advisor or assistant or a student who monitors access to dormitories.
- A coordinator of [fraternity and sorority affairs].
- A physician in a campus health center, a counselor in a campus counseling center or a victim advocate or sexual assault response team in a campus rape crisis center if they are identified by [an Institution] as someone to whom crimes should be reported or if they have significant responsibility for student and campus activities. . . .[rr]

## B. Collecting Crime Statistics

The Clery Act requires Institutions to collect information about all Clery Crimes,[ss] which include forcible and non-forcible sex offenses,[tt] so that the information

---

[qq]34 C.F.R. § 668.46(a).

[rr]While the above citation is from 2011, the Department of Education has had similar guidance in place setting forth its interpretation of the definition of Campus Security Authorities since at least 1999. United States Department of Education, Handbook for Campus Safety and Security Reporting (hereinafter U.S. Dept. of Education Clery Handbook) (Washington D.C., February 2011), 75. *See* 64 F.R. 59060, 59063 (November 1, 1999).

[ss]20 U.S.C. § 1092(f)(1)(F)(i).

can be used for reporting statistics to the public on an annual basis and determining whether to issue timely warnings to the campus community. Institutions are required to report Clery Crimes that are "reported to campus security authorities or local police agencies" on an annual basis.[uu] Institutions are required to include any Clery Crime in their collected statistics, even if there is no criminal charge filed or arrest made. The Institution must collect and report the crime if the information is reported to a CSA who believes that the allegation was made to him or her "in good faith."[vv]

### C. Issuance of Timely Warnings

The Clery Act requires an institution to issue "timely warnings" of Clery Crimes if the crime is reported to a CSA and is "considered by the Institution to represent a threat to students and employees."[ww] If the Institution, in the exercise of its judgment, determines that the reported crime poses an ongoing threat to students and employees, the Institution must utilize appropriate procedures to notify students and employees of the threat "in a manner that is timely and will aid in the prevention of similar crimes."[xx]

### D. Preparation of an Annual Safety Report

The Clery Act requires Institutions to prepare and distribute an annual safety report ("ASR") to the campus community, which includes, among other things, the annual Clery Act crime statistics described above. The Clery Act and accompanying regulations set forth in detail what the ASR must include, including where and how crimes should be reported, crime prevention policies, alcohol and drug information, and emergency response and evacuation information.[yy]

---

[tt]Clery Crimes include: murder, manslaughter, forcible and non-forcible sex offenses, robbery, aggravated assault, motor vehicle theft, arson, and certain drug and alcohol violations. 20 U.S.C. § 1092(f)(1)(F)(i).

[uu]20 U.S.C. § 1092(f)(1)(F)(i).

[vv]"If a campus security authority receives the crime information and believes it was provided in good faith, he or she should document it as a crime report. In 'good faith' means there is a reasonable basis for believing that the information is not simply rumor or hearsay. That is, there is little or no reason to doubt the validity of the information." U.S. Dept. of Education, Clery Handbook, 73.

[ww]34 C.F.R. § 668.46(e); see 20 U.S.C. § 1092(f)(3).

[xx]34 C.F.R. § 668.46(e).

[yy]20 U.S.C. § 1092(f).

## II. The University's Failure To Implement the Clery Act

The Clery Act was passed in 1990 and became effective in 1991. From approximately 1991 until 2007, University officials delegated Clery Act compliance to the University Police Department's Crime Prevention Officer ("CPO").[630] The CPO was not provided any formal training before taking over the position nor does he recall receiving any Clery Act training until 2007.[631] The CPO was supervised by others in the University Police Department, including, ultimately, then Chief Thomas Harmon.[632] Before 2007, the CPO was unaware that the Clery Act included the concept of CSAs or that the University had an obligation to collect crime data from student organizations, coaches, and others who have regular contact with students. To the CPO's knowledge, his supervisors were also unaware of these requirements.[633] In fact, according to the CPO, he told one of his supervisors in 2007 that there was a need for additional personnel to assist with the Clery Act and "we could get hurt really bad here."[634] The supervisor responded by saying "we really don't have the money."[635]

In 2007, the Director of the University Police Department, Stephen Shelow, transferred the Clery Act compliance responsibility from the CPO to a departmental sergeant, because he believed that compliance with the Clery Act had not been handled well in the past.[636] However, the sergeant in the University Police Department was only able to devote minimal time to Clery Act responsibilities.

Shelow also directed a number of University police department employees to attend a training program on the Clery Act. When the trainers discussed the requirements to identify and train CSAs, the attendees realized that the University did not have a sufficient process for those tasks.[637] In fact, Shelow does not believe that anyone at the University understood, before that conference, that the Clery Act requires that information be gathered from outside the University Police Department.[638]

Realizing that the University had serious deficiencies in the way that it gathered Clery Crime information,[639] the University Police Department began to provide training and conduct outreach to the broader group of CSAs to gather crime data. They developed a crime report form to be completed by any CSA to whom a crime was reported and made the form available on the internet.[640] The sergeant created PowerPoint materials and provided some training and information sessions for groups at University Park and some of the Commonwealth campuses.[641] The University Police

Department also held meetings with faculty and staff members involved in athletics, student activities and the fraternity and sorority system to increase awareness of the Clery Act and to explain the obligations of some of these individuals as CSAs.[642]

Despite the efforts of the University Police Department, awareness and interest in Clery Act compliance remained lacking throughout the University.[643] Since making the report form available electronically in 2007, the University Police Department has received only one completed form through 2011.[644] No record reflects that any Commonwealth campus used the form until 2009.[645] The training sessions and outreach efforts were conducted primarily for just one or two years, were "sporadic" and were not well attended.[646]

The Director and the sergeant's intention to properly follow Clery Act regulations also were stymied by their own lack of time and resources. The sergeant, in addition to her Clery Act responsibilities, also was in charge of all criminal investigations and was only able to devote minimal time to Clery Act compliance.[647] The Director suggested to the then Senior Vice President Finance and Business that the University appoint a "compliance coordinator" to assist with Clery Act implementation.[648] The Director was told that while the need for the position existed, the University had other priorities that needed attention first.[649]

In April 2009, the University's outside legal counsel provided information to the University about Clery Act compliance.[650] The Director, the sergeant and others created a "draft" Clery Act policy that would have required written notification to all CSAs of their roles and responsibilities.[651]

As of November 2011, the University's Clery Act policy was still in draft form and had not been implemented.[652] Many University employees interviewed were unaware of their CSA status or responsibilities under the Clery Act. In an interview with the Special Investigative Counsel, Spanier said that he was not aware that the Clery Act policy had not been implemented and remained in draft form.[653] Spanier said no one at Penn State had ever informed him that the University was not in compliance with the Clery Act.[654] Spanier also stated that there had been no internal or external audits for Clery Act compliance.[655] He also said he had never briefed the Board on Clery Act compliance, nor had the Board asked him questions on this issue.[656] Spanier emphasized that Penn State "was big on compliance, more than other universities."[657]

## III. Pennsylvania Child Sexual Abuse Reporting Requirements

The Commonwealth of Pennsylvania charged Curley and Schultz in November 2011 with violating Pennsylvania's statute, 23 Pa. C.S. § 6311, relating to the mandatory reporting of child abuse in 2002. That statute requires certain individuals who are "mandatory reporters" to report suspected child abuse to the appropriate state agency. The statute has been amended several times but the relevant provision in effect in 2001 states:

> Persons who, in the course of their employment, occupation or practice of their profession, come into contact with children shall report or cause a report to be made in accordance with section 6313 (relating to reporting procedure) when they have reasonable cause to suspect, on the basis of their medical, professional or other training and experience, that a child coming before them in their professional or official capacity is an abused child. . . .

The 2012 version of the statute states:

> A person who, in the course of employment, occupation or practice of a profession, comes into contact with children shall report or cause a report to be made in accordance with section 6313 (relating to reporting procedure) when the person has reasonable cause to suspect, on the basis of medical, professional or other training and experience, that a child under the care, supervision, guidance or training of that person or of an agency, institution, organization or other entity with which that person is affiliated is a victim of child abuse, including child abuse by an individual who is not a perpetrator.

Both the 2001 and 2012 versions of the law also state:

> In addition to those persons and officials required to report suspected child abuse, any person may make such a report if that person has reasonable cause to suspect that a child is an abused child.[zz]

---

[zz] 23 Pa. C.S. § 6312.

## IV. Implications of The University's Failure to Report Allegations of Child Sexual Abuse

McQueary testified at the preliminary hearing on December 16, 2011 that he described the 2002[658] incident involving Sandusky and a child in the Lasch Building to Paterno as "a young boy in the shower and it was way over the lines" and "extremely sexual in nature."[659] McQueary testified at that same hearing that he later met with Curley and Schultz, and told them that he observed Sandusky in the shower with a young boy and that he "thought that some kind of intercourse was going on."[660] While Curley and Schultz dispute McQueary's version of what he told them about the incident, Paterno testified to the Grand Jury on January 12, 2011 that McQueary described the incident to him as "fondling" and "a sexual nature."[661] The conduct described by McQueary and Paterno constitutes the Clery Crime of sexual assault.

Based on the facts uncovered by the Special Investigative Counsel, Paterno, Curley and McQueary were obligated as CSAs to report this incident to the University Police Department for inclusion in Clery Act statistics and for determining whether a timely warning should be issued to the University community. The Special Investigative Counsel found no indication that Paterno, Curley and McQueary met their responsibilities as CSAs by reporting, or ensuring that someone reported, this incident to the University Police Department. As a result, no timely warning could have been issued to the University community and the incident was not included in the University's Clery Crime statistics for 2001.[662]

McQueary, Paterno and Curley did report the incident to Schultz who, as SVP-FB, was ultimately in charge of the University Police Department. However, Schultz was not a law enforcement officer and was not the person designated to receive Clery Crime reports or to collect Clery Crime statistics for the University.[aaa] Arguably, as the most senior leaders of the University, Schultz and Spanier should have ensured compliance with the Clery Act regarding this incident. There is no record that Spanier or Schultz reported, or designated someone to report, the incident to the University Police Department, which should have caused the incident to be included in the

---

[aaa] 34 C.F.R. § 668.46(b)(2) requires the University to include in its ASR a statement setting forth to whom individuals should report crimes. The University's ASR for 2001 did not contain any such statement; however, it generally states that the police department investigates crimes.

University's Clery Crime statistics and may have triggered the issuance of a timely warning to the University community.

## V. Improvements in Clery Act Compliance
## Since November 2011

After the criminal charges against Sandusky, Curley and Schultz became known, the University assessed its implementation and compliance with the Clery Act. Notwithstanding an investigation begun on November 9, 2011 by the Department of Education concerning the same issues,[bbb] the University moved forward by hiring a reputable national consultant to conduct this assessment. The consultant's study identified several shortcomings in the University's Clery Act procedures, including those cited above.[663]

On January 19, 2012, the Special Investigative Counsel recommended several actions relative to compliance with the Clery Act's training and reporting requirements. As described in Chapter 10 of this report, some of the recommended actions were already in place and the others have now been implemented or are underway,[664] including the appointment of a full-time Clery Compliance Officer on March 26, 2012.

---

[bbb] As of the date of this report, the Department of Education's investigation is ongoing.

# CHAPTER 9
# THE PROTECTION OF CHILDREN IN UNIVERSITY FACILITIES AND PROGRAMS

## KEY FINDINGS

- The University had two main policies, *Background Check Process*, and *Protection of Minors Involved in University Sponsored Programs*, that were designed to protect children using University facilities and participating in University-supported programs. The policies for background checks on employees and volunteers were significantly inadequate.
- University staff involved with youth programs said that some persons serving as volunteer coaches and counselors "fell through the cracks" and were allowed to participate in youth programs or events without appropriate clearances.
- Factors in the inconsistent application of these policies and procedures include confusion among University staff members about what the background process entails and who is subject to the process.
- The University historically has not trained administrators of youth programs on the policies. The University also has not consistently required timely submission of background applications so as to allow sufficient time for background checks.

## I. University Policies for the Protection of Non-Student Minors

The Special Investigative Counsel found that The Pennsylvania State University's ("Penn State" or "University") system for implementing the child protection policies was inadequate, but that corrective efforts are underway. While the identified deficiencies historically may not have had a direct impact on Sandusky's crimes, the issues are serious and reflect that the University has not sufficiently focused on the protection of children in the past.

University programs for youth are diverse and are held at nearly every Commonwealth campus. Youth programs range from summer academic and sport camps that can be day or overnight, to year-round activities and events in arts, theatre, science, sports, adventure, nature, and leadership. Penn State Outreach plays a prominent role in the youth programming offered by the University as does the Intercollegiate Athletics Department ("ICA").[665] At University Park alone, more than 20,000 non-student minors are now attending the 2012 summer sport camps offered by the ICA.[666]

Two University policies – AD 39, *Minors Involved in University-Sponsored Programs or Programs Held at the University and/or Housed in University Facilities (formerly Programs Involving Minors Housed in University Facilities)* [667] and HR 99, *Background Check Process*, are the core policies the University relies on to help protect the many thousands of children who visit its campuses each year.

All 20 Penn State campuses offer an "open-campus" environment, sharing academic and recreational facilities with the local community. The largest campus located at University Park annually invites hundreds of thousands of minors to participate in University sponsored educational, recreational, cultural and sports programs.

### A. AD 39, *Minors Involved in University-Sponsored Programs or Programs held at the University and/or Housed in University Facilities*

The Penn State policy on minors involved in University-sponsored programs or youth programs held at the University or housed in University facilities was created in October 1992 and is closely aligned with the nationally accepted American Camping Association Standards.[668] The policy was revised several times over the years and on

April 11, 2012, the University issued another revision. The purpose of the revision is "[t]o provide for appropriate supervision of minors who are involved in University-sponsored programs, programs held at the University and/or programs housed in University facilities at all geographic locations."[669] The policy addresses background clearances; codes of conduct; legal consents; medical information; counselor/staff member training/orientation; adult-to-participant ratios; and child abuse and mandated reporting procedures.[670] Policy AD 39 also applies to any external organization that utilizes University facilities for youth activities through a Memorandum of Agreement ("MOA").[671]

Recent revisions made to Policy AD 39 are intended to strengthen the University's internal controls and procedures for the protection of non-student minors on University campuses. The revised policy expands mandatory background checks for all individuals, paid or unpaid, working with minors.[672] The policy requires self-disclosure of arrests and convictions. The Office of Human Resources ("OHR") must review and approve all background check verifications. The policy also requires mandatory annual training on child protection and reporting incidents of possible abuse to appropriate authorities.

### B. HR-99, *Background Check Process*

Historically, background checks at Penn State have been conducted under two policies, Policies HR-95 and HR-96.[673] Policy HR-96 for "other-than-academic appointments," had been the governing policy for those participating in youth programs. The University also developed an implementation guide, the *Reference and Background Check Process Guideline*.

On July 5, 2012, the University implemented Policy HR-99, *Background Check Process*, which supersedes and consolidates the prior policies HR-95 and HR-96.[674] HR-99 establishes "a process for ensuring background checks are completed for any individual who is engaged by the University in any work capacity including employees, volunteers, adjunct faculty, students, consultants, contractors or other similar positions."[675] The revised background check process will require an additional 23,650 background checks to be conducted annually.[ccc]

The new policy requires any individual engaged by the University in any work capacity to have a University background check and/or verification of successful completion of Pennsylvania Act 34 (background check) and Act 151 (child abuse clearance). Covered staff must provide notice to the University of any criminal charges within 72 hours of their arrest.[676] The new policy also defines key terms such as "minor," "sex and violent offender registry check," and "sensitive/critical positions."[677]

## II. Implementation of the University's Child Protection Policies

Penn State staff involved with youth programs explained to the Special Investigative Counsel that some persons serving as volunteer coaches and counselors were "slipping through the cracks"[678] and were allowed to participate in youth programs or events without appropriate clearances. An Outreach employee involved in University summer sport camps stated that participation by unscreened individuals occurred "every year and all the time."[679] One senior Outreach employee described the background check process as a "sieve."[680] A report prepared by an employee in the Outreach Finance Office in May 2010 revealed that 234 of the 735 coaches paid to work at the summer sports camps in 2009 did not have a background check completed before the start of the sport camp for which they worked.[681]

When interviewed by the Special Investigative Counsel, the director of the Sport Camps Office denied that there had ever been any issues or incidents with the summer sport camps.[682] Other interviews conducted and documents reviewed, however, pointed to several instances of unauthorized participation in summer youth camps.[683] For example, in 2010, at least five coaches or counselors with criminal records were allowed to work at University Park summer youth programs.[684] One individual who registered for a coaching position for the University Park Football I camp in 2010 indicated in his self-disclosure statement that he had no criminal history, and camp personnel "cleared" him to participate in the camp. A background check initiated a day later and completed

---

[ccc] This number is Penn State's estimate of the total number of background checks that the University would need to complete annually if it implemented a policy that required a background check for every category of employee and volunteers, attached hereto as Appendix B.

the following day revealed that the man had a criminal record for child endangerment. The man had already stayed overnight in a Penn State residence hall with minors.[685]

Several significant factors contributed to the inconsistent implementation of Policy AD39 and the background check process. For example, some University staff members appeared confused about the background check and child welfare policies.[686] Even those familiar with the policies had different interpretations of what the background process entailed and who was subject to the process.[687] One HR employee who was involved in the process said the policies are "clear as mud."[688] The University historically has not trained administrators of youth programs on the policies.[689] The University also has not consistently required timely submission of applications so as to allow sufficient time for background checks.[690]

Application of the background check process is not uniform across the Commonwealth campuses. The process varies from the use of a web-based computer application to conduct background checks [691] and background checks using fingerprints,[692] to campuses that never required any background check until the Sandusky charges became public, and now use only a free internet search of questionable accuracy.[693]

In past years, problems with the background check process have been brought to the attention of Penn State administrators and those responsible for overseeing youth programs at Penn State.[694] One employee who presented reports concerning shortcomings in the process felt "like [she] wasn't being heard," but did not pursue the matter because the employee "didn't feel like it was [her] place to say anything." She further stated, "I have to be careful, I had my job [to lose]."[695] Another employee who prepared the May 2010 report on background checks expressed concern for the degree of risk to the University.[696] When the employee voiced concerns to the director of the Sports Camps Office, the director dismissed the issue and said that other matters were more pressing.[697]

The Special Investigative Counsel found only one instance where a University employee was held accountable for not complying with Policy AD39 and the background check process. After multiple failures to enforce the policies in the summer of 2010, a "Memorandum of Conversation" was placed in the personnel file of a senior Sports Camp employee that states, "any future failure…might result in disciplinary action up to and including termination." The memorandum addressed only one of multiple incidents.[698]

Some Penn State staff expressed concerns with the complexity of the revised policies.[699] According to one employee "[w]e all understand why [a background check process is needed] but the issue now is how are we going to do this?"[700]

## III. Use of University Facilities by Third Parties for Youth Programs

Under the University's standard MOAs for use of University facilities by third parties,[701] the party contracting with the University has the duty to ensure that its counselors and staff possess the appropriate background clearances.[702] The revised Policy AD39 provides that non-University groups using University facilities "must provide to the sponsoring unit satisfactory evidence of compliance with all of the requirements of this Policy at least (30) days prior to the scheduled use of University facilities."

# CHAPTER 10
# RECOMMENDATIONS FOR UNIVERSITY GOVERNANCE, ADMINISTRATION, AND THE PROTECTION OF CHILDREN IN UNIVERSITY FACILITIES AND PROGRAMS

The failure of President Graham B. Spanier ("Spanier"), Senior Vice President – Finance and Business ("SVP-FB") Gary C. Schultz ("Schultz"), Head Football Coach Joseph V. Paterno ("Paterno") and Athletic Director ("AD") Timothy M. Curley ("Curley") to protect children by allowing Gerald A. Sandusky ("Sandusky") unrestricted and uncontrolled access to Pennsylvania State University ("Penn State" or "University") facilities reveals numerous individual failings, but it also reveals weaknesses of the University's culture, governance, administration, compliance policies and procedures for protecting children. It is critical for institutions and organizations that provide programs and facilities for children to institute and adhere to practices that have been found to be effective in reducing the risk of abuse. Equally important is the need for the leaders of those institutions and organizations to govern in ways that reflect the ethics and values of those entities.

The Special Investigative Counsel provided several recommendations to the Board and the University in January 2012 to address exigent needs to reform policies and procedures, particularly those involving upcoming activities, such as summer camps. Before, but especially since November 2011, the Board and University administrators have reviewed, modified, or added relevant policies, guidelines, practices and procedures relating to the protection of children and University governance. Consistent with the recommendations in this report, members of the Board, University administrators, faculty and staff have:

- Strengthened security measures and policies to safeguard minors, students and others associated with the University and its Outreach programs.
- Improved the organization and procedures of the Board to better identify, report, and address issues of significance to the University and members of its community.

- Increased compliance with The Jeanne Clery Disclosure of Campus Security Policy and Campus Crime Statistics Act, 20 U.S.C. § 1092(f) ("Clery Act") training, information collection and reporting requirements.
- Encouraged prompt reporting of incidents of abuse and sexual misconduct.
- Conducted abuse-awareness training for many University areas, including its top leadership.
- Provided better oversight and governance of the University's educational, research and athletic compliance programs.

One of the most challenging tasks confronting the University community – and possibly the most important step in ensuring that the other recommended reforms are effectively sustained, and that public confidence in the University and its leadership is restored – is an open, honest, and thorough examination of the culture that underlies the failure of Penn State's most powerful leaders to respond appropriately to Sandusky's crimes.

The following recommendations are intended to assist University administrators, faculty, staff and the Board, in improving how they govern and provide protection for children in University facilities and programs. These recommendations relate to the University's administrative structure, policies and procedures and the Office of General Counsel; the responsibilities and operations of the Board; the identification of risk; compliance with federal and state statutes and reporting misconduct; the integration of the Athletic Department into the greater University community; the oversight, policies and procedures of the University's Police Department; and the management of programs for non-student minors and access to University facilities. In addition, recommendations are included that will assist the University in monitoring change and measuring future improvement. [ddd]

---

[ddd] Recommendations accompanied by an asterisk are being implemented or have been completed as of June 2012.

## 1.0 – Penn State Culture

The University is a major employer, landholder and investor in State College, and its administrators, staff, faculty and many of its Board members have strong ties to the local community. Certain aspects of the community culture are laudable, such as its collegiality, high standards of educational excellence and research, and respect for the environment. However, there is an over-emphasis on "The Penn State Way" as an approach to decision-making, a resistance to seeking outside perspectives, and an excessive focus on athletics that can, if not recognized, negatively impact the University's reputation as a progressive institution.

University administration and the Board should consider taking the following actions to create a values- and ethics-centered community where everyone is engaged in placing the needs of children above the needs of adults; and to create an environment where everyone who sees or suspects child abuse will feel empowered to report the abuse.

1.1 Organize a Penn State-led effort to vigorously examine and understand the Penn State culture in order to: 1) reinforce the commitment of all University members to protect children; 2) create a stronger sense of accountability among the University's leadership; 3) establish values and ethics-based decision making and adherence to the Penn State Principles as the standard for all University faculty, staff and students; 4) promote an environment of increased transparency into the management of the University; and 5) ensure a sustained integration of the Intercollegiate Athletics program into the broader Penn State community.

This effort should include the participation of representatives from the Special Faculty Committee on University Governance; Penn State's Coalition on Intercollegiate Athletics; Penn State's Rock Ethics Institute; students, alumni, faculty and staff; as well as representatives from peer institutions with experience in reviewing and improving institutional culture in academic settings.

| | | |
|---|---|---|
| 1.2 | | Appoint a University Ethics Officer to provide advice and counsel to the President and the Board of Trustees on ethics issues and adherence to the Penn State Principles; develop and provide, in conjunction with the Rock Ethics Center, leadership and ethics training modules for all areas of the University; and coordinate ethics initiatives with the University's Chief Compliance Officer.* (See also Recommendation 4.0) |
| | 1.2.1 | **Establish an "Ethics Council" to assist the Ethics Officer in providing advice and counsel to the President and the Board on ethical issues and training.** |
| | 1.2.2 | **Finalize and approve the proposed modifications to the Institutional Conflict of Interest Policy; identify the senior administrative and faculty positions to which the policy should apply, and implement the policy throughout the University.** |
| 1.3 | | Conduct open and inclusive searches for new employees and provide professional training for employees who undertake new responsibilities. |
| 1.4 | | Continue to benchmark the University's practices and policies with other similarly situated institutions, focus on continuous improvement and make administrative, operational or personnel changes when warranted. |
| 1.5 | | Communicate regularly with University students, faculty, staff, alumni and the community regarding significant University policies and issues through a variety of methods and media. |
| 1.6 | | Emphasize and practice openness and transparency at all levels and within all areas of the University. |

## 2.0 – Administration and General Counsel: Structure, Policies and Procedures

In various ways the University's administrative structure, the absence or poor enforcement of policies relating to the protection of children and employee misconduct,[eee] and the lack of emphasis on values and ethics-based action created an

---

[eee] The University has policies for investigating employee misconduct: HR-78 created in 1974, and HR-70, created in 2005; and a whistleblower policy, AD67 created in 2010.

environment in which Spanier, Schultz, Paterno and Curley were able to make decisions to avoid the consequences of bad publicity. Standard personnel practices were ignored or undermined by the lack of centralized control over the human resources functions of various departments – most particularly, the Athletic Department.

University administrators, faculty, staff and the Board should consider taking the following actions to create an atmosphere of values and ethics-based decision making.

2.1 Review organizational structures and make adjustments for greater efficiency and effectiveness.

    **2.1.1 Evaluate the span of control of the University President and make adjustments as necessary to ensure that the President's duties are realistic and capable of the President's oversight and control.**

    **2.1.2 Evaluate the span of control and responsibility of the Senior Vice President – Finance and Business ("SVP-FB") and make adjustments as necessary to ensure that the SVP-FB's duties are realistic and capable of the SVP-FB's oversight and control.**

    **2.1.3 Upgrade the position of the Associate Vice President for Human Resources to a Vice President position reporting directly to the University President.**

    **2.1.4 Evaluate the size, composition and procedures of the President's Council and make adjustments as necessary.**

2.2 Review administrative processes and procedures and make adjustments for greater efficiency and effectiveness.

    **2.2.1 Separate the University's Office of Human Resources ("OHR") from the University's Finance and Business organization.**

    **2.2.2 Assign all human resources ("HR") policy making responsibilities to the OHR and limit the ability of individual departments and campuses to disregard the University's human resources policies and rules.**

2.2.3 Centralize HR functions, where feasible, such as background checks, hiring, promotions, terminations, on-board orientation and management training, while recognizing the unique requirements of University components and Commonwealth campuses, and their need for measured autonomy.*

2.2.4 Designate the Vice President for Human Resources ("VP-HR") as the hiring authority for HR representatives throughout the University and establish a "dotted-line" reporting relationship between the HR representatives and the VP-HR similar to that used in the Finance and Audit areas.

2.2.5 Develop job descriptions for all new key leadership positions and incumbent positions if none exist.

2.2.6 Evaluate the size of the OHR staff, benchmark its human capital capacity against public universities of similar size and scope of responsibility, and modify as necessary.

2.2.7 Adopt a Human Resource Information/Capital Management System ("HRIS/HCM") with sufficient growth capacity for use at University Park and all Commonwealth campuses.

2.2.8 Engage external HR professionals to assist in the development of the University's next performance management system.

2.2.9 Provide the OHR with complete access to executive compensation information and utilize the OHR, in conjunction with the University Budget Office, to benchmark and advise the administration and the Board of Trustees on matters of executive compensation.

2.2.10 Develop a mechanism to provide and track all employee training mandated by state and federal law and University policies.

2.2.11 Update, standardize, centralize, and monitor background check procedures.*

2.2.12 Require updated background checks for employees, contractors and volunteers at least every five years.*

2.2.13 Audit periodically the effectiveness of background check procedures and the University's self-reporting system for employees.*

2.2.14 Update computer-use policies and regularly inform employees of the University's expectations and employee responsibilities with regard to electronic data and materials.

2.2.15 Develop a procedure to ensure that the University immediately retrieves keys and access cards from unauthorized persons.*

2.3 Complete the development of the University's Office of General Counsel ("OGC").

2.3.1 Develop a mission statement for the OGC that clearly defines the General Counsel's responsibilities and reporting obligations to the University and the Board of Trustees.

2.3.2 Select and hire a permanent General Counsel ("GC").*

2.3.3 Expand the GC's office staff to provide broader coverage of routine legal issues including employment law.

2.3.4 Appropriate sufficient budget to the OGC to hire specialized outside counsel when needed.

2.4 Advertise all senior executive positions externally and engage educational search experts to broaden the talent pools for senior executive positions.*

2.5 Integrate faculty and staff from different disciplines and areas in University-wide professional development/leadership training to increase their exposure to other University personnel, programs, challenges and solutions.*

2.6 Implement consistent, state-of-the art records management and retention procedures.

2.7 Provide sufficient support and oversight of the Office of Student Affairs to make certain that all students follow the same standards of conduct.*

> 2.8 Designate an individual, administrative entity or committee to approve and review all new and modified University policies.
>
> **2.8.1 Develop guidelines for creating, standardizing, approving, reviewing and updating University policies.**
>
> **2.8.2 Review periodically all University policies for relevance, utility and necessity, and modify or rescind as appropriate.**

## 3.0 – Board of Trustees: Responsibilities and Operations

Spanier and other University leaders failed to report timely and sufficiently the incidents of child sexual abuse against Sandusky to the Board of Trustees in 1998, 2001 and 2011. Nonetheless, the Board's over-confidence in Spanier's abilities, and its failure to conduct oversight and responsible inquiry of Spanier and senior University officials, hindered the Board's ability to deal properly with the most profound crisis ever confronted by the University.

The Board should consider taking the following actions to increase public confidence and transparency, realign and refocus its responsibilities and operations, improve internal and external communications and strengthen its practices and procedures.

> 3.1 Review the administrative and governance issues raised in this report, particularly with regard to the structure, composition, eligibility requirements and term limits of the Board, the need to include more members who are not associated with the University, and the role of the Emeriti. In conducting this review, the Board should seek the opinions of members of the Penn State community, as well as governance and higher education experts not affiliated with the University. The Board should make public the results and recommendations generated from the review.
>
> 3.2 Review, develop and adopt an ethics/conflict of interest policy for the Board that includes guidelines for conflict management and a commitment to transparency regarding significant issues.

3.2.1 Include training on ethics and oversight responsibilities in the current regulatory environment in Board member orientation.

3.2.2 Require full and public disclosure by Board members of financial relationships between themselves and their businesses and the University.

3.3 Implement the Board's proposals for revised committee structures to include a committee on Risk, Compliance, Legal and Audit and subcommittees for Audit and Legal matters; and a subcommittee for Human Resources as part of the Committee on Finance, Business and Capital Planning.*fff

3.3.1 **Rotate Committee Chairs every five years or sooner.**

3.4 Increase and improve the channels of communication between the Board and University administrators.

3.4.1 Ensure that the University President, General Counsel and relevant members of senior staff thoroughly and forthrightly brief the Board of Trustees at each meeting on significant issues facing the University.*

3.4.2 **Require regular Risk Management, Compliance and Internal Audit reports to the Board on assessment of risks, pending investigations, compliance with federal and state regulations as well as on measures in place to mitigate those risks.**

3.4.3 Require that the SVP-FB, the GC and/or their designee to provide timely briefings to the Board on potential problem areas such as unusual severance or termination payments, Faculty and staff Emeriti appointments, settlement agreements, government inquiries, important litigation and whistleblower complaints.

3.4.4 Use the Board's Executive Session/Question Period with the President to make relevant and reasonable inquiry into substantive matters and to facilitate sound decision-making.

---

fff Exhibit 10-A, Pennsylvania State University Board of Trustees, Organizational Chart.

3.4.5 Review annually the University's *Return of Organization's Exempt from Income Tax Form (990)*, Clery Act reports, and the compensation and performance of senior executives and leaders.*

3.4.6 Conduct an informational seminar for the Board and senior administrators on Clery Act compliance and reporting procedures.

3.4.7 Continue to provide all Board members with regular reports of local, national and academic media coverage of the University.*

3.5 Increase and improve the channels of communication between the Board and the University community.

3.5.1 Establish and enforce rules regarding public and press statements made by Board members and Emeriti regarding confidential University matters.

3.5.2 Increase and publicize the ways in which individuals can convey messages and concerns to Board members.

3.5.2.1 Provide Board members with individual University email addresses and make them known to the public.

3.5.2.2 Use common social media communications tools to communicate with the public on various Board matters.

3.6 Develop a critical incident management plan, including training and exercises, for the Board and University administrators.

3.7 Continue to conduct and publicize periodic internal and external self-assessments of Board performance.*

## 4.0 – Compliance: Risk and Reporting Misconduct

The University's incomplete implementation of the Clery Act was a contributing factor in the failure to report the 2001 child sexual abuse committed by Sandusky. A strong compliance function, much like exists in the University's financial area, should encourage individuals to report misconduct more readily in the future. A regularized risk identification and management system is as prudent and consistent with best business practices.

University administrators and the Board should consider taking the following actions to ensure compliance with the multiple laws, regulations, rules and mandates that effect its operations, risk management and national reputation.

4.1 Establish and select an individual for a position of "Chief Compliance Officer,"* The Chief Compliance Officer should:

    4.1.1 **Head an independent office equivalent to the Office of Internal Audit.**

    4.1.2 **Chair a Compliance Council.**

    4.1.3 **Coordinate compliance functions in a manner similar to the Office of Internal Audit.**

    4.1.4 **Have similar access to, and a reporting relationship with the Board, as does the Internal Auditor.**

    4.1.5 **Coordinate the Chief Compliance Officer's responsibilities with the Office of General Counsel, the Director of Risk Management and the Director of Internal Audit.**

    4.1.6 **Direct further review of any incidents or risks reported to the Compliance Officer.**

4.2 Assign full-time responsibility for Clery Act compliance to an individual within the University Police Department and provide the individual with sufficient resources and personnel to meet Clery Act regulations.*

The individual responsible for Clery Act compliance should:

4.2.1 Establish a University policy for the implementation of the Clery Act.

4.2.2 Create a master list of names of those persons with Clery Act reporting responsibilities, notify them annually of the Clery Act responsibilities and publish the list to the University community.

4.2.3 Require, monitor and track training, and periodic retraining for Campus Security Authorities ("CSAs") on Clery Act compliance.

4.2.4 Provide information to the OHR on Clery Act responsibilities, reporting suspicious activity to CSAs and whistleblower protection for inclusion in the general training for all employees.

4.2.5 Coordinate timely notices of incidents and threat warnings with the Vice President for Student Affairs, the Chief Compliance Officer and the General Counsel.

4.2.6 Review annual Clery Act reports with the President's Council, the Board of Trustees and the Compliance Officer.

4.2.7 Coordinate Clery Act training and compliance with responsible officials at the Commonwealth campuses.

4.2.8 Arrange for periodic internal and external audits of Clery Act compliance.

4.3 Update regularly and prioritize the University's list of institutional risks; determine the appropriate implementation and audit schedule for those risks; and present the results to the Board.

4.4 Send a communication to all University students, faculty and staff at the beginning of each academic term: that encourages the reporting of misconduct; describes the channels for direct or anonymous reporting; and the University's whistleblower policy and protection from retaliation.

4.5 Publicize the employee misconduct hotline regularly and prominently throughout the University on a variety of platforms including social media networks and the webpages of individual University components.*

## 5.0 – Athletic Department: Integration and Compliance

For the past several decades, the University's Athletic Department was permitted to become a closed community. There was little personnel turnover or hiring from outside the University and strong internal loyalty. The football program, in particular, opted out of most of the University's Clery Act, sexual abuse awareness and summer camp procedures training. The Athletic Department was perceived by many in the Penn State community as "an island," where staff members lived by their own rules.

University administrators and the Board of Trustees should consider taking the following actions to more fully involve the Athletic Department within the broader University community; provide relevant training and support to the Athletic Department staff to ensure compliance with external regulations and University policies; and maintain a safe environment for those who use the University's recreational facilities, especially children.

| | | |
|---|---|---|
| 5.1 | | Revise the organizational structure of the Athletic Department to clearly define lines of authority, responsibilities and reporting relationships. |
| 5.2 | | Evaluate security and access protocols for athletic, recreational and camp facilities and modify as necessary to provide reasonable protections for those using the facilities.* |
| 5.3 | | Conduct national searches for candidates for key positions, including head coaches and Associate Athletic Director(s) and above. |
| 5.4 | | Integrate, where feasible, academic support staff, programs and locations for student-athletes.* |
| 5.5 | | Provide the University's Athletic Compliance Office with additional staff and adequate resources to meet its many responsibilities.* |
| | 5.5.1 | **Benchmark against peer institutions to determine an appropriate staffing level for the office.** |
| | 5.5.2 | **Establish an effective reporting relationship with the University Compliance Officer.** |

> **5.5.3** Realign the compliance-related responsibilities of Athletic Department staff members to ensure that the Athletic Compliance Office has oversight of the entire program.
>
> **5.5.4** Ensure that new hires and incumbent compliance personnel have requisite working knowledge of the NCAA, Big Ten Conference and University rules.
>
> 5.6 Ensure that Athletic Department employees comply with University-wide training mandates.
>
> **5.6.1** Provide and track initial and on-going training for athletic staff in matters of leadership, ethics, the Penn State Principles and standards of conduct, abuse awareness, and reporting misconduct pursuant to the Clery Act and University policy.
>
> **5.6.2** Include Athletic Department employees in management training programs provided to other University managers.

## 6.0 – University Police Department: Oversight, Policies and Procedures

The University Police Department promptly responded to the 1998 complaint about Sandusky's conduct, but the sensitivity of the investigation and the need to report on its progress to a senior administrator could have compromised the extent of its inquiry. The independence of the University's law enforcement function is essential to providing unbiased service and protection to the University community. The University Police Department's recent restructuring and additional training for its employees is an important step in the continuous improvement of the Department.

The University Police Department and/or University administrators should consider taking the following additional actions to improve the functions and oversight of the University's law enforcement services:

6.1 Arrange for an external examination of the University Police Department's structure, organization, policies and procedures through a professionally recognized accreditation body, [ggg] with a particular emphasis on the University Police Department's training for and qualifications of sex abuse investigators.*

6.2 Review the organizational placement of the University Police Department in the University's Finance and Business area in conjunction with the review of the span of control of the SVP-FB. (See Section 2.0)

6.3 Provide the Vice President/Director of Public Safety with sufficient administrative authority and resources to operate effectively and independently.

6.4 Review records management procedures and controls and revise where needed.*

**6.4.1 Establish a policy to ensure that all police reports alleging criminal conduct by Penn State students, faculty and staff are reported to the OHR.[hhh]**

**6.4.2 Establish or reinforce protocols to assign a timely incident number and proper offense classification to all complaints received.[iii]***

**6.4.3 Include the final disposition of each complaint in the original or follow-up report (e.g., founded, unfounded, exceptionally cleared).**

6.5 Establish a policy to request assistance from other law enforcement agencies in sensitive or extraordinary cases or where a conflict of interest may exist.

---

[ggg] The University Police Department has engaged the Pennsylvania State Police Chiefs Association to conduct an external review. For a more expansive review, the University should utilize an organization that has extensive experience in reviewing and accrediting college and university police departments, such as the Commission on the Accreditation on Law Enforcement ("CALEA").

[hhh] Notifications regarding students, faculty and staff who are confirmed suspects of allegations of criminal conduct are made to the OHR as a standard practice, but there is no departmental policy to confirm or guide the practice.

[iii] The University Police Department has established an automatic system to assign timely incident numbers and eliminated the "Administrative" category of offenses.

| | | |
|---|---|---|
| 6.6 | Implement consistent law enforcement standards and practices, through regular training at all Penn State campuses. |
| 6.7 | Review and update, with the GC, the current policies pertaining to the investigation of various categories of offenses involving Penn State employees. |
| 6.8 | Provide specialized training to investigators in the area of sexual abuse of children. |

## 7.0 – Management of University Programs for Children and Access to University Facilities

Over the years, University policies regarding programs for non-student minors were inconsistently implemented throughout the University. Enforcement of those policies was uneven and uncoordinated and, as a result, Sandusky was allowed to conduct football camps at University Park and three Commonwealth campuses without any direct oversight by University officials. The University's background check process also was arbitrarily applied and on-site supervision at camps was sometimes provided by staff members who had not been fully vetted.

University administrators and the Board of Trustees should consider taking the following actions to create a safer environment for children involved in University programs, activities, and who use its facilities. University administrators must provide better oversight of staff members responsible for youth programs and increase abuse awareness through training of responsible adults.

| | | |
|---|---|---|
| 7.1 | Increase the physical security and access procedures in areas frequented by children or used in camps and programs for children.* |
| 7.2 | Require and provide abuse awareness and mandatory reporter training to all University leaders, including faculty, coaches and other staff, volunteers and interns.[iii] |

---

[iii] On June 6, 2012, the University implemented AD72, *Reporting Suspected Child Abuse*, requiring all University personnel to report incidents or allegations of suspected abuse or be subject to disciplinary action, up to, and including, dismissal.

> **7.2.1** Consolidate the responsibility for abuse awareness training and mandatory reporting in the OHR and coordinate an abuse awareness training program throughout the University's campuses.*

**7.3** Consolidate oversight of the University's policies and procedures for programs involving non-student minors in the OHR and appoint a coordinator to oversee the implementation of those policies. The Coordinator should have sufficient authority to:

> **7.3.1** Develop and maintain an inventory of all University programs for children.*
>
> **7.3.2** Update, revise or create policies for unaccompanied children at University facilities, housing and University programs.*
>
> **7.3.3** Enforce all policies relating to non-student minors involved in University programs at all Penn State campuses.
>
> **7.3.4** Assist the University's camp and youth program administrators in ensuring that staff and volunteers are appropriately supervised.
>
> **7.3.5** Provide information to parents of non-student minors involved in University programs regarding the University's safety protocols and reporting mechanisms for suspicious or improper activity.

## 8.0 – Monitoring Change and Measuring Improvement

The Pennsylvania State University has taken several significant steps to improve its governance and more adequately protect the hundreds of thousands of children who use its facilities and participate in its programs every year. However, restoring confidence in the University's leadership and the Board will require greater effort over a prolonged period of time. As the institution moves forward, it is incumbent upon its leaders to monitor those changes, make adjustments as necessary and communicate their progress to the Penn State community as well as to the public.

University administrators and the Board of Trustees should consider taking the following actions to ensure that their initiatives to prevent and respond to incidents of sexual abuse of children and to improve University governance are duly enforced, monitored, measured and modified as needed:

8.1 Designate an internal monitor or coordinator to oversee the implementation of recommendations initiated, or adopted, by the Board and/or the University administration. The monitor/coordinator would:

8.1.1 **Chair a panel of the individuals responsible for developing and implementing these and other approved recommendations and for establishing realistic milestones.**

8.1.2 **Select a practical and diverse number of members of the University community and solicit input from the larger University community, to provide insights and recommendations to the monitor. (See Recommendation 1.0)**

8.1.3 **Report actions and accomplishments regularly to the Board of Trustees and University administration.***

8.2 Provide the monitor, or the Chief Compliance Officer, with the authority and resources to hire appropriate external evaluators/compliance auditors to certify that milestones for implementation of these recommendations are being met.

8.3 Conduct a review of the University's progress 12 months from the acceptance of this report using internal and external examiners and provide the findings to University administrators, the Board and the public.

8.4 Conduct a second review of the University's progress 24 months from the acceptance of this report using internal and external examiners and provide the findings to University administrators, the Board and the public.

# ENDNOTES

[1] Presentment of Statewide Grand Jury, November 4, 2011.
[2] http://034fccc.netsolhost.com/WordPress/.
[3] Sally Jenkins, "Joe Paterno's Last Interview," *The Washington Post* (1-14-12).
[4] [-] Interview (7-6-12).
[5] http://www.budget.psu.edu/FactBook/StudentDynamic/UGGREnrollSummary.aspx?YearCode=2011Enr&FBPlusIndc=N.
[6] http://www.budget.psu.edu/factbook/StateAppropriation/TtlOperBudget1112.asp.
[7] http://www.psu.edu/Trustees/pdf/march2012agendafppappendix2.12.pdf; http://www.controller.psu.edu/Divisions/ControllersOffice/docs/FinStmts/2011FinStmts.pdf.
[8] Penn State is accredited by The Middle States Commission on Higher Education, which contacted the University about concerns relating to the Sandusky investigation on November 11, 2011. The University responded in its *Informational Report to the Middle States Commission on Higher Education* on December 21, 2011.
[9] http://www.research.psu.edu/about/documents/strategicplan.pdf.
[10] Standing Orders of the Penn State Board of Trustees, Order IX(1)(b)(1).
[11] Standing Orders of the Penn State Board of Trustees, Order IX(1)(b)(2).
[12] http://www.psu.edu/ur/about/administration.html.
[13] http://president.psu.edu/.
[14] http://www.psu.edu/provost/provost.htm.
[15] http://president.psu/edu/biography.
[16] http://www.psu.edu/provost/provost.htm.
[17] [-] Interview (6-12-12).
[18] [-] Interview (6-12-12).
[19] [-] Interview (6-12-12).
[20] Board of Trustees Minutes of Meeting at 7 (1-22-10).
[21] http://www.psu.edu/ur/about/administration.html.
[22] Although not further described here, the Office of Research Programs manages the University's Conflict of Interest policies.
[23] See Chapter 8, *Federal and State Child Sexual Abuse Reporting Requirements*.
[24] http://www.police.psu.edu/aboutus/.
[25] http://www.police.psu.edu/cleryact/documents/116593_PolicySafety_Up.pdf.
[26] [-] Interview (4-9-12); [-] Interview (2-29-12).
[27] http://www.psu.edu/ur/archives/intercom_1998/May21/partings.html.
[28] *See* Organizational Chart for the Pennsylvania State University Administrative Organization, http://www.psu.edu/provost/assets/President_organizational_chart%2008.pdf.
[29] [-] Interview (2-29-12); [-] Interview (2-1-12).
[30] *See* Organizational Chart for the Pennsylvania State University Administrative Organization, http://www.psu.edu/provost/assets/President_organizational_chart%2008.pdf. [-] Interview (3-1-12).
[31] Office of Human Resources website, http://ohr.psu.edu/; [-] Interview (1-4-12).
[32] *See* Organizational Chart for the Pennsylvania State University Administrative Organization, http://www.psu.edu/provost/assets/President_organizational_chart%2008.pdf.
[33] [-] Interview (12-8-11).
[34] [-] Interview (12-15-11).
[35] [-] Interview (4-11-12).

[36] http://www.gopsusports.com/compliance/psu-compliance.html.
[37] http://www.gopsusports.com/genrel/curley_tim00.html.
[38] http://www.gopsusports.com/genrel/111611aaa.html.
[39] www.gopsusports.com/sports/m-footbl/mtt/paterno_joe00.html.
[40] http://www.gopsusports.com/sports/m-footbl/mtt/obrien_bill00.html.
[41] [-] Interview (12-19-11).
[42] www.outreach.psu.edu/crai-weidemann.html; [-] Interview (1-5-12).
[43] [-] Interview (12-19-11); [-] Interview (1-5-12).
[44] http://guru.psu.edu/policies/.
[45] http://www.psu.edu/ur/2001/principles.html.
[46] [-] Interview (1-4-12); [-] Interview (1-5-12).
[47] [-] Interview (1-10-12).
[48] [-] Interview (1-5-12).
[49] http://live.psu.edu/story/58968.
[50] http://www.controller.psu.edu/divisions/RiskManagement/indexRM.html.
[51] [-] Interview (1-5-12).
[52] [-] Interview (1-4-12).
[53] http://www.internalaudit.psu.edu/.
[54] [-] Interview (1-4-12).
[55] [-] Interview (1-4-12).
[56] [-] Interview (1-4-12).
[57] [-] Interview (1-4-12).
[58] [-] Interview (1-4-12); [-] Interview (1-12-12).
[59] [-] Interview (1-4-12).
[60] Sara Ganim, "Jerry Sandusky Trial: Coaching colleagues describe Sandusky as busy, involved with children," *Patriot-News* (6-18-12).
[61] Amended Bill of Particulars, *Commonwealth v. Sandusky*, CP-14-CR-2421-2011; CP-14-CR-2422-2011 (5-18-12); Bill of Particulars, *Commonwealth v. Sandusky*, CP-14-CR-2421-2011; CP-14-CR-2422-2011 (2-21-12).
[62] Jeremy Roebuck, "Alleged Sandusky victim tells NBC: 'He knows what he did,'" *Philadelphia Inquirer*, (6-12-12).
[63] The Special Investigative Counsel did not interview the boy involved in the Lasch Building incident. The details of the incident are described as found in the Penn State University Police Department report and the Grand Jury report.
[64] Penn State University Police Report 41-98-1609 at 27.
[65] *Id*. at 26.
[66] *Id*. at 2.
[67] *Id*. at 29.
[68] *Id*. at 23.
[69] *Id*.
[70] *Id*. at 30.
[71] *Id*.
[72] *Id*.
[73] *Id*. at 30, 52.
[74] *Id*. at 40.
[75] *Id*. at 31, 44.
[76] *Id*. at 45.

[77] *Id.* at 45-46.
[78] *Id.* at 46, 52.
[79] *Id.* at 22.
[80] *Id.*
[81] [-] Interview (4-18-12).
[82] Penn State University Police Report 41-98-1609 at 22.
[83] *Id.* at 22.
[84] *Id.* at 3.
[85] *Id.* at 3-4.
[86] Details regarding the investigation come from the University Police Department records and his interview; [-] Interview (1-27-12).
[87] Penn State University Police Report 41-98-1609 at 3-4.
[88] *Id.* at 21.
[89] *Id.* at 22.
[90] *Id.*
[91] *Id.* at 23.
[92] *Id.*
[93] *Id.*
[94] *Id.* at 5; http://www.co.centre.pa.us/511.asp.
[95] [-] Interview (4-11-12); Penn State University Police Report 41-98-1609 at 9.
[96] [-] Interview (4-26-12); [-] Interview (1-27-12).
[97] [-] Interview (4-26-12).
[98] Penn State University Police Report 41-98-1609 at 19-20; [-] Interview (4-11-12).
[99] [-] Interview (4-11-12); Id. at 41-98-1609 at 9.
[100] Penn State University Police Report 41-98-1609 at 6.
[101] [-] Interview (1-27-12).
[102] Penn State University Police Report 41-98-1609 at 7.
[103] *Id.* at 41-98-1609 at 7.
[104] *Id.*
[105] *Id.*
[106] *Id.* at 10.
[107] *Id.* at 21.
[108] *Id.* at 10.
[109] [-] Interview (4-11-12).
[110] [-] Interview (4-11-12).
[111] Penn State University Police Report 41-98-1609 at 11; [-] Interview (1-27-12).
[112] [-] Interview (4-26-12); [-] Interview (4-13-12).
[113] Penn State University Police Report 41-98-1609 at 87-88.
[114] *Id.* at 88.
[115] *Id.*
[116] *Id.* at 90.
[117] *Id.* at 12.
[118] *Id.*; [-] Interview (1-27-12).
[119] Penn State University Police Report 41-98-1609 at 12.
[120] Email from [-] (5-31-12), included in Controller Records relating to [-] payments [Box.net].
[121] Email from [-] (5-31-12), included in Controller Records relating to [-] payments [Box.net].

[122] [-] File Memo (3-5-12).
[123] Penn State University Police Report 41-98-1609 at 14.
[124] Penn State University Police Report 41-98-1609 at 14.
[125] Id. at 14.
[126] Id.
[127] Id. at 15.
[128] Id.
[129] Id. at 16.
[130] Id.
[131] Id.
[132] Id. at 17.
[133] [-] Interview (4-18-12).
[134] [-] Interview (4-11-12).
[135] [-] Interview (4-11-12).
[136] [-] Interview (1-27-12).
[137] [-] Interview (4-11-12).
[138] Penn State University Police Report 41-98-1609 at 18.
[139] Id. at 41-98-1609 at 015_0000018.
[140] [-] Interview (4-11-12).
[141] [-] Interview (4-11-12).
[142] Penn State University Police Report at 18.
[143] [-] Interview (1-27-12).
[144] Exhibit 2-H.
[145] The May 5, 1998 notes refer to a meeting that was scheduled to take place at 9:00 a.m. on May 5 with the "local child abuse people." This reference supports the inference that these notes were taken before 9:00 a.m. on May 5.
[146] Exhibit 2-I.
[147] Exhibit 2-I.
[148] [-] Interview (7-6-12).
[149] Control Number 00649354.
[150] Control Number 00649354.
[151] [-] Interview (1-27-12).
[152] [-] Interview (1-27-12).
[153] Penn State University Police Report at 2-18.
[154] [-] Interview (1-27-12).
[155] [-] Interview (1-27-12).
[156] [-] Interview (2-2-12).
[157] [-] Interview (2-2-12).
[158] [-] Interview (2-2-12).
[159] Schultz confidential file notes (5-1-12).
[160] Control Number 3009518.
[161] Control Number 00641616.
[162] Control Number 00648360.
[163] Exhibit 2-C (Control Number 00644098).
[164] Control Number 644098.
[165] Preliminary Hearing Trans. at 120 (12-16-11).

[166] *See* Exhibits 2-A and 2-B.
[167] [-] Interview (5-1-12); [-] Interview (12-6-11); [-] Interview (4-11-12).
[168] [-] Interview (7-6-12).
[169] [-] Interview (7-6-12).
[170] Michael Raphael, "Penn State Wants Agent Prosecuted," AP News Archive (1-6-98).
[171] *Id.*
[172] *Id.*
[173] Control Number 00644972.
[174] [-] Interview (1-27-12).
[175] Preliminary Hearing Trans. at 219 (12-16-11).
[176] Control Number 06018018.
[177] Preliminary Hearing Trans. at 190 (12-16-11).
[178] Preliminary Hearing Trans. at 177-78 (12-16-11).
[179] Sara Ganim, "Jerry Sandusky book 'Game Over' angers Joe Paterno's family," *Patriot-News* (4-18-12).
[180] [-] Interview (7-6-12).
[181] [-]Notes (3-22-11).
[182] [-] Interview (7-9-12).
[183] [-] Interview (7-9-12).
[184] Control Number 09354508.
[185] Amended Bill of Particulars, *Commonwealth v. Sandusky*, CP-14-CR-2421-2011; CP-14-CR-2422-2011 (May 18, 2012); Bill of Particulars, *Commonwealth v. Sandusky*, CP-14-CR-2421-2011; CP-14-CR-2422-2011 (Feb. 21, 2012).
[186] Control Number 00644655.
[187] Control Number 03008143.
[188] Control Number 03008143.
[189] *"30-and-Out Window Closing,"* SERSNews (Spring 1999), www.portal.state.pa.us/portal/server.pt/document/1079979/1999_q2_pdf; [-] Interview (1-4-12).
[190] *"30-and-Out Window Closing,"* SERSNews (Spring 1999), www.portal.state.pa.us/portal/server.pt/document/1079979/1999_q2_pdf; [-] Interview (1-4-12).
[191] Control Number 00643981.
[192] Control Number JVP-000021.
[193] Control Number JVP-000021.
[194] Control Number 00642802.
[195] [-] Interview (2-2-12).
[196] [-] Interview (2-2-12).
[197] Control Number 03013385.
[198] Control Number 03013385.
[199] Documents provided by Wick Sollers to Special Investigative Counsel.
[200] Control Number JVP000025-26.
[201] Control Number JVP000025-26.
[202] Control Number JVP000025-26.
[203] Exhibit 3-F (Control Number JVP000027).
[204] Exhibit 3-F (Control Number JVP000027).
[205] Exhibit 3-F (Control Number JVP000027).
[206] [-] Interview (7-3-12).
[207] Exhibit 3-G (Control Number 03014658).

[208] Exhibit 3-G (Control Number 03014658).
[209] Control Number 00650775.
[210] Control Number 00650174.
[211] Control Number 00650174.
[212] Control Number 00650174.
[213] Control Number JVP-000023.
[214] Control Number 006_0000014.
[215] Control Number 006_0000014.
[216] Control Number 006_0000011.
[217] Control Number 006_0000005.
[218] [-] Interview (1-12-12).
[219] [-] Interview (1-12-12).
[220] [-] Interview (4-30-12).
[221] Control Number 006_0000029.
[222] Control Numbers 006_0000035, 014_0000127.
[223] Control Number 014_0000133.
[224] Penn State Policy HR-25 (Control Number 014_0000034).
[225] *Id.*
[226] *Id.*
[227] *Id.*
[228] Control Number 014_0000136.
[229] Control Number 014_0000136.
[230] [-] Interview (2-22-12).
[231] [-] Interview (3-14-12).
[232] Control Number RAE_000001.
[233] Control Number RAE_000001.
[234] Control Number RAE_000001.
[235] Control Number RAE_000001.
[236] [-] Interview (4-12-12).
[237] [-] Interview (7-2-12).
[238] [-] Interview (4-15-12).
[239] [-] Interview (7-2-12).
[240] [-] Interview (7-2-12).
[241] [-] Interview (7-2-12).
[242] [-] Interview (7-2-12).
[243] [-] Interview (7-2-12).
[244] [-] Interview (7-2-12).
[245] [-] Interview (7-2-12).
[246] [-] Interview (7-2-12).
[247] [-] Interview (7-2-12).
[248] [-] Interview (7-2-12).
[249] [-] Interview (7-2-12).
[250] [-] Interview (7-2-12).
[251] Email from [-] to [-] (3-21-12); Penn State University Press Release, *"Former FBI director Freeh to conduct independent investigation"* (11-21-11) (Judge Freeh noted, "We will cooperate fully with the law enforcement authorities, will defer to them, and will not impede their work in any way").

[252] Preliminary Hearing Trans. at 10 (12-16-11).
[253] *Id.* at 9-10.
[254] *Id.* at 10, 14.
[255] *Id.* at 13.
[256] *Id.*
[257] *Id.* at 13-14, 16-17.
[258] *Id.* at 17.
[259] *Id.* at 17, 19.
[260] *Id.* at 19.
[261] *Id.* at 20-21.
[262] *Id.* at 22.
[263] *Id.* at 22-23.
[264] *Id.*
[265] *Id.* at 23.
[266] *Id.* at 23-24.
[267] [-] Interview (3-1-12).
[268] Preliminary Hearing Trans. at 24-25 (12-16-11).
[269] *Id.* at 176.
[270] *Id.* at 175-76.
[271] *Id.* at 176.
[272] *Id.* at 25-26.
[273] *Id.* at 26.
[274] Sally Jenkins, "Joe Paterno's Last Interview," *Washington Post* (1-14-12).
[275] Preliminary Hearing Trans. at 177 (12-16-11).
[276] *Id* at 177.
[277] *Id.* at 177.
[278] *Id.* at 180, 202.
[279] *Id.*
[280] *Id.* at 181.
[281] *Id.* at 229.
[282] *Id.* at 206.
[283] *Id.* at 211.
[284] *Id.*
[285] *Id.* at 229.
[286] Exhibit 5-A.
[287] Control Number 11118161.
[288] [-] Interview (1-12-12); [-] Interview (4-12-12).
[289] [-] File Memo (5-1-12).
[290] Exhibit 5-C.
[291] Exhibit 2-J.
[292] *Id.*
[293] *Id.*
[294] *Id.*
[295] *Id.*
[296] *Id.*
[297] *Id.*

[298] *Id.*
[299] *Id.*
[300] [-] Notes (12-28-10).
[301] [-] Notes (12-28-10).
[302] [-] Notes (12-28-10).
[303] Schultz confidential file notes (5-1-12).
[304] Schultz confidential file notes (5-1-12).
[305] Exhibit 2-J; [-] Interview (7-6-12).
[306] Exhibit 5-A.
[307] Exhibit 5-C.
[308] Exhibit 5-D (Control Number 00675162).
[309] Exhibit 5-C.
[310] Schultz confidential file notes (5-1-12).
[311] Preliminary Hearing Trans. at 30 (12-16-11).
[312] *Id.* at 202-03.
[313] *Id.* at 32-33.
[314] *Id.* at 35.
[315] *Id.* at 183.
[316] *Id.* at 225.
[317] *Id.*
[318] Control Number 00681288.
[319] Control Number 03030942.
[320] Preliminary Hearing Trans. at 30 (12-16-11).
[321] Spanier 2001 Calendar.
[322] [-] Interview (7-6-12).
[323] [-] Interview (7-6-12).
[324] [-] Interview (7-6-12).
[325] [-] Interview (7-6-12).
[326] [-] Interview (7-6-12).
[327] [-] Interview (7-6-12).
[328] Exhibit 5-F (Control Number 00677433).
[329] Exhibit 5-G (Control Number 00679428).
[330] Exhibit 5-G (Control Number 00679428); Exhibit 5-H (Control Number 00676529).
[331] Exhibit 5-G (Control Number 00679428).
[332] Exhibit 5-G (Control Number 00679428).
[333] *See* Control Number 00642973 (6-9-1998) (email subject is "*Jerry*"); Control Number 00645223 (6-1-1998) ("The DPW investigator and our officer met discreetly with *Jerry* this morning"); Control Number 00646346 (6-9-1998)(" They met with *Jerry* on Monday and concluded that there was no criminal behavior and the matter was closed as an investigation"); Control Number 00647284 (5-19-1998)(email subject is "*Jerry*"); Control Number 00648360 (5-14-1998) ("Tim, I understand that a DPW person was here last week; don't know for sure if they talked with *Jerry*").
[334] Control Numbers 00650775, 00650174, 00650775, 03014658, 03013385.
[335] Control Numbers 09302202, 09350582; [-] Notes of meeting with Graham Spanier (3-22-11).
[336] [-] Notes of meeting with Graham Spanier (3-22-11).
[337] [-] Notes of meeting with Graham Spanier (3-22-11).
[338] [-] Interview (2-1-12); [-] Interview (1-23-12); [-] Interview (12-12-11); [-] Interview (1-3-12).

[339] [-] Interview (4-12-12).
[340] [-] Interview (2-6-12); [-] Interview (4-17-12).
[341] [-] Interview (2-6-12); [-] Interview (4-25-12); [-] Interview (1-24-12); [-] Interview (1-3-12); [-] Interview (2-7-12); [-] Interview (1-23-12); [-] Interview (12-12-11).
[342] Exhibit 5-G (Control Number 00679428).
[343] *See* Exhibit 2-J.
[344] *See* Exhibit 2-J.
[345] Exhibit 5-H (Control Number 00676529).
[346] Preliminary Hearing Trans. at 185-86 (12-16-11).
[347] Preliminary Hearing Trans. at 185-86 (12-16-11).
[348] Preliminary Hearing Trans. at 182 (12-16-11).
[349] [-] File Memo (2-28-12).
[350] [-] File Memo (2-28-12).
[351] [-] File Memo (2-28-12).
[352] [-] File Memo (2-28-12).
[353] [-] File Memo (2-28-12).
[354] [-] File Memo (2-28-12).
[355] Schultz confidential file notes (5-1-12).
[356] Control Number 00680519.
[357] Preliminary Hearing Trans. at 215 (12-16-11).
[358] [-]Notes of meeting with Graham Spanier (3-22-11).
[359] Exhibit 2-J.
[360] [-] Interview (7-6-12).
[361] Sally Jenkins, "Joe Paterno's Last Interview," *Washington Post* (1-14-12).
[362] [-] File Memo (4-9-12).
[363] [-] File Memo (3-22-12).
[364] [-] File Memo (3-22-12).
[365] [-] File Memo (3-22-12).
[366] [-] File Memo (3-22-12).
[367] [-] File Memo (3-22-12).
[368] [-] File Memo (3-22-12).
[369] [-] File Memo (3-22-12).
[370] [-] File Memo (3-22-12).
[371] Control Number 03036051.
[372] Control Number 03036051.
[373] Control Number 00684991.
[374] Control Number 00684991.
[375] Preliminary Hearing Trans. at 191-92 (12-16-11).
[376] [-] Interview (7-6-12).
[377] Subpoena from Statewide Investigating Grand Jury, Supreme Court of Pennsylvania, 190 M.D. Misc. Dkt. 2001, Dauphin County Common Pleas, No. 1430, M.D. 2008, Notice 29, Subpoena 671 (1-7-10).
[378] [-] Interview (3-6-12); [-] Interview (2-21-12).
[379] [-] Interview (3-6-12).
[380] [-] Interview (3-6-12); Control Number 09327800 ("The specifics of the investigation were not disclosed to us"); Control Number 09369385 (the prosecutor "kept the core of the issue very close to her vest").
[381] Notes of [-] (2-8-10); [-] Interview (3-6-12).

[382] Notes of [-] (3-1-10); [-] Interview (3-6-12).
[383] Control Number 09327800.
[384] Control Number 09327800.
[385] [-] Notes (12-28-10).
[386] [-] Interview (11-23-11).
[387] [-] Interview (11-23-11); [-] Notes (12-28-10).
[388] [-] Notes (12-28-10).
[389] [-] Notes (12-28-10).
[390] [-] Notes (12-28-10).
[391] [-] Notes (12-28-10).
[392] [-] Notes (12-28-10).
[393] Control Number 11117847.
[394] Control Number 11117847.
[395] [-] Notes (1-3-11).
[396] [-] Notes (1-3-11).
[397] [-] Notes (1-3-11).
[398] [-] Interview (2-29-12).
[399] Control Number 09354508.
[400] Control Number 09354508.
[401] Control Number 09354508.
[402] Control Number 09354508.
[403] Control Number 09361218.
[404] [-] Interview (11-23-11).
[405] Control Number 09382271.
[406] Control Number 04065904.
[407] Control Number 04065904.
[408] Control Number 166851.
[409] [-] Interview (2-29-12).
[410] [-] Interview (2-29-12).
[411] [-] Interview (2-29-12).
[412] [-] Interview (2-29-12).
[413] Control Number 06633947; [-] Notes of [-] Interviews (1-15-11).
[414] Control Number 00045093.
[415] Control Number 09405967.
[416] Spanier was questioned about a 2002 incident that was later determined to have occurred in 2001.
[417] [-] Notes of meeting with Graham Spanier (3-22-11); Control Number 09302202.
[418] Subpoena 92. Spanier suggested in recent court filings that he appeared before the Grand Jury "voluntarily and without subpoena." *Spanier v. Pennsylvania State University*, Verified Complaint in Equity (5-25-12).
[419] Control Number 00035001.
[420] Control Number 00043675.
[421] [-] Interview (1-25-12); Control Number 04046135.
[422] Control Number 4046135.
[423] Sara Ganim, "Jerry Sandusky, former Penn State football staffer, subject of Grand Jury investigation," *Patriot-News* (3-31-11).
[424] *Id.*

[425] *Id.*
[426] *Id.*
[427] Control Number 1096008.
[428] Control Number 1096008.
[429] Control Number 9341973.
[430] Control Number 9365024.
[431] Control Number 9365024.
[432] Control Number 9365024.
[433] Control Number 9365024.
[434] [-] Interview (7-6-12).
[435] [-] Notes (4-13-11).
[436] Control Number 9365024.
[437] [-] Interview (2-29-12).
[438] [-] Interview (2-20-12).
[439] [-] Interview (2-20-12).
[440] [-] Interview (2-29-12).
[441] [-] Interview (7-6-12).
[442] [-] Interview (7-6-12).
[443] [-] Interview (7-6-12); [-] Interview (7-6-12).
[444] [-] Interview (4-20-12); [-] Interview (3-13-12).
[445] Exhibit 6-A (Baldwin affidavit).
[446] Exhibit 6-A (Baldwin affidavit).
[447] Exhibit 6-A (Baldwin affidavit).
[448] [-] Interview (2-29-12).
[449] [-] Interview (2-29-12).
[450] *See, e.g.,* [-] Interview (3-22-12); [-] Interview (4-16-12); [-] Interview (4-12-12); [-] Interview (5-3-12); [-] Interview (4-16-12); [-] Interview (3-13-12); [-] Interview (3-15-12); [-] Interview (4-5-12); [-] Interview (4-16-12).
[451] *See, e.g.,* [-] Interview (3-15-12); [-] Interview (3-22-12); [-] Interview (3-15-12); [-] Interview (4-12-12); [-] Interview (4-16-12); [-] Interview (5-3-12); [-] Interview (4-16-12); [-] Interview (3-13-12); [-] Interview (3-15-12); [-] Interview (3-15-12).
[452] *See, e.g.,* [-] Interview (3-22-12); [-] Interview (4-16-12); [-] Interview (4-12-12); [-] Interview (4-16-12); [-] Interview (5-3-12); [-] Interview (3-15-12); [-] Interview (3-15-12).
[453] [-] Interview (3-13-12); [-] Interview (3-13-12); [-] Interview (4-16-12).
[454] *See, e.g.,* [-] Interview (3-8-12); [-] Interview (3-13-12); [-] Interview (4-11-12); [-] Interview (3-15-12); [-] Interview (3-22-12); [-] Interview (4-16-12); [-] Interview (3-15-12); [-] Interview (4-12-12); [-] Interview (4-16-12); [-] Interview (4-16-11); [-] Interview (5-3-12); [-] Interview (4-20-12); [-] Interview (4-16-12); [-] Interview (3-13-12); [-] Interview (3-15-12); [-] Interview (3-15-12); [-] Interview (4-5-12); [-] Interview (3-13-12).
[455] Control Number 12005881; [-] Interview (4-6-12); [-] Interview (3-15-12); [-] Interview (3-14-12); [-] Interview (3-15-12); [-] Interview (5-3-12); [-] Interview (4-11-12); [-] Interview (3-15-12).
[456] Control Numbers 06633947, 00045093, 09405967, 10615894, 06630379; [-] Notes of [-] Interviews (1-15-11); [-] Notes of [-] Interviews of [-] and [-] (1-17-11).
[457] Grand Jury Subpoena 109 (3-24-11).
[458] Grand Jury Subpoena 191 (5-11-11).
[459] Grand Jury Subpoena 183 (5-9-11); Grand Jury Subpoena 185 (5-10-11).

[460] [-] Interview (4-20-12); [-] Interview (3-15-12).
[461] [-] Interview (4-20-12); [-] Interview (3-13-12).
[462] [-] Interview (3-8-12).
[463] [-] Interview (4-12-12).
[464] [-] Interview (3-14-12).
[465] [-] Interview (3-22-12); [-] Interview (3-15-12); [-] Interview (3-13-12); [-] Interview (3-8-12); [-] Interview (4-16-12); [-] Interview (3-14-12).
[466] [-] Interview (4-16-12).
[467] *See, e.g.,* [-] Interview (3-8-12); [-] Interview (3-15-12); [-] Interview (3-15-12); [-] Interview (5-3-12).
[468] [-] Interview (4-16-12).
[469] [-] Interview (11-25-11).
[470] [-] Interview (11-25-11).
[471] Control Number 00039079.
[472] [-] Interview (7-6-12).
[473] Spanier Calendar 2011; Control Number 01000672.
[474] [-] Interview (1-25-12).
[475] Control Number 01001160.
[476] Control Numbers 01001782, 09377177, 09382920, 09388808, 09398766.
[477] [-] Interview (1-25-12).
[478] [-] Interview (1-25-12).
[479] [-] Interview (7-6-12).
[480] [-] Interview (7-6-12).
[481] Spanier Calendar 2011.
[482] [-] Interview (2 29 12).
[483] [-] Interview (2-20-12).
[484] [-] Interview (2-20-12).
[485] [-] Interview (2-20-12).
[486] [-] Interview (2-20-12).
[487] [-] Interview (7-6-12).
[488] [-] Interview (7-6-12).
[489] [-] Interview (7-6-12).
[490] [-] Interview (7-6-12).
[491] Control Number 00510882.
[492] Control Numbers 09361376, 09368381, 09361329.
[493] Control Numbers 10245114.
[494] Control Number 1001210.
[495] Control Number 1001203.
[496] Control Number 09347465.
[497] Control Number 09347465.
[498] Control Number 1001210.
[499] [-] Notes (11-5-11).
[500] [-] Notes (11-5-11).
[501] [-] Notes (11-5-11).
[502] [-] Notes (11-5-11).
[503] [-] Notes (11-5-11).
[504] Control Number 1001228.

[505] Control Number 1001228.
[506] [-] Interview (3-8-12); [-] Interview (3-13-12); [-] Interview (3-12-12).
[507] [-] Interview (3-8-12).
[508] [-] Notes (11-6-11).
[509] [-] Notes (11-6-11).
[510] [-] Notes (11-6-11).
[511] [-] Notes (11-6-11).
[512] Control Number 01035996.
[513] Control Number 01035996.
[514] [-] Notes (11-6-11).
[515] [-] Interview (4-16-12); [-] Interview (3-8-12).
[516] [-] Interview (4-13-12); [-] Interview (3-12-12); [-] Interview (4-16-12); [-] Interview (4-16-12); [-] Interview (3-13-12); [-] Interview (4-16-12); [-] Interview (3-8-12).
[517] [-] Interview (4-16-12); [-] Interview (3-13-12); [-] Interview (4-16-12); [-] Interview (3-8-12); [-] Interview (3-12-12); [-] Interview (4-13-12)
[518] [-] Interview (7-6-12).
[519] [-] Interview (3-13-12).
[520] [-] Interview (3-13-12).
[521] Control Number 1001535.
[522] [-] Notes (11-8-11).
[523] [-] Notes (11-8-11).
[524] [-] Notes (11-8-11).
[525] [-] Notes (11-8-11).
[526] [-] Notes (11-8-11).
[527] http://live.psu.edu/story/56285.
[528] http://live.psu.edu/story/56285.
[529] http://live.psu.edu/story/56285.
[530] [-] Notes (11-9-11).
[531] [-] Notes (11-9-11).
[532] [-] Notes (11-9-11).
[533] [-] Interview (5-16-12).
[534] [-] Interview (4-23-12).
[535] [-] Interview (4-16-12); [-] Interview (4-16-12); [-] Interview (3-13-12).
[536] [-] Interview (4-16-12); [-] Interview (3-12-12).
[537] [-] Interview (4-16-12); [-] Interview (3-15-12); [-] Interview (4-16-12); [-] Interview (3-13-12).
[538] [-] Interview (3-15-12); [-] Interview (5-16-12).
[539] [-] Interview (4-16-12).
[540] [-] Interview (4-16-12).
[541] [-] Interview (4-16-12).
[542] [-] Interview (4-16-12).
[543] [-] Interview (4-23-12); [-] Interview (4-18-12).
[544] [-] Interview (4-23-12).
[545] [-] Interview (4-23-12).
[546] [-] Interview (4-23-12).
[547] [-] Notes (11-9-11).
[548] [-] Notes (11-9-11).

[549] Jessica VanderKolk, "King says PSU Gave Little Warning," *Center Daily Times* (11-16-11).
[550] [-] Interview (5-9-12); [-] Interview (4-16-12); [-] Interview (4-6-12); [-] Interview (4-11-12); [-] Interview (4-18-12).
[551] [-] Interview (4-6-12); [-] Interview (4-16-12).
[552] Standing Orders of the Penn State Board of Trustees, Order IX(1)(a).
[553] http://www.psu.edu/trustees/selection.html.
[554] *See* Board of Trustees Minutes of Meeting at 208-12 (5-16-03).
[555] Standing Orders of the Penn State Board of Trustees, Order XI.
[556] http://www.psu.edu/trustees/membership.html.
[557] *See* Standing Orders of the Penn State Board of Trustees, Order IX. This statement on the general policies of the Board of Trustees was initially set forth and approved by the Board on June 11, 1970 and amended from time, the most recent being January 19, 1996. www.psu.edu/Trustees/governance.html.
[558] Board of Trustees Corporate By-Laws, Art. 4, Sections 7-9 (2010).
[559] Board of Trustees Minutes of Meeting, March 19, 2004 and September 19, 2008, http://www.psu.edu/trustees/archives.html#2008.
[560] Standing Orders of the Penn State Board of Trustees, Order III. During the period 1998-2002, the Board met six times per year.
[561] *See* 15 Pa. Cons. Stat. § 5712; *In re Caremark International, Inc. Derivative Litigation*, 698 A.2d 959, 970-71 (Del. Ch. 1996).
[562] Standing Orders of the Penn State Board of Trustees, Order IX(1)(b)(2).
[563] *See Stone v. Ritter*, 911 A.2d 362, 370 (Del. Ch. 2006).
[564] *See Caremark*, 698 A.2d at 970-971.
[565] [-] Interview (3-22-12); [-] Interview (3-15-12); [-] Interview (3-13-12); [-] Interview (3-8-12); [-] Interview (4-16-12); [-] Interview (3-14-12).
[566] [-] Interview (4-16-12); [-] Interview (3-8-12).
[567] [-] Interview (4-16-12).
[568] Control Number 12005881; [-] Interview (4-6-12); [-] Interview (3-15-12); [-] Interview (3-14-12); [-] Interview (3-15-12); [-] Interview (5-3-12); [-] Interview (4-11-12); [-] Interview (3-15-12); [-] Interview (3-22-12); [-] Interview (3-15-12); [-] Interview (4-12-12); [-] Interview (4-16-12); [-] Interview (4-16-12); [-] Interview (3-13-12); [-] Interview (3-15-12).
[569] Control Number 9365024.
[570] Standing Orders of the Penn State Board of Trustees, Order IX(1)(b)(2).
[571] Standing Orders of the Penn State Board of Trustees, Order IX(1)(b)(2).
[572] Control Number 9365024.
[573] Control Number 1001203.
[574] Control Number 1001203.
[575] [-] Notes (11-5-11).
[576] Control Number 006_0000043.
[577] Penn State Policy HR-25 (Control Number 014_0000034).
[578] [-] Interview (2-15-12); [-] Interview (12-7-11); [-] Interview (12-5-11); [-] Interview (12-12-11); [-] Interview (12-16-11).
[579] [-] Interview (12-15-11); [-] Interview (1-25-12).
[580] [-] Interview (1-25-12); keylist.xls.
[581] Penn State Policy HR-25 (Control Number 014_0000034); Control Number 006_0000043.
[582] [-] Interview (12-07-11).

[583] The Special Investigative Counsel and investigators with the Attorney General's Office found Sandusky's documents in April 2012.
[584] Id.
[585] [-] Interview (4-19-12).
[586] [-] Interview (1-5-12); [-] Interview (1-10-12); [-] Interview (2-8-12).
[587] Nittany Lion Club Records (7-8-11); [-] Interview (1-5-12); [-] Interview (2-8-12).
[588] [-] Interview (1-5-12); [-] Interview (2-8-12).
[589] Nittany Lion Club Records, November 2011; [-] Interview (1-5-12); [-] Interview (2-8-12).
[590] Letterman Club Records, Nittany Lion Club Records.
[591] Nittany Lion Club Records, September-October 2011.
[592] [-] Interview (2-8-12).
[593] [-] Interview (3-14-12); [-] Interview (12-19-11).
[594] Sandusky was scheduled to conduct a camp in 2009, but his wife called the campus and cancelled the camp.
[595] Penn State Policy AD39.
[596] *See* [-] Interview (4-24-12); [-] Interview (4-24-12).
[597] [-] Interview (4-24-12).
[598] *See, e.g.,* [-] Interview (4-24-12); [-] Interview (4-24-12).
[599] XL spreadsheet of PSU payments to Sandusky provided by the Controller's Office.
[600] XL spreadsheet of PSU payments to Sandusky provided by the Controller's Office.
[601] Control Number 014_0000054.
[602] XL spreadsheet of PSU payments to Sandusky provided by the Controller's Office.
[603] XL spreadsheet of PSU payments to Sandusky provided by the Controller's Office.
[604] XL spreadsheet of PSU payments to Sandusky provided by the Controller's Office.
[605] *See e.g.,* [-] Interview (2-1-12).
[606] [-] Interview (12-5-11); (12-5-11); [-] Interview (12-6-11).
[607] Control Number 00033853; [-] Interview (2-29-12).
[608] [-] Interview (2-22-12).
[609] [-] Interview (2-29-12).
[610] [-] Interview (2-15-12); [-] Interview (2-14-12).
[611] [-] Interview (2-29-12).
[612] [-] Interview (12-16-11); [-] Interview (1-18-12).
[613] [-] Interview (12-16-11); [-] Interview (1-18-12).
[614] Armen Keteyian, "Sandusky's Second Mile charity probed for clues," *CBS Evening News* (11-11-11).
[615] [-] Interview (4-11-12).
[616] http://www.psu.edu/dept/psusportsinfo/football/profiles/sanduskyretires.html.
[617] Id.
[618] Memorandum from [-] to The Board of Directors (8-23-1999).
[619] Control Number 006_0000044.
[620] Second Mile Golf Tournament documents provided by Controller's Office (2-9-12).
[621] Control Number 00555509.
[622] Control Number 04122803.
[623] [-] Interview (4-24-12); [-] Interview (4-24-12); Exhibit 3-F.
[624] http://www.foxnews.com/us/2011/11/19/penn-state-paid-by-sanduskys-charity-for-use-facilities-as-recently-as-2009/.
[625] [-] Interview (4-19-12).

[626] [-] Interview (4-19-12).
[627] [-] Interview (4-19-12).
[628] [-] Interview (3-6-12); [-] Interview (4-11-12); [-] Interview (4-11-12).
[629] [-] Interview (4-11-12).
[630] [-] Interview (1-13-12).
[631] [-] Interview (1-13-12).
[632] [-] Interview (1-13-12).
[633] [-] Interview (1-13-12).
[634] [-] Interview (1-13-12).
[635] [-] Interview (1-13-12).
[636] In its 2002 ASR, for example, the University mistakenly reported that there were no sexual assaults in its Clery Act statistics. A watchdog organization noticed the discrepancy; the University discovered that it had made a mistake in its calculation and reissued the statistics. The incident resulted in negative publicity in the local newspaper. *See* Email of 1-12-2004 at 3:47:09 p.m.
[637] [-] Interview (2-1-12); [-] Interview (1-5-12).
[638] [-] Interview (2-1-12).
[639] [-] Interview (1-5-12).
[640] [-] Interview (1-5-12).
[641] [-] Interview (1-5-12).
[642] [-] Interview (1-5-12); [-] Interview (2-1-12); *e.g.,* Control Number 09503459.
[643] [-] Interview (1-5-12); [-] Interview (2-1-12).
[644] [-] Interview (1-5-12).
[645] Control Number 09528529.
[646] [-] Interview (2-1-12); [-] Interview (1-5-12).
[647] [-] Interview (1-5-12).
[648] Control Number 08036801.
[649] [-] Interview (2-1-12).
[650] Control Number 09618422.
[651] [-] Interview (2-1-12).
[652] [-] Interview (2-1-12).
[653] [-] Interview (7-6-12).
[654] [-] Interview (7-6-12).
[655] [-] Interview (7-6-12).
[656] [-] Interview (7-6-12).
[657] [-] Interview (7-6-12).
[658] The Special Investigative Counsel determined that this incident occurred in 2001.
[659] Preliminary Hearing Trans. at 24-25 (12-16-11).
[660] Preliminary Hearing Trans. at 34 (12-16-11).
[661] Preliminary Hearing Trans. at 175-76 (12-16-11).
[662] The University Police Department recently surveyed everyone who worked there in February 2001. None of those employees had ever been informed of this incident. The incident was not included in Penn State's Clery statistics and no timely warning was made about it. [-] Interview (6-1-12).
[663] Report prepared by [-] for Penn State, November 27, 2011.
[664] *See Chapter 9, The Protection of Children in University Facilities and Programs.*
[665] Outreach consists of five major units: Continuing Education, Cooperative Extension, Economic and Workforce Development, Public Broadcasting and Online Education.

[666] Email from [-] to [-] (8-6-10).
[667] *See* Appendix (2), Penn State Policy AD39.
[668] Control Number 09341611.
[669] *See* Appendix (2), Penn State Policy AD39.
[670] *See id.*
[671] Additional clarifications, added June 7, 2012, include updated requirements for high school students visiting on pre-enrollment visits with Penn State students, clarification of reporting process and exclusion of client representation clinics in Dickinson School of Law from policy.
[672] Although Policy AD39 first took effect in 1992, it was not until April 28, 2010 that the Policy addressed background checks. Under the revised Policy AD39, the background check consists of a University background check or evidence of completion of Pennsylvania Act 34 (background check), Pennsylvania Act 151 (child abuse clearance) and FBI background history report clearance before being hired and/or interacting with minors.
[673] *See* Appendix (2), Penn State Policies HR-95 and HR-96.
[674] *See* Appendix (2), Penn State Policy HR-99, *Background Check Process.*
[675] *See* Appendix (2), Penn State Policy HR-99, *Background Check Process.*
[676] *See* Appendix (2), Penn State Policy HR-99, *Background Check Process.*
[677] *See* Appendix (2), Penn State Policy HR-99, *Background Check Process.*
[678] [-] Interview (3-8-12).
[679] [-] Interview (3-12-12).
[680] [-] Interview (2-23-12).
[681] [-] Interview (2-23-12).
[682] [-] Interview (12-19-11).
[683] *See, e.g.* [-] Interview (3-6-12) (stating that, "it has happened here [at Altoona]" on a number of occasions over the years and coaches have always just been told not to do it again); [-] Interview (3-8-12) (stating that the use of individuals that were not registered or subjected to background checks happened once or twice each year. When those in her office would discover such individuals their response was, "guess what happened again?").
[684] [-] Interview (3-8-12).
[685] [-] Interview (2-23-12).
[686] *See, e.g.,* [-] Interview (2-23-12); [-] Interview (3-24-12) (stating that such unauthorized participation occurred every year, "all the time"); [-] Interview (3-6-12)(stating that "it has happened here [at Altoona] and on a number of occasions over the years and coaches have always just been told not to do it again); [-] Interview (3-8-12) (stating that the use of individuals that were not registered or subjected to background checks happened once or twice each year).
[687] Email from [-] to [-] (8-6-10).
[688] [-] Interview (3-1-12).
[689] *See e.g.,* [-] Interview (3-1-12); [-] Interview (3-5-12); [-] Interview (4-25-12); [-] Interview (3-6-12); [-] Interview (4-24-12).
[690] [-] Interview (3-1-12); [-] Interview (3-8-12).
[691] [-] Interview (4-16-12).
[692] [-] Interview (4-25-12).
[693] [-] Interview (4-24-12); [-] Interview (3-6-12); [-] Interview (3-21-12). Using E-PATCH, a coach or counselor can apply for a criminal background check online and, most of the time, a "no record" result is returned immediately. [-] Interview (3-5-12); see also, www.portal.state.pa.us. The coach or counselor requesting the background check bears the cost of this search. If a result of "no record" is returned, the

coach or counselor is allowed to work with youth with the limitation that the coach or counselor is not allowed to stay overnight with youth in a residence hall until the University background check is completed. [-] Interview (3-6-12).

[694] [-] Interview (4-16-12). Senior administrator interviewers were unaware that fingerprinting was being utilized at this campus.

[695] [-] Interview (3-24-12).

[696] [-] Interview (3-8-12).

[697] [-] Interview (3-12-12).

[698] [-] Interview (3-23-12).

[699] [-] Interview (3-23-12).

[700] [-] Interview (3-23-12); [-] Interview (12-19-11).

[701] [-] Interview (3-23-12); [-] Interview (12-19-11).

[702] [-] Interview (3-23-12); [-] Interview (12-19-11).

# APPENDICES

# APPENDIX A
# EXHIBITS

# EXHIBIT LIST

| | |
|---|---|
| 2A: | EMAIL, SCHULTZ TO CURLEY, 5.6.98; RE: JOE PATERNO |
| 2B: | EMAIL, SCHULTZ TO HARMON, 5.14.98; RE: JERRY |
| 2C: | EMAIL, SCHULTZ TO HARMON, 6.9.98; EMAIL RE: JERRY; EMAIL SCHULTZ TO CURLEY 6.8.98 |
| 2D: | EMAIL, SCHULTZ TO HARMON, 6.9.98; RE: CONFIDENTIAL |
| 2E: | EMAIL, SCHULTZ TO CURLEY, SPANIER, HARMON, 6.9.98; RE: JERRY |
| 2F: | EMAIL, SCHULTZ TO SPANIER, CURLEY, 2.28.01; RE: MEETING |
| 2G: | NOTE, TYPED FORM/ HANDWRITTEN NOTES; SANDUSKY RETIREMENT REQUESTS |
| 2H: | NOTE, SCHULTZ HANDWRITTEN NOTES, 5.4.98 @ 5:00PM |
| 2I: | NOTE, SCHULTZ HANDWRITTEN NOTES, 5.5.98; RE: LAST EVENING |
| 2J: | NOTE, SPANIER STATEMENT |
| 3A: | EMAIL, CURLEY TO SPANIER, 2.8.99; RE: SANDUSKY UPDATE |
| 3B: | EMAIL, SPANIER TO CURLEY, SCHULTZ, 2.10.98; RE: SANDUSKY UPDATE; EMAIL, CURLEY, 2.9.98 |
| 3C: | EMAIL, SPANIER TO CURLEY, 1.19.99; RE: JERRY |
| 3D: | INTERPRETATION OF JVP HANDWRITTEN NOTES, FROM PATERNO RESIDENCE; RE: MEETING WITH JERRY AND TIM C |
| 3E: | LETTER, SANDUSKY TO CURLEY, 5.28.99; RE: RETIREMENT OPTIONS |
| 3F: | NOTE, TYPED FORM/ HANDWRITTEN NOTES; SANDUSKY RETIREMENT REQUESTS |
| 3G: | EMAIL, CURLEY TO SPANIER, 6.13.99; RE: JERRY |
| 3H: | LETTER, CURLEY TO SANDUSKY, 6.29.99; RE: RETIREMENT PREREQUISITES |
| 3I: | EMAIL, ERICKSON TO SECOR; RE: EMERITUS QUESTION; EMAIL, REBECCA YOUNG TO SECOR, 8.30.99; RE: EMERITUS QUESTION |
| 5A: | TIMESHEET, MCQUAIDE BLASKO, INC., COURTNEY, 2.1.01 TO 4.30.01 |
| 5B: | EMAIL, SCHULTZ TO COURTNEY, 1.10.11; RE: JSRECE; EMAIL COURTNEY TO SCHULTZ, 1.10.11; RE: JS |
| 5C: | NOTE, SCHULTZ CONFIDENTIAL HANDWRITTEN NOTE, 2.12.01 |
| 5D: | EMAIL, HARMON TO SCHULTZ, 2.12.01; RE: INCIDENT IN 1998 |
| 5E: | NOTE, SCHULTZ HANDWRITTEN NOTES, 2.25.01 |
| 5F: | EMAIL, SCHULTZ TO CURLEY, COBLE, 2.26.01; RE: CONFIDENTIAL |
| 5G: | EMAIL, SCHULTZ TO SPANIER, CURLEY, 2.28.01; RE: MEETING; EMAIL, SPANIER, 2.27.01; RE: MEETING; EMAIL, CURLEY, 2.27.01 |
| 5H: | EMAIL, SCHULTZ TO CURLEY, 3.1.01; RE: SCHEDULE |
| 5I: | EMAIL, COBLE TO CURLEY, 3.7.01; RE: CONFIDENTIAL; EMAIL SCHULTZ TO CURLEY, 2.26.01; RE: CONFIDENTIAL |
| 6A: | AFFIDAVIT, BALDWIN, 1.16.12 |
| 10A: | COMMITTEE LIST, ORGANIZATION CHART BOARD OF TRUSTEES AS OF FEBRUARY 1998, FEBRUARY 2001, JULY 1, 2012 |

# Exhibit 2A

**From:** Gary C. Schultz <gcs2@psu.edu>
**Sent:** Wednesday, May 06, 1998 2:06 PM
**To:** Tim Curley
**Cc:** Spanier-Graham (GBS)
**Subject:** Re: Joe Paterno

Will do. Since we talked tonight I've learned that the Public Welfare people will interview the individual Thursday.

At 05:24 PM 5/5/98 -0400, Tim Curley wrote:
>I have touched base with the coach. Keep us posted. Thanks.
>_____
>Tim Curley
>Tmc3@psu.edu
>
>
>

# Exhibit 2B

**From:** Gary C. Schultz <gcs2@psu.edu>
**Sent:** Thursday, May 14, 1998 8:55 AM
**To:** Thomas Harmon
**Subject:** Re: Jerry

Good, Tom. Thanks for the update and I agree that we want to resolve quickly.

At 04:48 PM 5/13/98 EST, Thomas Harmon wrote:
>The psychologist from DPW spoke with the child. They have not spoken
>to him. It is still my understanding that they intend to do this. I
>have also been advised that they want to resolve this quickly.
>
>> Date:      Thu, 14 May 1998 04:11:19 -0400
>> To:        Tim Curley <tmc3@psu.edu>
>> From:      "Gary C. Schultz" <gcs2@psu.edu>
>> Subject:   Re: Jerry
>
>> Tim, I understand that a DPW person was here last week; don't know
>> for sure if they talked with Jerry. They decided to have a child
>> psychologist talk to the boys sometime over the next week. We won't know anything before then.
>>
>> At 02:21 PM 5/13/98 -0400, Tim Curley wrote:
>> >Anything new in this department? Coach is anxious to know where it stands.
>> >_____
>> >Tim Curley
>> >Tmc3@psu.edu
>> >
>> >
>> >
>> Gary C. Schultz
>> Sr. V.P. for Finance and Business/Treasurer
>> 208 Old Main
>> Phone: 865-6574
>> Fax:   863-8685
>>
>>
>Thomas R. Harmon
>Director of Police Services
>The Pennsylvania State University
>30-B Eisenhower Parking Deck
>University Park, PA 16802
>(814) 865-1864
>harmon@police.psu.edu
>
>

# Exhibit 2C

**From:** Gary C. Schultz <gcs2@psu.edu>
**Sent:** Tuesday, June 09, 1998 2:03 AM
**To:** Harmon-Thomas (TRH)
**Subject:** Re: Jerry

Tom, I've been holding some "catch up time" on my calendar on Monday and I'd suggest that we use a piece of it to meet and discuss the status (I also recall the last time we talked you indicated that there was some aspects of this that you felt you should review with me when we had a chance to talk). Please get ahold of Joan and see what time will work. thanks

>Date: Mon, 08 Jun 1998 21:59:42 -0400
>To: Tim Curley <tmc3@psu.edu>
>From: "Gary C. Schultz" <gcs2@psu.edu>
>Subject: Re: Jerry
>
>Tim, I don't have an update at this point. Just before I left for vac, Tom told me that the DPW and Univ Police services were planning to meet with him. I'll see if this has happened and get back to you.
>
>At 10:27 AM 5/30/98 -0400, Tim Curley wrote:
>>Any further update?
>>
>>
>>
>>
>>At 09:46 AM 5/19/98 -0400, you wrote:
>>>No, but I don't expect we'll hear anything prior to the end of this week.
>>>
>>>At 09:37 PM 5/18/98 -0400, Tim Curley wrote:
>>>>Any update?
>>>>
>>>>
>>>>At 04:11 AM 5/14/98 -0400, you wrote:
>>>>>Tim, I understand that a DPW person was here last week; don't know
>>>>>for sure if they talked with Jerry. They decided to have a child
>>>>>psychologist talk to the boys sometime over the next week. We won't know anything before then.
>>>>>
>>>>>At 02:21 PM 5/13/98 -0400, Tim Curley wrote:
>>>>>>Anything new in this department? Coach is anxious to know where it stands.
>>>>>>_____
>>>>>>Tim Curley
>>>>>>Tmc3@psu.edu
>>>>>>
>>>>>>
>>>>>>
>>>>>Gary C. Schultz
>>>>>Sr. V.P. for Finance and Business/Treasurer
>>>>>208 Old Main
>>>>>Phone: 865-6574

>>>>>Fax: 863-8685
>>>>>
>>>>>
>>>>>
>>>>_____
>>>>Tim Curley
>>>>Tmc3@psu.edu
>>>>
>>>>
>>>>
>>>Gary C. Schultz
>>>Sr. V.P. for Finance and Business/Treasurer
>>>208 Old Main
>>>Phone: 865-6574
>>>Fax: 863-8685
>>>
>>>
>>>
>>_____
>>Tim Curley
>>Tmc3@psu.edu
>>
>>
>>
>

# Exhibit 2D

**From:** Gary C. Schultz <gcs2@psu.edu>
**Sent:** Tuesday, June 09, 1998 2:04 AM
**To:** Thomas Harmon
**Subject:** Re: Confidential

Tom, you can ignore my earlier email, unless you feel that we should talk some more about this. thanks

At 01:11 PM 6/1/98 EST, Thomas Harmon wrote:
>Gary,
>
>The DPW investigator and our officer met discreetly with Jerry this
>morning. His account of the matter was essential the same as the
>child's. He also indicated that he had done this with other children
>in the past. He was advised since there was no criminal behavior
>established that the matter was closed as an investigation.
>He was a little emotional and expressed concern as to how this might
>have adversely affected the child.
>
>Tom
>
>
>
>
>Thomas R. Harmon
>Director of Police Services
>The Pennsylvania State University
>30-B Eisenhower Parking Deck
>University Park, PA 16802
>(814) 865-1864
>harmon@police.psu.edu
>
>

# Exhibit 2E

| | |
|---|---|
| **From:** | Gary C. Schultz <gcs2@psu.edu> |
| **Sent:** | Tuesday, June 09, 1998 2:09 AM |
| **To:** | Curley-Tim (TMC) |
| **Cc:** | Spanier-Graham (GBS); Harmon-Thomas (TRH) |
| **Subject:** | Re: Jerry |

They met with Jerry on Monday and concluded that there was no criminal behavior and the matter was closed as an investigation. He was a little emotional and expressed concern as to how this might have adversely affected the child. I think the matter has been appropriatedly investigated and I hope it is now behind us.

>Date: Mon, 08 Jun 1998 21:59:42 -0400
>To: Tim Curley <tmc3@psu.edu>
>From: "Gary C. Schultz" <gcs2@psu.edu>
>Subject: Re: Jerry
>
>Tim, I don't have an update at this point. Just before I left for vac, Tom told me that the DPW and Univ Police services were planning to meet with him. I'll see if this has happened and get back to you.
>
>At 10:27 AM 5/30/98 -0400, Tim Curley wrote:
>>Any further update?
>>
>>
>>
>>
>>At 09:46 AM 5/19/98 -0400, you wrote:
>>>No, but I don't expect we'll hear anything prior to the end of this week.
>>>
>>>At 09:37 PM 5/18/98 -0400, Tim Curley wrote:
>>>>Any update?
>>>>
>>>>
>>>>At 04:11 AM 5/14/98 -0400, you wrote:
>>>>>Tim, I understand that a DPW person was here last week; don't know
>>>>>for sure if they talked with Jerry. They decided to have a child
>>>>>psychologist talk to the boys sometime over the next week. We won't know anything before then.
>>>>>
>>>>>At 02:21 PM 5/13/98 -0400, Tim Curley wrote:
>>>>>>Anything new in this department? Coach is anxious to know where it stands.
>>>>>>_____
>>>>>>Tim Curley
>>>>>>Tmc3@psu.edu
>>>>>>
>>>>>>
>>>>>>
>>>>>Gary C. Schultz
>>>>>Sr. V.P. for Finance and Business/Treasurer
>>>>>208 Old Main
>>>>>Phone: 865-6574

>>>>>Fax:    863-8685
>>>>>
>>>>>
>>>>>
>>>> _____
>>>>Tim Curley
>>>>Tmc3@psu.edu
>>>>
>>>>
>>>>
>>>Gary C. Schultz
>>>Sr. V.P. for Finance and Business/Treasurer
>>>208 Old Main
>>>Phone: 865-6574
>>>Fax:    863-8685
>>>
>>>
>>>
>> _____
>>Tim Curley
>>Tmc3@psu.edu
>>
>>
>>
>

# Exhibit 2F

**From:** Gary C. Schultz <gcs2@psu.edu>
**Sent:** Wednesday, February 28, 2001 2:13 PM
**To:** Graham Spanier; Tim Curley
**Subject:** Re: Meeting

Tim and Graham, this is a more humane and upfront way to handle this. I can support this approach, with the understanding that we will inform his organization, with or without his cooperation (I think that's what Tim proposed). We can play it by ear to decide about the other organization.

At 10:18 PM 2/27/01 -0500, Graham Spanier wrote:

> Tim: This approach is acceptable to me. It requires you to go a step further and means that your conversation will be all the more difficult, but I admire your willingness to do that and I am supportive. The only downside for us is if the message isn't "heard" and acted upon, and we then become vulnerable for not having reported it. But that can be assessed down the road. The approach you outline is humane and a reasonable way to proceed.
>
> At 08:10 PM 2/27/01 -0500, Tim Curley wrote:
>
>> I had scheduled a meeting with you this afternoon about the subject we discussed on Sunday. After giving it more thought and talking it over with Joe yesterday-- I am uncomfortable with what we agreed were the next steps. I am having trouble with going to everyone, but the person involved. I think I would be more comfortable meeting with the person and tell him about the information we received. I would plan to tell him we are aware of the first situation. I would indicate we feel there is a problem and we want to assist the individual to get professional help. Also, we feel a responsibility at some point soon to inform his organization and and maybe the other one about the situation. If he is cooperative we would work with him to handle informing the organization. If not, we do not have a choice and will inform the two groups. Additionally, I will let him know that his guests are not permitted to use our facilities.
>>
>> I need some help on this one. What do you think about this approach?
>
> ---------------------------------------
> Graham B. Spanier
> President
> The Pennsylvania State University
> 201 Old Main
> University Park, Pennsylvania  16802
>
> Phone:  814-865-7611
> email:  gspanier@psu.edu

# Exhibit 2G

Retirement Requests

1. An office and telephone

2. $20,000/year annuity that includes protection for Dottie. *Please refer to the enclosed economic justification for this request.

3. A title that reflects my relationship with Penn State.

4. To maintain my option to purchases tickets for games for fund-raising.

5. Access to training and workout facilities

6. The opportunity to run a football camp for middle school youth.

7. Discuss ways of maintaining visibility.

# Exhibit 2H

5/4/98
5:00 pm

Name
Hamilton
Mrs. G_____
T_____

to fill he _____
Behavior - at best unprepared to
_____ _____
Police involved

- Maybe _____ of the _____
- Statement _____ _____
  _____ through _____ stuff

- wheeled out on stretcher / etc
- jaw - intake + chin -
  - _____ 0 - 710 other
  Shiver ? 4 in head

Shampoo
  came up behind &
  hit _____ bar -
  small wound
  _____ out - all

- keep clothes - socks SUP's
- hat
- tooth _____

Mother concerned about boy
mom - kid took another
shiver last night after a.m.

Mother — asked how old
to guess him.
had to be age-ful catch
because of age difference
but the outfall of boy —
he guessed 10 - NO

- Fred ( Brother, age 10.
also @ Military Garden's -
Claims doing things went
on with him

- Mother also has to —
- Clothes? If this broke
unhyped had enough to
left to the room - thought

—4—

1 Mother over worthy — NO
 Serious — Credible
 2 Claim — Does go past
 ───────────────
 Critical onset — surface
  w gentals?

 ────────────
 Accusing some aspects —
 w/3rd claim? Not cases?

# Exhibit 2I

Tom Harmon
Last Evening

- At interview 11½ yr old
- Only change added what happened in Shower demonstrated on chair how Jerry hugged him back hands around abdomen + closer to thighs-pulled him up + held him at shower head - rinse soap out of hair
 observed at PSU FB + several school & FB & Jerry on trips - getting FB tickets

-2-

- Kid has been seeing Psychologist
 Probably emotional Battles but articulate + believable
- Mother → Psychol. said she would call child abuse hotline
 will speak w/ needed / no - with Dept of Public Welfare Office of Children & Youth — interviewed kid
 Similar acct
 Between months
 kissed on head

- 3 -

Hoping from Dahlil
Sylvia
No allegation beyond that

Kob chus changes &
shoes room
he initially went down to
shower & got shots
away o Jerry followed
him the conversation
to shower next to his
Least Chief other people
Mtg at 700 today to
decide what to do

- 4 -

Esther was, Caseworker
felt they would intervene
Jerry

Is this opening of problems
how? Other children?

# Exhibit 2J

## Initial Heads Up

More than a decade ago, Tim Curley and Gary Schultz asked to catch me after another meeting to give me a "heads up" about a matter. Looking back at my calendar for what is now presumed to be February, 2001, I surmise that meeting to have been on Monday, February 12, at about 2:30pm, following a scheduled meeting of the President's Council. It was common that members of the council would catch me individually for brief updates following such meetings.

The meeting lasted perhaps 10-15 minutes. Curley and Schultz shared that they had received a report that a member of the athletic department staff had reported something to Joe Paterno, and that Joe had passed that report on to Tim and Gary. The report was that Jerry Sandusky was seen in an athletic locker room facility showering with one of his Second Mile youth, after a workout, and that they were "horsing around" (or "engaged in horseplay"). It was reported that the staff member was not sure what he saw because it was around a corner and indirect.

I recall asking two questions:

"Are you sure that is how it was described to you, as horsing around"? Both replied "yes."

"Are you sure that that is all that was reported?" Both replied "yes."

We then agreed that we were uncomfortable with such a situation, that it was inappropriate, and that we did not want it to happen again. I asked that Tim meet with Sandusky to tell him that he must never again bring youth into the showers. We further agreed that we should inform the Second Mile president that we were directing Jerry accordingly and furthermore that we did not wish Second Mile youth to be in our showers.

## Notes:

There was no mention of anything abusive, sexual, or criminal.

At no time was it said who had made the report to Joe Paterno. (I never heard Mike McQuery's name associated with this episode until November 7, 2011, when I read it in a newspaper story.)

The hour of the day was not mentioned.

The specific building and locker room were not mentioned.

The age of the child was not mentioned. I had presumed it was a high school age child under Jerry's guardianship or sponsorship, since that is all I knew about the Second Mile.

There was no mention in that meeting of any prior shower incident, and I had no recollection of having heard of a prior incident.

## Follow Up

In reviewing my calendar for February, 2001, I note a double entry for Sunday, February 25. I had been out of town for several days and was scheduled to return in time to see a Penn State women's basketball game at 2pm. My assistant noted on the calendar that I should stop in to see Tim Curley briefly in my way into the game. I have no recollection of that meeting other than that Tim was worried about how he should handle things if he informed Sandusky that we were forbidding him from bringing Second Mile youth into our facilities and then Sandusky disagreed with this directive. I do not recall knowing about any prior incidents, but it is apparent from emails recently released to the media that Tim also indicated that there had been an earlier occasion when Sandusky had showered with a minor. We also now know that I was copied on two emails in 1998 that may have alerted me to that (the first one being a vague reference with no individual named) and the second essentially saying that the matter had been closed. I had absolutely no recollection of that history in 2001 nor do I recall it today. I don't believe I replied to those emails nor was I briefed verbally.

Tim Curley sent me a follow up email that has recently been shared with the news media. My use of the word "humane" refers specifically and only to my thought that it was humane of Tim to wish to inform Sandusky first and to allow him to accompany Tim to the meeting with the president of the Second Mile. Moreover, it would be humane to offer counseling to Sandusky if he didn't understand why this was inappropriate and unacceptable to us. My comment that we could be vulnerable for not reporting it further relates specifically and only to Tim's concern about the possibility that Jerry would not accept our directive and repeat the practice. Were that the outcome of his discussion I would have worried that we did not enlist more help in enforcing such a directive. I suggested that we could visit that question down the road, meaning after Curley informed Sandusky of our directive and learning of his willingness to comply and after talking with Second Mile executives who had responsibility for the Second Mile youth.

A few days after the brief Sunday interaction, I saw Tim Curley and he reported that both of the discussions had taken place, that those discussions had gone well and our directive accepted, and that the matter was closed.

I never heard another word about this from any individual until I learned of the investigation into Sandusky. I was eager to assist the attorney general and was completely honest to the best of my recollection. I had absolutely no idea until midway through my voluntary grand jury testimony that this inquiry was about anything more than the one episode in the shower.

**Notes:**

I do not recall that I was privy to any follow up discussions between Curley, Schultz, legal counsel, or others. February 2001 was an extraordinarily pressured period for Penn State and me: I had five out of town trips that month, my appropriations hearings, THON, a packed calendar with 164 appointments, an average of 100 incoming and 50 outgoing emails a day, and the turmoil of the Black Caucus disruption and the takeover of the student union.

I do not recall being involved in any discussions about DPW or the police, although I now assume that DPW is the "other organization" being referenced by Curley and Schultz in their emails.

# Exhibit 3A

## Shared Mailbox

**From:** Tim Curley <tmc3@psu.edu>
**Sent:** Sunday, February 08, 1998 11:19 AM
**To:** gspanier@psu.edu; gcs2@psu.edu
**Subject:** Sandusky update

Jerry and I had several conversations this past week about the Assistant AD position. He visited with Joe last week and is to let me know early this week if he is interested. I told him he would continue with his base salary and that he would give up his camp and bowl compensation. Also, I indicated that his dealer car may be a concern since Sue Scheetz is not provided one.
We talked about his involvement with the Second Mile and my expectations for the position. I did not get any indication which way he was leaning. I will keep you informed as the week progresses. Thanks.

Tim Curley
Tmc3@psu.edu

# Exhibit 3B

## Shared Mailbox

**From:** Graham Spanier <gspanier@psu.edu>
**Sent:** Tuesday, February 10, 1998 9:40 PM
**To:** Curley, Tim
**Cc:** Schultz, Gary C.
**Subject:** Re: Sandusky update

Thanks for this update. We are looking for a dean of the Eberly College Science. Does Joe Sarra have any background there?

At 08:51 PM 2/9/98 -0500, Tim Curley wrote:
>Jerry is not interested in the Assistant AD position. Joe and Jerry
>have agreed that he will continue in the coaching capacity for the next year.
>Jerry will have 30 years in the system next year, which will give him
>some options after next season. Joe tells me he made it clear to Jerry
>he will not be the next head coach. Joe did indicate that he still
>plans to make a change on the defensive side of the ball. He wants to
>talk to me at a later date about what might be available for Joe Sarra.
>Do you two need an administrative assistant?
>_____
>Tim Curley
>Tmc3@psu.edu
>
>
>
----------------------------------
Graham B. Spanier
President
The Pennsylvania State University
201 Old Main
University Park, Pennsylvania 16802

Phone: 814-865-7611
email: gspanier@psu.edu

# Exhibit 3C

## Shared Mailbox

**From:** Graham Spanier <gspanier@psu.edu>
**Sent:** Tuesday, January 19, 1999 11:12 PM
**To:** Curley, Tim
**Subject:** Re: Jerry

Thanks. Let me know if I can be helpful as this moves forward.

At 10:14 PM 1/19/99 -0500, Tim Curley wrote:
>I had a good meeting with Jerry today. He is interested in going one
>more year and then transition into a spot that handles our outreach
>program. We talked about his benefits situation and his expectations
>about salary. I told him that we needed to get with Billie about his
>benefits and that I would take a look at what kind of position we could
>develop and how we might handle his salary situation. Additionally, we
>need to have Joe in support. I plan to follow-up and will keep you in the loop. PS--He is not pleased about
>the entire situation as you might expect.
>_____
>Tim Curley
>Tmc3@psu.edu
>
>
>

------------------------------------
Graham B. Spanier
President
The Pennsylvania State University
201 Old Main
University Park, Pennsylvania  16802

Phone: 814-865-7611
email: gspanier@psu.edu

# Exhibit 3D

The following is typewritten interpretation of handwritten notes of JVP on document JVP- 000017 from Sandusky file kept at Paterno residence.

Meeting with Jerry and Tim C

Jerry

We know this isn't easy for you and it isn't easy for us or Penn State. Part of the reason it isn't easy is because I allowed and at times tried to help you with your developing the 2nd Mile. If there were no 2nd Mile then I believe you belief (sp?) that you probably could be the next Penn State FB Coach. But you wanted the best of two worlds and I probably should have sat down with you 6 or 7 years ago and said "look Jerry if you want to be the Head Coach at Penn State, give up your association with the 2nd Mile and concentrate on nothing but your family and Penn State. Don't worry about the 2nd Mile – you don't have the luxury of doing both. One will always demand a decision of preference. You are too deeply involved in both.

(Interpretation of notes by T. Cloud)

# Exhibit 3E

May 28, 1999

Attention: Tim Curley

As I struggle with the difficult decision of a career change, many factors enter my mind. Foremost, I am concerned about my mental health, the financial security of my family and Mother, and the well-being of The Second Mile.

Based on my conversations with Coach Paterno, his concern with the inevitable transition into a new era of Penn State football, the realization that I am not going to be the next head coach, and the opportunity that exists with a thirty-year window, the timing may be right for me to retire from the University and work for The Second Mile. I also appreciate the help that the University has offered to me during this process. However, there are questions that I am struggling to answer.

> What impact will my retirement have on The Second Mile's growth and development? Can a relationship be maintained between Penn State (Athletics) and The Second Mile? Is there a way for me to maintain visibility with Penn State? Is my active involvement in developing an outreach program featuring Penn State Athletes a possibility? Are there ways for me to continue to work with young people through Penn State? What is a fair financial arrangement?

I believe that Penn State football has played a significant role in the foundation of The Second Mile. Additionally, The Second Mile has promoted and enhanced Penn

State football. This is a unique situation and an attempt to satisfy my desire to maintain an long-term relationship with the University.

Many factors have played a significant role in my decisions to stay at Penn State and forego other more lucrative options. One element that was important was the probability of becoming the next head football coach at Penn State. In addition to the personal satisfaction that this would have afforded me this would have also enabled me to better secure my family's economic future. As I have been informed that this will not happen, I continue to make an effort to find avenues of fulfillment and to remain positive about a tremendous experience. With all of this in consideration I enclose a list of requests. Thank you!

*Jerry*
Jerry Sandusky

# Exhibit 3F

Retirement Requests

1. An office and telephone

2. $20,000/year annuity that includes protection for Dottie. *Please refer to the enclosed economic justification for this request.

3. A title that reflects my relationship with Penn State.

4. To maintain my option to purchases tickets for games for fund-raising

5. Access to training and workout facilities.

6. The opportunity to run a football camp for middle school youth.

7. Discuss ways of maintaining visibility.

# Exhibit 3G

**Shared Mailbox**

**From:** Tim Curley <tmc3@psu.edu>
**Sent:** Sunday, June 13, 1999 8:19 PM
**To:** Spanier, Graham
**Cc:** Schultz, Gary C.
**Subject:** Jerry

Jerry just called and said he is leaning towards the retirement window option if we will agree to the $20,000 annuity and two basketball tickets in addition to the other items he requested. I am at home and do not have the projected costs for the annuity, but my recollection was it would cost us about $268,000. Joe did give him the option to continue to coach as long as he was the coach. I am not comfortable with the $20,000 annuity, but wanted to check to see if you feel the same way. Perhaps we could suggest another option of him coaching three more seasons and we get creative with his base salary or some other scheme that makes him whole and then some, but doesn't cost us an arm and a leg. Since Joe is okay with him continuing to coach this might make more sense to all concerned. I do need some help on what this third option might be if you agree. Also, I need to run it by Joe. I can get with Gary and Billie first thing tomorrow to see what we can work out if you are in agreement.. We need to respond to him asap since
time is running out. I need some help on this one. Thank you.

# Exhibit 3H

Rec'd
2-28-11
6:28 p.m.

June 29, 1999

<u>CONFIDENTIAL - HAND DELIVERED</u>

Gerald A. Sandusky
130 Grandview Road
State College, PA 16801

IN RE: Retirement Perquisites

Dear Mr. Sandusky:

In accordance with our discussions regarding your retirement from University service effective June 29, 1999, and in recognition of your many contributions to the University and its Intercollegiate Athletics Program during the tenure of your employment, I am pleased to confirm the following perquisites to be extended to you upon and after your retirement on June 29, 1999:

1. The University will pay you the amount of One Hundred Sixty-eight Thousand and 00/100 ($168,000.00) Dollars in lump sum, less applicable withholdings as required by law, on or before July 31, 1999.

2. The University will give you four (4) complimentary football season tickets in your current location, and in addition, you will be given the option to purchase four (4) more football season tickets within the thirty-five yard lines and below the walkway. This benefit will continue for the balance of your lifetime.

3. The University will give you two (2) complimentary men's basketball season tickets and two (2) complimentary women's basketball season tickets. The location of these tickets will be within the normal Football Staff ticket location. This benefit will continue for the balance of your lifetime.

4. The University will permit you to use, at no charge, a locker, weight rooms, fitness facilities and training room in the East Area locker room complex. This benefit will continue for the balance of your lifetime.

006_0000043

PSU_000001

Gerald A. Sandusky
June 29, 1999
Page 2

5. For a period of five (5) years commencing July 1, 1999, and subject to renewal upon concurrence of both parties, you and the University agree to work collaboratively with each other in the future in community outreach programs, such as the Second Mile, and other programs which provide positive visibility to the University's Intercollegiate Athletics Program. It is understood that the nature and extent of such collaborative efforts, which will include continuation of the Nittany Lion TIPS and PEAK Programs and occasional recognitions of the Second Mile in the Beaver Stadium Pictorial and the Penn State Football Story Show, will be as mutually agreed by you and me.

6. For a period of ten (10) years, commencing July 1, 1999, and subject to renewal upon concurrence of both parties, you will be given an office and a phone in the East Area locker room complex for purposes of the collaborative arrangements referenced in no. 5 above.

If the foregoing understandings are agreeable, kindly indicate your acceptance by signing on the line below and returning a copy to me.

Sincerely,

Timothy M. Curley
Director of Athletics

APPROVED BY UNIVERSITY OFFICER:

Gary C. Schultz, Senior Vice President for Finance and Business/Treasurer

I hereby accept the above-mentioned terms on June 29, 1999.

Gerald A. Sandusky

# Exhibit 3I

To: Robert Secor[rxs2@psu.edu]
From: Rodney A. Erickson
Subject: Re: Fwd: Re: Emeritus Question

Bob,

Let's go ahead and grant it if Graham has already promised it. We can hope that not too many others take that careful notice. These requests would have to come through the deans in any case, and I can't imagine many deans lobbying for assistant professors.

Rod

At 10:23 AM 8/31/99 -0400, you wrote:
>In addition to the exchange below, I've talked with Billie Willits.
>Although she said we have made exceptions in the past for assistant profs,
>she could not give any particulars because any information would have been
>filed with the faculty member's file and she wouldn't know where to look.
>In other words, if this really happened (and without particulars it is hard
>to know), it may have been way past, and so not terribly helpful if we
>don't have a specific precedent to point to. But we are in a bind.
>Apparently, Graham told ▮▮▮▮▮ that we would do this--he was wholly
>within his rights here since the policy says "The President may grant (or
>deny) Emeritus Rank on an exception basis"--then informed Tim, who
>suggested going through the college and went to Barbara, who then made the
>request of us. (I had wrongly assumed all along that the request
>originated with Barbara.) ▮▮▮▮ is also going to be honored by the college
>as an Alumni Fellow this fall, and I think they may want to present the
>emeritus status to him on that occasion (or at least announce it then,
>although I'm not positive about this connection). I'm not sure what our
>best options are at this point. Maybe we need to go along with the
>Assistant Professor Emeritus of Physical Education/Assistant Coach
>recommendation, since by tying the two there is nobody else with that
>double designation who can claim they have the exact same credentials and
>are not being given the emeritus title.
>
>>X-Sender: ray2@mail.psu.edu
>>X-Mailer: Windows Eudora Pro Version 2.2 (32)
>>Date: Mon, 30 Aug 1999 09:07:06 -0400
>>X-PH: V4.1@f04n07
>>To: rxs2@psu.edu
>>From: Rebecca Young <ray2@psu.edu>
>>Subject: Re: Emeritus Question
>>
>>Dr. Secor,
>>
>>Here are Jeanie's comments regarding emeritus rank for ▮▮▮▮ ▮▮▮▮▮▮. All
>>good points she raises. --Becky
>>
>>
>>>X-Sender: jsa3@email.psu.edu
>>>Date: Mon, 30 Aug 1999 08:39:34 -0400
>>>X-PH: V4.1@f04n01
>>>To: Rebecca Young <ray2@psu.edu>
>>>From: Janine Andrews <jsa3@psu.edu>
>>>Subject: Re: Emeritus Question
>>>
>>>Hi Becky. I had an opportunity to look into your question from a previous
>>>e-mail with regard to exceptions for Assistant Professors. Historically,

>>>we have made exceptions, although not for this exact title, i.e., Assistant
>>>Professor Emeritus of Physical Education/Assistant Coach! In my opinion,
>>>given the circumstances, the most appropriate title would be the one
>>>requested -- Assistant Professor Emeritus of Physical Education/Assistant
>>>Coach. I say this because if we keep the professorial connection out of
>>>the title and just use something like Assistant Coach Emeritus, we then
>>>establish a new precedence by giving someone a "Coach" emeritus status --
>>>which we have never done based on what I could gather. So . . . the
>>>requested title serves two purposes: it keeps the professorial connection,
>>>yet is very inclusive by adding in the "coach" connection.
>>>
>>>Please let me know if you need anything else. Have a great day.
>>>
>>>Jeanie
>>>
>>>
>>>At 01:20 PM 8/25/99 -0400, you wrote:
>>>>Hi, Jeanie. Just wanted to update you on the ████████ question. Dr.
>>>>Spanier has received the request, as we anticipated. It's for the title
>>>>Assistant Professor Emeritus of Physical Education/Assistant Coach.
>>>>
>>>>Another thought from here. If it's not well advised to grant the
>>>>professorial emeritus rank, how about Assistant Coach Emeritus? We'll wait
>>>>to hear from you. --Becky
>>>>
>>>>********************************************************************
>>>>Rebecca A. Young
>>>>Office of the Provost
>>>>201 Old Main
>>>>University Park, PA 16802
>>>>(814) 863 7494 (Telephone)
>>>>(814) 863-8583 (FAX)
>>>>
>>>>********************************************************************
>>>>
>>>
>>>Janine S. Andrews
>>>Assistant Manager
>>>Employee Relations Division
>>>Office of Human Resources
>>>Penn State University
>>>(814) 865-1412
>>>e-mail: jsa3@psu.edu
>>>
>>>
>>>>>                  ("/").___.--"""--
>>>>>                  '9 9 ) `.  (    ).`-.__.`)
>>>>>                  (_Y_.) ' ._  )  `._  `. ``-..-'
>>>>>                _..`--'_..-_/ /--'_.' ,'
>>>>>               (ii).-'' (((.' (((.-'
>>>>>
>>>>>           We ARE..............Penn State!!!
>>>
>>>
>>>
>>>
>>
>>********************************************************************
>>Rebecca A. Young

>>Office of the Provost
>>201 Old Main
>>University Park, PA 16802
>>(814) 863-7494 (Telephone)
>>(814) 863-8583 (FAX)
>>
>>****************************************************************
>>
>
>Robert Secor
>Vice Provost for Academic Affairs
>201 Old Main
>(814) 863-7494

# Exhibit 5A

| Matter I.D. | Description | Task Activity | Hours | |
|---|---|---|---|---|
| 02-08-01 | | | | |
| | 4000-465063 PSU - Labor - Human Resources PS010 | | 0.60 | |
| | Conference with J Purdum re holiday pay issue; Conference with R Maney re same | | | |
| | 4000-490106 PSU - Personnel - Continuing & Distance Educat | | 0.50 | |
| | Conference with J Elliott re J Marshall; Conference with G Schultz | | | |
| | 4000-490143 PSU - Personnel - Mont Alto Campus | | 2.20 | |
| | Conference with J Leathers re D Goldenberg; Preparation of correspondence to G Spanier; Review of files; Preparation of correspondence to G Spanier et al; Conference with J Leathers | | | |
| | 4000-481582 PSU - Students - Student Affairs | | 2.90 | |
| | Interoffice conference re camping policy; Legal research re same | | | |
| | 4000-481582 PSU - Students - Student Affairs | | 1.70 | |
| | Study/analyze documents re LGB tenant; Interoffice conference re same; Legal research; Preparation of correspondence to G Spanier et al re same | | | |
| | 4000-490163 PSU - Personnel - Human Resources | | 0.30 | |
| | Conference with R Maney re R Khalliq | | | |
| | 4000-465026 PSU - Labor - COM - General | | 1.50 | |
| | Preparation of documents re HMC parking | | | |
| ** Total for 2/8/2001 ** | | | 9.70 | 0.00 |
| 02-09-01 | | | | |
| | 4000-490143 PSU - Personnel - Mont Alto Campus | | 1.60 | |
| | Review of documents re D Goldenberg; Preparation of correspondence to G Spanier; Preparation of correspondence to J Leathers; Legal research | | | |
| | 4000-451558 PSU - Gifts & Grants - Develop and Alumni Rela | | 0.20 | |
| | Review of files re Hagan estate | | | |
| | 4000-490117 PSU - Personnel - College of Liberal Arts | | 1.10 | |
| | Conference with J Battista re R Echemendia; Interoffice conference | | | |
| | 4000-425562 PSU - Contracts - Hershey Medical Center | | 0.80 | |
| | Review of documents re Purchase of Services Agreement; Interoffice conference re same | | | |
| | 4000-465026 PSU - Labor - COM - General | | 2.60 | |
| | Conference with L Kushner re HMC parking fees; Preparation of correspondence to L Kushner re same; Preparation of documents; Legal research | | | |
| | 4000-465063 PSU - Labor - Human Resources PS010 | | 0.70 | |
| | Review Schaeffer brief | | | |
| ** Total for 2/9/2001 ** | | | 7.00 | 0.00 |
| 02-11-01 | | | | |
| | 4000-450061 PSU - General - Finance/Business - Central | | 2.90 | |
| | Conference with G Schultz re reporting of suspected child abuse; Legal research re same; Conference with G Schultz | | | |
| 02-12-01 | | | | |

# Exhibit 5B

| | |
|---|---|
| From: | Schultz, Gary C. |
| Sent: | Monday, January 10, 2011 8:34 PM |
| To: | First Administrative Group/cn=Recipients/cn=WVCOURTNEY; GCS2@psu.edu |
| Subject: | Re: JSRece |

Thanks for letting me know.

Gary

*Sent via DROID on Verizon Wireless*


-----Original message-----
**From:** Wendell Courtney <WVCourtney@mqblaw.com>
**To:** "Schultz, Gary C." <GCS2@psu.edu>
**Sent:** Mon, Jan 10, 2011 23:59:28 GMT+00:00
**Subject:** JS

Gary-Cynthia Baldwin called me today to ask what I remembered about JS issue I spoke with you and Tim about circa 8 years ago. I told her what I remembered. She did not offer why she was asking, nor did I ask her. Nor did I disclose that you and I chatted about this.

Wendell V. Courtney, Esquire
McQuaide Blasko Law Offices
811 University Drive
State College, Pa. 16801
wvcourtney@mqblaw.com
Phone: (814) 238-4926
Fax: (814) 234-5620

This electronic mail transmission may contain privileged or confidential information intended only for the individual person(s) identified as addressee(s). Any use, distribution, copying, or disclosure by another person is strictly prohibited. If you have received this transmission in error, please reply to the sender indicating this error and delete the transmission from your system immediately.

This electronic mail transmission may be protected by the attorney-client privilege and/or may contain privileged or confidential information intended only for the individual person(s) identified as addressee(s). Any use, distribution, copying, or disclosure by another person is strictly prohibited. If you have received this transmission in error, please reply to the sender indicating this error and delete the transmission from your system immediately.

Tax Advice Disclosure: Pursuant to requirements imposed under the U.S. Treasury Department Circular 230, we hereby inform you that any U.S. federal tax advice contained in this communication (including any attachments), unless otherwise specifically stated, was not intended or written to be used, and cannot be used, for the purpose of (1) avoiding penalties under the Internal Revenue Code; or (2) promoting, marketing or recommending to another party any matters addressed herein.

# Exhibit 5C

# PENN STATE

**Confidential**

Date: 2/12/01
From: Gary C. Schultz
To:

Talked w/ TMC
- reviewed 1998 history
- agreed TMC will discuss w/ JVP + advise. We think TMC should meet w/ JS on Friday.
- unless he "confesses" to having a problem, TMC will indicate we need to have DPW review the matter as an independent agency concerned w/ child welfare.
- TMC will keep me posted.

Senior Vice President for Finance and Business/Treasurer

The Pennsylvania State University
208 Old Main
University Park, PA 16802-1503
(814) 865-6574
Fax: (814) 863-7188

**Exhibit 5D**

**From:** Thomas R. Harmon <HARMON@SAFETY-1.SAFETY.PSU.EDU>
**Sent:** Monday, February 12, 2001 4:57 PM
**To:** gcs2@psu.edu
**Subject:** Incident in 1998

Regarding the incident in 1998 involving the former coach, I checked and the incident is documented in our imaged achives.
Thomas R. Harmon
Director, University Police
The Pennsylvania State University
30-B Eisenhower Parking Deck
University Park, PA 16802
(814) 865-1864
harmon@police.psu.edu

# Exhibit 5E

2/25/01

③ ○ Tell Chair* Board of Second Mile

② ○ Report to Dept of Welfare.

① ○ Tell J.S to avoid bringing children alone into Lasch Bldg.

*who's the chair??

… **Exhibit 5F**

**From:** Gary C. Schultz <gcs2@psu.edu>
**Sent:** Monday, February 26, 2001 1:57 PM
**To:** TMC3@psu.edu
**Cc:** Coble-Joan (JLC)
**Subject:** Confidential

Tim, I'm assuming that you've got the ball to 1) talk with the subject ASAP regarding the future appropriate use of the University facility; 2) contacting the chair of the Charitable Organization; and 3) contacting the Dept of Welfare. As you know I'm out of the office for the next two weeks, but if you need anything from me, please let me know.

# Exhibit 5G

**From:** Gary C. Schultz <gcs2@psu.edu>
**Sent:** Wednesday, February 28, 2001 2:13 PM
**To:** Graham Spanier; Tim Curley
**Subject:** Re: Meeting

Tim and Graham, this is a more humane and upfront way to handle this. I can support this approach, with the understanding that we will inform his organization, with or without his cooperation (I think that's what Tim proposed). We can play it by ear to decide about the other organization.

At 10:18 PM 2/27/01 -0500, Graham Spanier wrote:

> Tim: This approach is acceptable to me. It requires you to go a step further and means that your conversation will be all the more difficult, but I admire your willingness to do that and I am supportive. The only downside for us is if the message isn't "heard" and acted upon, and we then become vulnerable for not having reported it. But that can be assessed down the road. The approach you outline is humane and a reasonable way to proceed.
>
> At 08:10 PM 2/27/01 -0500, Tim Curley wrote:
>
>> I had scheduled a meeting with you this afternoon about the subject we discussed on Sunday. After giving it more thought and talking it over with Joe yesterday-- I am uncomfortable with what we agreed were the next steps. I am having trouble with going to everyone, but the person involved. I think I would be more comfortable meeting with the person and tell him about the information we received. I would plan to tell him we are aware of the first situation. I would indicate we feel there is a problem and we want to assist the individual to get professional help. Also, we feel a responsibility at some point soon to inform his organization and and maybe the other one about the situation. If he is cooperative we would work with him to handle informing the organization. If not, we do not have a choice and will inform the two groups. Additionally, I will let him know that his guests are not permitted to use our facilities.
>>
>> I need some help on this one. What do you think about this approach?
>
> ------------------------------------
> Graham B. Spanier
> President
> The Pennsylvania State University
> 201 Old Main
> University Park, Pennsylvania  16802
>
> Phone: 814-865-7611
> email: gspanier@psu.edu

# Exhibit 5H

**From:** Gary C. Schultz <gcs2@psu.edu>
**Sent:** Thursday, March 01, 2001 4:06 PM
**To:** Tim Curley
**Subject:** Re: Fwd: Re: Schedule

OK, Tim. You can reach me anytime thru my office.

At 07:34 AM 3/1/01 -0500, Tim Curley wrote:

> Gary: I will be sure to keep in touch with you on the basketball situation.
>
>> X-Sender: gspanier@mail.psu.edu
>> X-Mailer: QUALCOMM Windows Eudora Pro Version 4.2.0.58
>> Date: Wed, 28 Feb 2001 21:18:24 -0500
>> X-PH: V4.1@f04n01
>> To: Tim Curley <tmc3@psu.edu>
>> From: Graham Spanier <gspanier@psu.edu>
>> Subject: Re: Schedule
>>
>> Tim: I'll be in Australia, and it might be difficult to reach me--a 15 hour time difference. But call if you need me--Carolyn has my phone numbers. I will try to check email from time to time, but who knows how easy that will be. I will return late Saturday night (but that involves starting my return sometime on Friday, US time), so you might try calling me at home on Sunday afternoon if we haven't communicated earlier via email. If you need to start in one direction without me, do so. I think we are on the same wavelength and I will support you.
>>
>> At 08:19 PM 2/28/01 -0500, Tim Curley wrote:
>>> Graham: I know you are going out of town. When will you be returning? I may need to touch base with you regarding the basketball situation towards the end of next week. We will play next Thursday and pending the outcome of the next two games I will need to make a recommendation to you next Friday. I am planning to meet with the person next Monday on the other subject. Have a great trip!! You sure deserve a break!!!
>>
>> ------------------------------------
>> Graham B. Spanier
>> President
>> The Pennsylvania State University
>> 201 Old Main
>> University Park, Pennsylvania 16802
>>
>> Phone: 814-865-7611
>> email: gspanier@psu.edu

# Exhibit 5I

| | |
|---|---|
| **From:** | Joan Coble <jlc9@psu.edu> |
| **Sent:** | Wednesday, March 07, 2001 8:54 AM |
| **To:** | TMC3@psu.edu |
| **Cc:** | gcs2@psu.edu |
| **Subject:** | Fwd: Confidential |

Tim - Have you updated Gary lately? Before he left for FL, he asked me to ck. w/you re this.

Pls. know that he is doing e-mail, but will not be reading until Sun., 3/11. He is spending a few days with Dave Schuckers and you may either phone him on his cellphone at 777-7393 or @ Schuckers at 941/388-3034. Pls. know that the Schuckers live in a Condominium & you may have to go through some referrals to get to speak w/them, so be patient if you go that route.

Thx. Joan


X-Sender: gcs2@imap.cac.psu.edu
X-Mailer: QUALCOMM Windows Eudora Version 4.3.2
Date: Mon, 26 Feb 2001 08:57:16 -0500
X-PH: V4.1@f04n01
To: TMC3@psu.edu
From: "Gary C. Schultz" <gcs2@psu.edu>
Subject: Confidential
Cc: jlc9@psu.edu

Tim, I'm assuming that you've got the ball to 1) talk with the subject ASAP regarding the future appropriate use of the University facility; 2) contacting the chair of the Charitable Organization; and 3) contacting the Dept of Welfare. As you know I'm out of the office for the next two weeks, but if you need anything from me, please let me know.
Gary C. Schultz
Senior Vice President for
   Finance & Business/Treasurer
Penn State University
208 Old Main
University Park, PA 16802
814/865-6574
814/863-8685 (fax)
http://www.psu.edu/dept/fab


Joan L. Coble
Administrative Assistant
Office of the Senior Vice President for
   Finance & Business/Treasurer
208 Old Main
University Park, PA 16802

814/865-6574 (phone)
814/863-8685 (fax)
http://www.psu.edu/dept/fab

# Exhibit 6A

## AFFIDAVIT OF CYNTHIA A. BALDWIN

The undersigned, Cynthia A. Baldwin, having been duly sworn according to law, hereby states that the following is true and correct to the best of her knowledge, information and belief:

1. I have been employed with The Pennsylvania State University as Vice President and General Counsel since February, 2010.

2. I was asked to brief the Board of Trustees by President Graham Spanier who was also a member of the Board of Trustees in the month of April, 2011.

3. On Thursday, May 12, 2011, I presented a report on an investigation by The Pennsylvania Office of Attorney General into allegations of child sexual abuse by Jerry Sandusky, an employee who had retired from Penn State in 1999, to the Trustees who were in attendance. (See Attachment I)

4. The following items were included in my report:

- Definition and description of a Grand Jury and how it works;

- That the Grand Jury process was confidential, but those who testified before the Grand Jury are free to divulge their testimony;

- That Tim Curley, Gary Schultz and Joe Paterno had been interviewed in January and Graham Spanier had been interviewed in April;

- That the people who had testified had been asked about a 2002 incident in the football building;

- The fact that there had been a 1998 incident involving Mr. Sandusky that had been investigated by the University Police, the District Attorney's Office and Children and Youth Services and that no charges had been filed against Mr. Sandusky; and
- That the University did not appear to be a focus of the investigation;

After the report, I responded to several questions. At that point Dr. Spanier said that he would take over. I left and the Board continued in Executive Session.

The undersigned hereby verifies that the facts set forth in the foregoing Affidavit are true and correct to the best of her knowledge, information and belief and that false statements herein are made subject to penalties of 18 Pa.C.S. § 4094, relating to unsworn falsification to authorities.

Date: January 16, 2012

COMMONWEALTH OF PENNSYLVANIA }
} ss
COUNTY OF CENTRE }

On this 16th day of January, 2012, before me, the undersigned notary public, personally appeared, known to me or satisfactorily proven to be the person whose name is subscribed to the within instrument, and acknowledged the same for the purposes therein contained.

In witness whereof, I hereunto set my hand and official seal.

Notary Public

# Exhibit 10A

# FEBRUARY 1998 COMMITTEE LIST

## ORGANIZATION OF THE BOARD OF TRUSTEES OF THE PENNSYLVANIA STATE UNIVERSITY

Edward P. Junker III, President
Edward R. Hintz, Vice President
Graham B. Spanier, Secretary
Gary C. Schultz, Treasurer

*The President of the Board of Trustees, Edward P. Junker III, and the President of the University, Graham B. Spanier, are, according to the Bylaws, ex officio members of all standing and special committees and subcommittees.*

---

### COMMITTEE ON EDUCATIONAL POLICY

Joel N. Myers, Chairman
Mary G. Beahm, Vice Chairwoman

### COMMITTEE ON FINANCE AND PHYSICAL PLANT

L. J. Rowell, Jr., Chairman
Robert D. Metzgar, Vice Chairman

↓

### SUBCOMMITTEE ON ARCHITECHT/ ENGINEER SELECTION

### COMMITTEE ON CAMPUS ENVIRONMENT

Cynthia A. Baldwin, Chairwoman
Anne Riley, Vice Chairwoman

### COMMITTEE ON MILTON S. HERSHEY MEDICAL CENTER

William L. Weiss, Chairman
Boyd E. Wolff, Vice Chairman

### EXECUTIVE COMMITTEE

*Elected by the Board of Trustees on January 16, 1998*

Mary G. Beahm
Alvin H. Clemens
Edward R. Hintz
David R. Jones
David A. Morrow
Anne Riley
Barry K. Robinson
L. J. Rowell, Jr.
William L. Weiss

### NOMINATING COMMITTEE

David A. Morrow, Chair

*The President of the Board of Trustees is chairman of the Executive Committee, and the Secretary of the Board is the recording secretary of the Executive Committee.*

# FEBRUARY 2001 COMMITTEE LIST

## ORGANIZATION OF THE BOARD OF TRUSTEES OF THE PENNSYLVANIA STATE UNIVERSITY

Edward R. Hintz, Jr., President

Cynthia A. Baldwin, Vice President
Graham B. Spanier, Secretary
Gary C. Schultz, Treasurer

*The President of the Board of Trustees, Edward R. Hintz, Jr., and the President of the University, Graham B. Spanier, are, according to the Bylaws, ex officio members of all standing and special committees and subcommittees.*

### COMMITTEE ON EDUCATIONAL POLICY

Joel N. Myers, Chairman
David R. Jones, Vice Chairman

### COMMITTEE ON FINANCE AND PHYSICAL PLANT

L. J. Rowell, Jr., Chairman
Robert D. Metzgar, Vice Chairman

↓

#### SUBCOMMITTEE ON ARCHITECHT/ ENGINEER SELECTION

### COMMITTEE ON CAMPUS ENVIRONMENT

Anne Riley, Chairwoman
Mary G. Beahm, Vice Chairwoman

### COMMITTEE ON MILTON S. HERSHEY MEDICAL CENTER

William L. Weiss, Chairman
Steve A. Garban, Vice Chairman

### EXECUTIVE COMMITTEE
*Elected by the Board of Trustees on January 19, 2001*

Cynthia A. Baldwin
Charles C. Brosius
Steve A. Garban
David R. Jones
David A. Morrow
Joel N. Myers
Anne Riley
L. J. Rowell, Jr.
Carl T. Shaffer
William L. Weiss

### NOMINATING COMMITTEE

Edward P. Junker III, Chair

*The President of the Board of Trustees is chairman of the Executive Committee, and the Secretary of the Board is the recording secretary of the Executive Committee.*

# JULY 1, 2012 COMMITTEE LIST

## ORGANIZATION OF THE BOARD OF TRUSTEES OF THE PENNSYLVANIA STATE UNIVERSITY

Karen B. Peetz, President

Keith E. Masser, Vice President
Rodney A. Erickson, Secretary
David J. Gray, Treasurer

*The President of the Board of Trustees, Edward R. Hintz, Jr., and the President of the University, Graham B. Spanier, are, according to the Bylaws, ex officio members of all standing and special committees and subcommittees.*

---

### COMMITTEE ON ACADEMIC AFFAIRS AND STUDENT LIFE

Marianne E. Alexander, Chair
Peter A. Khoury, Vice Chair

### COMMITTEE ON GOVERNANCE AND LONG-RANGE PLANNING

James S. Broadhurst, Chair
John P. Surma, Vice Chair

### COMMITTEE ON FINANCE, BUSINESS, AND CAPITAL PLANNING

Linda B. Strumpf, Chair
Paul H. Silvis, Vice Chair

### COMMITTEE ON OUTREACH, DEVELOPMENT AND COMMUNITY RELATIONS

Mark H. Dambly, Chair
Paul V. Suhey, Vice Chair

### COMMITTEE ON AUDIT, RISK, LEGAL AND COMPLIANCE

Keith W. Eckel, Chair
Ira M. Lubert, Vice Chair

### SUBCOMMITTEE ON ARCHITECT/ ENGINEER SELECTION

### EXECUTIVE COMMITTEE
*Elected by the Board of Trustees on March 16, 2012*

Marianne E. Alexander
James S. Broadhurst
Mark H. Dambly
Keith W. Eckel
Rodney A. Erickson, Ex Officio
Kenneth C. Frazier
Edward R. Hintz, Jr.
Keith E. Masser
Karen B. Peetz, Ex Officio
Linda B. Strumpf
John P. Surma

### SUBCOMMITTEE ON AUDIT
*(authorized by board in 2004)*

### SUBCOMMITTEE ON LEGAL
*(authorized by board in 2012)*

### SUBCOMMITTEE ON FINANCE
*(authorized by board in 2012)*

### SUBCOMMITTEE ON HUMAN RESOURCES
*(authorized by board in 2012)*

*The President of the Board of Trustees is chairman of the Executive Committee, and the Secretary of the Board is the recording secretary of the Executive Committee.*

# APPENDIX B
# PENNSYLVANIA STATE UNIVERSITY
# POLICIES: AD 67, AD 72, HR 99

**PENN STATE - ADMINISTRATIVE**

# Policy AD39 MINORS INVOLVED IN UNIVERSITY-SPONSORED PROGRAMS OR PROGRAMS HELD AT THE UNIVERSITY AND / OR HOUSED IN UNIVERSITY FACILITIES (Formerly *Programs Involving Minors Housed in University Facilities*)

## Contents:

- Purpose
- Definitions
- Policy
- Cross References

## PURPOSE:

To provide for appropriate supervision of minors who are involved in University-sponsored programs, programs held at the University and/or programs housed in University facilities at all geographic locations with the exception of the Penn State Hershey Medical Center campus (including the College of Medicine), the client representation clinics of the Dickinson School of Law, and University Health Services which will follow separate policies that reflect their unique activities. Supervision of minors who are involved in University research is addressed by Institutional Review Board processes as outlined in RA14, and is not addressed by this policy. This policy also does not apply to general public events where parents/guardians are invited/expected to provide supervision of minors.

## DEFINITIONS:

**Minor -**
> A person under the age of eighteen (18) who is not enrolled or accepted for enrollment at the University. Students who are "dually enrolled" in University programs while also enrolled in elementary, middle and/or high school are not included in this policy unless such enrollment includes overnight housing in University facilities.

**University Facilities -**
> Facilities owned by, or under the control of, the University with the exception of the Penn State Hershey Medical Center campus (including the College of Medicine) and the Student Health Center (University Park) which will follow separate policies that reflect the unique activities that occur in those locations.

**Programs -**
>Programs and activities offered by various academic or administrative units of the University, or by non-University groups using University facilities subject to Policies AD02 or AD03. This includes but is not limited to workshops, sport camps, academic camps, conferences, pre-enrollment visits, 4H or Cooperative Extension programs and similar activities.

**Sponsoring Unit-**
>The academic or administrative unit of the University which offers a program or gives approval for housing or use of facilities pursuant to AD02 or AD03.

**Authorized Adult-**
>Individuals, age 18 and older, paid or unpaid, who interact with, supervise, chaperone, or otherwise oversee minors in program activities, or recreational, and/or residential facilities. This includes but is not limited to faculty, staff, volunteers, graduate and undergraduate students, interns, employees of temporary employment agencies, and independent contractors/consultants. The Authorized Adults' roles may include positions as counselors, chaperones, coaches, instructors, etc. Authorized Adults are considered to be mandated reporters as defined by Pennsylvania law. Further guidance on mandated reporters is provided in University Human Resources policy(ies).

**Direct Contact -**
>Positions with the possibility of care, supervision, guidance or control of minors and/or routine interaction with minors.

**One-On-One Contact -**
>Personal, unsupervised interaction between any Authorized Adult and a participant without at least one other Authorized Adult, parent or legal guardian being present.

# POLICY:

A sponsoring unit offering or approving a program which involves minors or provides University housing for minors participating in a program, or a non-University group being sponsored for a program, whether utilizing University housing or not, shall:

>1. Establish a procedure for the notification of the minor's parent/legal guardian in case of an emergency, including medical or behavioral problem, natural disasters, or other significant program disruptions. Authorized Adults with the program, as well as participants and their parents/legal guardians, must be advised of this procedure in writing prior to the participation of the minors in the program.

>2. Provide a list of all program participants and a directory of program staff to the campus unit(s) responsible for police services (their contact information will be provided to the sponsors by the University). This list shall include participant's name; local room assignment (if applicable); gender, age, address, and phone number(s) of parent or legal guardian, as well as emergency contact information.

3. Provide information to parent or legal guardian detailing the manner in which the participant can be contacted during the program.

4. Provide a Medical Treatment Authorization form to the campus unit responsible for health services. Any request to amend the approved form must be approved by the Director of University Health Services prior to its distribution or use. All forms must include the following:

   a. A statement informing the parent/legal guardian that the University does (or does not, as applicable) provide medical insurance to cover medical care for the minor.
   b. A statement authorizing the release of medical information (HIPAA) and emergency treatment in case the parent/legal guardian/emergency contact cannot be reached for permission.
   c. A list of any physical, mental or medical conditions the minor may have, including any allergies that could impact his/her participation in the program.
   d. All emergency contact information including name, address and phone number of the emergency contact.

5. Follow guidance from University Health Services concerning communicable diseases.

6. University Policy SY21 shall be followed concerning first aid kits and epinephrine ("epi") pens. Participants' medicines may be distributed by program staff, under the following conditions:

   a. The participant's family provides the medicine in its original pharmacy container labeled with the participant's name, medicine name, dosage and timing of consumption. Over-the-counter medications must be provided in their manufacturers' container.
   b. Staff shall keep the medicine in a secure location, and at the appropriate time for distribution shall meet with the participant.
   c. The staff member shall allow the participant to self-administer the appropriate dose as shown on the container.
   d. Any medicine which the participant cannot self-administer, must be stored and administered by a licensed healthcare professional associated with the campus or, if no one is available, arrangements must be made with another health care professional in advance of the participant's arrival. The event coordinator should consult with the location's health service and the Office of Affirmative Action ADA Coordinator to discuss reasonable accommodations in the above situation.
   e. Personal "epi" pens and inhalers may be carried by the participant during activities.

7. Arrange to access emergency medical services at all locations and, for events at University Park, access to these services must be pursuant to ADG04. Medical care appropriate for the nature of the events, expected attendance and other variables should be discussed with the Director of University Health Services.

8. Follow appropriate safety measures approved by the Office of Environmental Health & Safety for laboratory and research work as outlined in SY01.

9. Ensure adequate supervision of minors while they are on University property. All activities involving minors must be supervised by at least two or more Authorized Adults or by their parent(s) or legal guardian(s) at all times. Some of the factors to consider in determining "adequate supervision" are the number and age of participants, the activity(ies) involved, type of housing if applicable, and age and experience of the counselors. See also, item 15 below.

When Penn State students are hosting High School students, including prospective athletes, participating in pre-enrollment visitation, the requirement for two Authorized Adults will be waived. The requirement also does not apply to licensed psychologists providing psychological and counseling services to minors.

All supervised participants in a University program or a program taking place on University property are permitted in the general use facilities [e.g. athletic fields, public spaces, academic buildings] but may be restricted from certain areas of the facilities [e.g. storage rooms, equipment rooms, athletic training rooms, staff/faculty offices] or from utilizing certain equipment.

10. Develop and make available to participants the rules and discipline measures applicable to the program. Program participants and staff must abide by all University regulations and may be removed from the program for non-compliance with rules. The following must be included in program rules:

   a. The possession or use of alcohol and other drugs, fireworks, guns and other weapons is prohibited.
   b. The operation of a motor vehicle by minors is prohibited while attending and participating in the program.
   c. The parking of staff and participant vehicles must be in accordance with University parking regulations.
   d. Rules and procedures governing when and under what circumstances participants may leave University property during the program.
   e. No violence, including sexual abuse or harassment, will be tolerated.
   f. Hazing of any kind is prohibited. Bullying including verbal, physical, and cyber bullying are prohibited.
   g. No theft of property regardless of owner will be tolerated.
   h. No use of tobacco products (smoking is prohibited in **all** University buildings) will be tolerated.
   i. Misuse or damage of University property is prohibited. Charges will be assessed against those participants who are responsible for damage or misusing University property.
   j. The inappropriate use of cameras, imaging, and digital devices is prohibited including use of such devices in showers, restrooms, or other areas where privacy is expected by participants.

11. Obtain all media and liability releases as part of the program registration process. All data gathered shall be confidential, is subject to records retention guidelines, and shall not be disclosed, except as provided by law.

12. Assign a staff member who is at least 21 years of age to be accessible to participants. The staff member must reside in the housing unit, if applicable. Additional Authorized Adults will be assigned to ensure one-on-one contact with minors does not occur and that appropriate levels of supervision are implemented. See also item 15 below.

When there are High School students, including prospective athletes, participating in pre-enrollment visitation, the hosting Penn State University student(s) will not be required to be at least 21 years of age and the requirement for two Authorized Adults will also be waived.

13. All Authorized Adults who have direct contact with minors are required to have a current background check on record with the University at the time of hire and/or beginning work with minors. This background check must be reviewed and approved by the applicable Human Resources department prior to being hired and/or working with minors.

When there are High School students, including prospective athletes, participating in pre-enrollment visitation, the hosting Penn State University student(s) will not be required to undergo a background check.

- New hires will be required to complete the University background check process at the time of hire.
- All other individuals must complete the University background check process **or** provide evidence of completion of PA State Criminal History Record, PA Department of Public Welfare Child Abuse Report and FBI criminal history report clearance dated within 6 months of the initial date of assignment. This includes current employees who have not previously had a background check completed, as well as all other individuals, paid or unpaid.
- If PA State Criminal History Record, PA Department of Public Welfare Child Abuse Report, and FBI criminal history report clearances are to be considered as a replacement for a University background check, verifications must be reviewed and approved by the applicable Human Resources department prior to being hired and/or interacting with minors.
- All Authorized Adults must also complete a self-disclosure form confirming that they have disclosed any arrests and/or convictions that have occurred since the date of a background check and/or clearance and will disclose any arrest and/or convictions within 72 hours of their occurrence. The cost for completion of PA State Criminal History Record, PA Department of Public Welfare Child Abuse Report, and FBI criminal history report clearances for non-employees will be the responsibility of the individual unless specifically authorized for processing and/or payment by the hiring unit.
- Overall guidance for background checks is provided in University Human Resources policy(ies).

14. If applicable, require the program to adopt and implement rules and regulations for proper supervision of minors in University housing. The following must be included:

   a. Written permission signed by the parent/guardian for the minor to reside in University housing.
   b. A curfew time which is age-appropriate for the participants, but in no case shall it be later than midnight.

c. In-room visitation to be restricted to participants of the same gender.
   d. Guests of participants (other than a parent/legal guardian and other program participants) are restricted to visitation in the building lobby and/or floor lounges, and only during approved hours specified by the program.
   e. The program must comply with all security measures and procedures specified by University Housing Services and Police Services.
   f. Pre-enrollment visit programs for high school students housed overnight in residence halls must be registered with the Office of Residence Life.

15. Require the program to provide and supervise trained counselors (also considered to be Authorized Adults) who must be at least 18 years of age, in accordance with the following:

   a. The ratio of counselors to program participants must reflect the gender distribution of the participants, and should meet the following:

      **Standards for resident camps are:**

      - One staff member for every five campers ages 4 and 5
      - One staff member for every six campers ages 6 to 8
      - One staff member for every eight campers ages 9 to 14
      - One staff member for every 10 campers ages 15 to 17

      **Standards for day camps are:**

      - One staff member for every six campers ages 4 and 5
      - One staff member for every eight campers ages 6 to 8
      - One staff member for every ten campers ages 9 to 14
      - One staff member for every twelve campers ages 15 to 17

   b. Training for the counselors must include, at a minimum, information about responsibilities and expectations; policies, procedures, and enforcement; appropriate crisis/emergency responses; safety and security precautions; confidentiality issues involving minors; and University responsibility/liability. Counselors must know how to request local emergency services and how to report suspected child abuse (counselors are considered to be mandatory reporters as defined by Pennsylvania law).
   c. Responsibilities of the counselors must include, at a minimum, informing program participants about safety and security procedures, University rules, rules established by the program, and behavioral expectations. Counselors are responsible for following and enforcing all rules and must be able to provide information included herein to program participants and be able to respond to emergency(ies).

16. Each Authorized Adult, who will be participating in a program covered by this Policy shall attend annual mandatory training on the conduct requirements of this Policy, on protecting participants from abusive emotional and physical treatment, and on appropriate or required reporting of incidents of improper conduct to the proper authorities including, but not limited to, appropriate law enforcement authorities. If a program participant discloses any type of assault or abuse (at any time previously or during the program), or an Authorized Adult has reason to

suspect that the participant has been subject to such assault or abuse, the Authorized Adult, as a mandatory reporter should inform the Program Director (Department Manager/Director for non-camp activities) immediately, unless the Authorized Adult believes that the Program Director (Department Manager/Director for non-camp activities) may be involved in the allegations of assault or abuse. The Program Director (Department Manager/Director for non-camp activities) and the Authorized Adult will then call the Commonwealth of Pennsylvania's reporting ChildLine (800-932-0313) together and provide written notification to the Department of Public Welfare within 48 hours of filing the oral report (utilizing form CY 47 available from the County Children and Youth agencies). In addition, the Program Director (Department Manager/Director for non-camp activities) will immediately notify University Police Services, Penn State's Office of General Counsel and Penn State's Risk Management Department. If the Program Director (Department Manager/Director for non-camp activities) is unavailable, or if the Program Director or his/her designee does not call Childline, the Authorized Adult should immediately call the Commonwealth of Pennsylvania's reporting ChildLine (800-932-0313). Authorized Adults must make all reasonable efforts to ensure the safety of minors participating in programs and activities covered by this Policy, including removal of minors from dangerous or potentially dangerous situations, irrespective of any other limitation or requirement. If a situation is felt to present imminent danger to a minor, University Police Services should be called immediately.

17. Authorized Adults participating in programs and activities covered by this Policy shall not:

   a. Have one-on-one contact with minors: there must be two or more Authorized Adults present during activities where minors are present. Authorized Adults also shall not have any direct electronic contact with minors without another Authorized Adult being included in the communication.
   b. In the case of adults supervising minors overnight, Authorized Adult should not enter a minor's room, bathroom facility, or similar area without another Authorized Adult in attendance, consistent with the policy of not having one-on-one contact with minors.
   c. Separate accommodations for adults and minors are required other than the minors' parents or guardians.
   d. Engage in abusive conduct of any kind toward, or in the presence of, a minor.
   e. Strike, hit, administer corporal punishment to, or touch in an inappropriate or illegal manner any minor.
   f. Pick up minors from or drop off minors at their homes, other than the driver's child(ren), except as specifically authorized in writing by the minor's parent or legal guardian.
   g. Authorized Adults shall not provide alcohol or illegal drugs to any minor. Authorized Adults shall not provide prescription drugs or any medication to any minor unless specifically authorized in writing by the parent or legal guardian as being required for the minor's care or the minor's emergency treatment. Participants' medicines may be distributed by program staff, following the conditions outlined in Policy IV. 5 in this document.
   h. Make sexual materials in any form available to minors participating in programs or activities covered by this Policy or assist them in any way in gaining access to such materials.

Items 17a, 17b, and 17c, do not apply when there are High School students, including prospective athletes, participating in pre-enrollment visitation, hosted by Penn State University student(s).

Item 17a does not apply to licensed psychologists providing psychological and counseling services to minors.

18. If an allegation of inappropriate conduct has been made against an Authorized Adult participating in a program, s/he shall discontinue any further participation in programs and activities covered by this Policy until such allegation has been satisfactorily resolved.

Authorized personnel/signatories for non-University groups using University facilities must provide to the sponsoring unit satisfactory evidence of compliance with all of the requirements of this Policy at least thirty (30) days prior to the scheduled use of University facilities, as well as sign an approved agreement for use of University facilities, if applicable.

19. Any exceptions to the application of the policy must be approved by the Office of Human Resources Recruitment and Compensation Division.

## CROSS REFERENCES:

Other Policies in this Manual should also be referenced, especially the following:

AD02 - Non-University Groups Using University Facilities,

AD03 - Conducting Educational Programs Using the Name of The University,

AD26 - Sales of Food and Beverages at University Locations,

AD27 - Commercial Sales Activities at University Locations,

AD34 - University Recycling Program,

AD42 - Statement on Nondiscrimination and Harassment,

AD72 - Reporting Suspected Child Abuse,

ADG04 - Providing Emergency Medical Services at University Events at University Park,

HR02 - Employment of Minors,

SY01 - Environmental Health and Safety Policy,

SY05 - Persons, Other Than Students or Employees, Who are Injured or Become Ill on University Property,

SY21 - First Aid Kits,

SY28 - Emergency Evacuations and Fire Drills - Residence Halls, and

RA14 - The Use of Human Participants in Research

Effective Date: June 7, 2012
Date Approved: May 14, 2012
Date Published: June 7, 2012

**Most Recent Changes:**

- June 7, 2012 - Additional clarifications, including update of requirements for high school students visiting on pre-enrollment visits with Penn State students, clarification of reporting process and exclusion of client representation clinics in Dickinson School of Law from policy.

**Revision History (and effective dates):**

- April 11, 2012 - Major revisions, reflecting improvements to the process. Revisions include clarifications about procedure, training, clearances, responsibilities and reporting of incidents for individuals who supervising minors that are participating in programs and activities covered by this policy.
- April 28, 2010 - Multiple changes, clarifying policy details pertinent to the administration of youth programs involving minors housed in University facilities.
- June 15, 2006 - Revision History added.
- June 1, 1998 - Added reference to Administrative Guideline ADG04, EMT Services.
- August 28, 1995 - Major Revisions.
- October 20, 1992 - New Policy.

**PENN STATE - ADMINISTRATIVE**

# Policy AD67 DISCLOSURE OF WRONGFUL CONDUCT AND PROTECTION FROM RETALIATION

## Contents:

- Purpose
- Policy
- Definitions
- Reporting Wrongful Conduct
- Investigating Allegations of Wrongful Conduct
- Protection From Retaliation
- Disciplinary Sanctions
- Cross References

## PURPOSE:

The University is committed to maintaining the highest standards of ethics and conduct, consistent with applicable legal requirements and University policies. Through the establishment of this policy, the University wishes to encourage and protect from **Retaliation** those who desire to report potential violations of these standards.

## POLICY:

It is the policy of the University to encourage and enable any member of the University faculty, staff, or student body to make **Good Faith Report**s of suspected **Wrongful Conduct**, and to protect such individuals from **Retaliation** for making such reports to the University or an **Appropriate Authority,** participating in any investigation, hearing, or inquiry by the University or an **Appropriate Authority** or participating in a court proceeding relating to an allegation of suspected **Wrongful Conduct** at the University.

## DEFINITIONS:

For purposes of this policy, the following definitions shall apply:

> **"Good Faith Report"** means any report, communication or other disclosure about actual or suspected **Wrongful Conduct** engaged in by a member of the University faculty, staff, or student body, which is made with a good faith reason to believe that **Wrongful Conduct** has occurred.

"**Wrongful Conduct**" includes a violation of University policy (including guidelines and codes of ethics or conduct which are available on GURU, or as hot links through a policy contained within GURU); a violation of a federal, state, and/or local law, rule, regulation, or ordinance; and the substantive use of University tangible and intangible assets, equipment, supplies and services for personal gain or for another purpose not authorized by the University.

"**Appropriate Authority**" means a federal, state or local government body, agency, or organization having jurisdiction over criminal law enforcement, regulatory violations, professional conduct or ethics, or waste; or a member, officer, agent, representative or supervisory employee of the body, agency or organization.

"**Retaliation**" means any adverse action taken by a member of the University faculty, staff, or student body against any individual on the basis of a **Good Faith Report** made by such individual, or on the basis of such individual's participation in an investigation, hearing, or inquiry by the University or an **Appropriate Authority,** or participation in a court proceeding relating to suspected **Wrongful Conduct** at the University. **Retaliation** shall include, but not be limited to, harassment, discrimination, threats of physical harm, job termination, punitive work schedule or research assignments, decrease in pay or responsibilities, or negative impact on academic progress.

## REPORTING WRONGFUL CONDUCT:

Any individual having reason to believe that a member of the University faculty, staff, or student body has engaged in **Wrongful Conduct** can report such suspected **Wrongful Conduct** to the designated contacts below. A report should include a description of the facts, avoid speculation and predetermined conclusions, and be based on a good faith reason to believe that suspected **Wrongful Conduct** has occurred.

An individual desiring to submit a **Good Faith Report** should contact the appropriate person as identified under the applicable University policy. Some key contacts are referenced on the University Ethics website. Members of the University community may also report suspected **Wrongful Conduct** on an anonymous, confidential basis through the University's Ethics and Compliance Hotline at 1-800-560-1637.

## INVESTIGATING ALLEGATIONS OF WRONGFUL CONDUCT:

Upon receiving a **Good Faith Report** of suspected **Wrongful Conduct**, the University will investigate and resolve the matter. The University may notify the individual suspected of **Wrongful Conduct** and may interview members of the faculty, staff and student body to gather all information necessary to resolve the matter. The University will make every reasonable effort to conduct all investigations in the most confidential manner possible.

## PROTECTION FROM RETALIATION:

No individual who makes or advises the University that he or she intends to make a **Good Faith Report** of suspected **Wrongful Conduct** to the University or an **Appropriate Authority,** participates in an investigation, hearing, or inquiry by the University or an **Appropriate Authority** or participates in a court proceeding involving suspected **Wrongful Conduct** at the University shall be subject to **Retaliation** from any member of the University faculty, staff, or student body. Any individual who believes that he or she may have been subject to prohibited **Retaliation** should notify one of the key contacts identified in the link above. Upon receiving a report of Retaliation, the University will investigate and resolve the matter. Protection from **Retaliation** for persons reporting under this policy is also provided by Pennsylvania's Whistleblower Law, 43 P.S. Section 1421 et seq.

## DISCIPLINARY SANCTIONS:

No member of the University faculty, staff, or student body may retaliate against any individual for making a **Good Faith Report** of suspected **Wrongful Conduct** to the University or an **Appropriate Authority**, for participating in an investigation, hearing, or inquiry by the University or an **Appropriate Authority** or for participating in a court proceeding involving suspected **Wrongful Conduct** at the University. Any member of the University who retaliates against any individual in violation of this policy will be subject to disciplinary sanctions, which may range from a disciplinary warning to termination or expulsion from the University.

In addition, any member of the University faculty, staff, or student body who knowingly, or with reckless disregard for the truth, provides false information in a report of **Wrongful Conduct**, or in a report of **Retaliation**, will be subject to disciplinary sanctions ranging from a disciplinary warning to termination or expulsion from the University. Allegations of suspected **Wrongful Conduct** or Retaliation that are not substantiated but are made in good faith are excused from disciplinary action.

## CROSS REFERENCES:

AD12 - Sexual Assault, Relationship and Domestic Violence, and Stalking

AD41 - Sexual Harassment

AD42 - Statement on Nondiscrimination and Harassment

FN19 - Policy for Handling and Distributing Confidential Internal Audit Reports and Other Documents

HR01 - Fair Employment Practices

HR11 - Affirmative Action in Employment at The Pennsylvania State University

HR76 - Faculty Rights and Responsibilities

HR79 - Staff Grievance Procedure

RA10 - Handling Inquiries / Investigations into Questions of Ethics in Research and in Other Scholarly Activities

---

Effective Date: June 22, 2010
Date Approved: June 14, 2010
Date Published: June 22, 2010

**Revision History (and effective dates):**

- June 22, 2010 - New Policy.

[top of this policy](#)    [GURU policy menu](#)    [GURU policy search](#)
[GURU home](#)    [GURU Tech Support](#)    [Penn State website](#)

**PENN STATE - ADMINISTRATIVE**

# Policy AD72 - REPORTING SUSPECTED CHILD ABUSE

## Contents:

- Purpose
- Definitions
- Policy
- Cross References

## PURPOSE:

To provide guidance to University employees, regarding mandated reporting requirements, per the University and the Pennsylvania Child Protective Services Law.

## DEFINITIONS:

**Child abuse** - is defined in Pennsylvania as a child under 18 years of age who has experienced:

- **Serious Physical Injury:** must cause the child severe pain or it must significantly impair functioning, either temporarily or permanently.
- **Serious Mental Injury:** a condition diagnosed by a physician or licensed psychologist that renders the child chronically and severely anxious, agitated, depressed, socially withdrawn, psychotic, or in reasonable fear that his/her safety is threatened, or seriously interferes with the child's ability to accomplish age-appropriate developmental and social tasks.
- **Sexual Abuse or Exploitation:** the use or coercion of any child to engage in any sexually explicit conduct, or any simulation of any sexually explicit conduct for the purpose of producing any visual depiction, or the rape, sexual assault, involuntary deviate sexual intercourse, aggravated indecent assault, molestation, incest, indecent exposure, prostitution, sexual abuse, or sexual exploitation of children.
- **Serious Physical Neglect:** any condition that arises from prolonged or repeated lack of supervision or the failure to provide essentials of life, including adequate medical care, which endangers a child's life or development or impairs the child's functioning.
- **Imminent Risk:** any act, or failure to act, that creates an imminent risk of serious physical injury or sexual abuse and exploitation of a child. (23 Pa.C.S. 6303)

## POLICY:

Pennsylvania law requires certain individuals to report child abuse, whenever they have reasonable suspicion of child abuse. However, ANY person may report abuse if they have reasonable suspicion that a child has been abused.

Pennsylvania law requires the following individuals to make a report about the suspected child abuse:

- A person who, in the course of employment comes into contact with children, and the person has reasonable cause to suspect that a child is a victim of child abuse.
- Specifically named professionals include, but are NOT limited to: any licensed physician, osteopath, medical examiner, coroner, funeral director, dentist, optometrist, chiropractor, podiatrist, intern, registered nurse, licensed practical nurse, hospital personnel engaged in the admission, examination, care or treatment of persons, Christian Science practitioner, member of the clergy, school administrator, school teacher, school nurse, social services worker, day-care center worker or any other child-care or foster-care worker, mental health professional, peace officer or law enforcement official. Two exceptions are made in the law for reporting requirement which involve confidential communications to a member of the clergy, and for confidential communications made to an attorney (23 Pa.C.S. § 6311).

Penn State University requires all University employees who have reasonable suspicion of abuse to make a report, with an exception to any confidential communications made to a University-employed attorney, or confidential communication made to University-employed member of the clergy.

As Penn State University is committed to research, Penn State policy (RA14) provides for ethical treatment and protection of human research participants. All human subjects research is safeguarded by the Institutional Review Board. The research environment presents unique circumstances related to reporting of child abuse, and reporting procedures must be reviewed, approved, and monitored by the IRB. The Principal Investigator is responsible for all aspects of the research, including reporting any child abuse identified through the research.

<u>How to make a report of suspected child abuse:</u>

1. If you suspect child abuse, immediately contact ChildLine, which is operated by the Pennsylvania Department of Public Welfare at 1-800-932-0313. This hotline is staffed at all times of day and night. If the call is not answered, then immediately contact the county child welfare agency in the county in which the incident occurred. If you do not reach an individual either through ChildLine or through the local county child welfare office, the reporter must continue calling until they reach an individual to complete the reporting process.
2. If a child is in imminent danger, the employee should contact police at 911 to obtain immediate protection for the child.
3. Finally, if you are considered to be an Authorized Adult as defined in policy AD39, follow the reporting procedure as described in AD39.

<u>Liability</u>

As per Pennsylvania law, any person or institution participating in good faith in the making of a report or testifying in any proceeding arising out of an instance of suspected child abuse shall have immunity from any liability, civil or criminal, that might otherwise result by reason of such actions.

Any person or official required by law to report a case of suspected child abuse who willfully fails to do so shall be guilty of a misdemeanor of the third degree for the first violation and a misdemeanor of the second degree for subsequent violations. Most importantly, without making a report, a child may continue to be at risk. *23 Pa.C.S. §6318 and §6319.*

Compliance

All University employees will be required to complete mandated reporter training annually through the Office of Human Resources, Center for Workplace Learning and Performance.

If any University employee willfully fails to report a case of suspected child abuse, it will result in disciplinary action, up to and including, dismissal.

## CROSS REFERENCES:

Other Policies in this Manual should also be referenced, especially the following:

AD39 - Minors Involved in University-Sponsored Programs or Programs Held at the University,

HR05 - "Regular" and "NonRegular" University Employees,

HR70 - Dismissal of Tenured or Tenured-eligible Faculty Members,

HR78 - Staff Employee Failure to Meet Acceptable Standards of Performance, and

RA14 - The Use of Human Participants in Research

Effective Date: June 7, 2012
Date Approved: May 14, 2012
Date Published: June 7, 2012

**Revision History (and effective dates):**

- May 14, 2012- New Policy.

top of this policy    GURU policy menu    GURU policy search
GURU home           GURU Tech Support   Penn State website

**PENN STATE - HUMAN RESOURCES**

# Policy HR99 Background Check Process

POLICY'S INITIAL DATE: July 5, 2012
THIS VERSION Effective: July 5, 2012

## Contents:

- Purpose
- Overview
- Individuals Covered by This Policy
- Definitions
- Background Check Inquiries
- Background Check Process
- Periodic Updates or Additional Background Checks
- Recruitment Notices
- Roles and Responsibilities
- Evaluation of Resulting Report
- Confidentiality
- Related Documents
- Cross-references

## PURPOSE:

This policy establishes a process for ensuring background checks are completed for any individuals, age 18 and over, (paid or unpaid) who are engaged by Penn State in any work capacity effective on or after the date of this policy. This includes employees; volunteers, working with minors; adjunct faculty; consultants; contractors; or other similar positions. In addition, it establishes a process requiring all individuals engaged by the University, including those engaged prior to, as of, or after, the effective date of this policy, to self-disclose criminal arrests and/or convictions as outlined in the Penn State Arrest and Conviction self-disclosure form within a 72-hour period of their occurrence.

Background checks will be used solely to evaluate candidates' eligibility to be engaged in any work capacity by the University, and will not be used to discriminate on the basis of race, color, national origin, ancestry, religious creed, gender, disability or handicap, age, veteran's status, gender identity or sexual orientation.

Criminal convictions will be reviewed with respect to the nature and gravity of the offense(s); time since conviction; completion of sentence or any other remediation; relevance to the position for which the candidate is being considered/employee is performing; and discrepancies between the background check and what the candidate/employee self-reported. When a finding adversely impacts eligibility to be engaged by the University in a specific position, the candidate will be notified of the decision and given associated information required by law.

(Note: Nothing herein is intended to contradict or lessen application of applicable federal or state laws or regulations.)

## OVERVIEW:

Penn State strives to provide the safest possible environment for its students, faculty, staff and visitors; to preserve University resources; and to uphold the reputation and integrity of the University. This policy supports the University's efforts to minimize institutional risk, provide a safe environment, and assist hiring authorities in making sound hiring decisions.

## INDIVIDUALS COVERED BY THIS POLICY:

Any individual engaged by Penn State in any work capacity beginning on or after the date of this policy including, but not limited to, the following positions:

- Staff
- Faculty (including Adjunct Faculty)
- Technical Service
- Temporary Employees not sponsored by a staffing agency (wage payroll)
- Administrators and Academic Administrators
- Executives
- Volunteers (if working with minors)
- Graduate Assistants
- Graduate and undergraduate student employees
- Work study students
- Interns (paid or unpaid)
- Third-party employees such as consultants, contractors and temporary staffing agency employees
- Any individual not previously described who is either paid directly by the University or who is working in a sensitive/critical position (defined below)

## DEFINITIONS:

### Consumer Report

Defined by the Fair Credit Reporting Act as: "Any communication of information by a Consumer Reporting Agency bearing on a consumer's credit worthiness, credit standing, credit capacity, character, general reputation, or personal characteristics." This includes background check information such as criminal history, child abuse checks, motor vehicle record checks, educational checks, etc. if provided by a Consumer Reporting Agency. Penn State's use of credit history checks will be limited to circumstances described below in "credit history check" definition.

### Consumer Reporting Agency

Defined by the Fair Credit Reporting Act as: "Any person or entity which, for a fee, dues or on a cooperative nonprofit basis, regularly engages in the practice of assembling or evaluating consumer credit information, or other information, on consumers for the purpose of furnishing Consumer Reports to third parties." For the purposes of this policy, a Consumer Reporting Agency refers to the vendor used by Penn State to conduct Background Checks.

## Credit History Check

Review of the individual's detailed credit history, as contained in a Consumer Report in accordance with the Fair Credit Reporting Act. Penn State's use of credit history checks will be consistent with Pennsylvania law that states "it shall be an unlawful discriminatory practice for any employer or any employer's agent, representative or designee to require an employee or prospective employee to consent to the creation of a credit report that contains information about the employee's or prospective employee's credit score, credit account balances, payment history, savings or checking account balances or savings or checking account numbers as a condition of employment unless one of the following applies: (1) Such report is substantially related to the employee's current or potential job. (2) Such report is required by law. (3) The employer reasonably believes that the employee has engaged in a specific activity that constitutes a violation of the law." Federal laws prohibit discrimination against an applicant or employee as a result of bankruptcy.

## Criminal Conviction

Being found guilty, entering a guilty plea or pleading no contest to a felony and/or misdemeanor as outlined in the Penn State Arrest and Conviction self-disclosure form. Convictions for which the individual's record has been expunged may not be considered.

## Criminal History Check

Verification that the individual does not have any undisclosed criminal convictions in any jurisdiction where he or she has resided or where he or she currently resides.

## Educational Verification

Confirmation of the individual's educational credentials listed on the application, resume or cover letter, or otherwise cited by the individual.

## Fair Credit Reporting Act (FCRA)

A Federal law designed to promote the accuracy, fairness and privacy of information in the files of Consumer Reporting Agencies, codified at 15 U.S.C. §1681 et seq.

## License Verification

Confirmation that the selected candidate or employee possesses all licenses listed on the application, resume or cover letter, or otherwise cited by the candidate or employee, including verification of the disposition of such licenses. This includes any motor vehicle driver's licenses required for a position.

## Minor

A person under the age of eighteen (18) who is not enrolled or accepted for enrollment at the University. Students who are "dually enrolled" in University programs while also enrolled in elementary, middle and/or high school are not included in this policy unless such enrollment includes overnight housing in University facilities.

**Penn State University**

Any campus, unit, program, association or entity of Penn State with the exception of the Penn State Hershey Medical Center campus (including the College of Medicine) which will follow a separate policy that reflects the unique activities that occur on that campus.

**Senior Leader**

For the purposes of this policy, the Senior Leader will be considered as one or more of the following:

- President
- Provost
- Vice Presidents
- Chancellors
- Assistant or Associate Vice Presidents
- Vice Chancellors
- Vice Provosts
- Deans
- Department Heads and Chairs

**Sensitive/Critical Positions**

Positions whose responsibilities may include the following:

- Master key access to all, or the majority of all, offices/facilities within buildings (including residences or other on-site or off-site facilities)
- Direct responsibility for the care, safety and security of people, or the safety and security of personal and University property (includes child care workers, physicians, student affairs officers, residence hall supervisors, coaches, transit drivers, etc.)
- Direct responsibility for the care, safety and security of animals
- Direct responsibility for providing legal counsel to the University and/or outside parties
- Direct access to or responsibility for cash, cash equivalents, checks, credit card account information, or University property disbursements or receipts
- Extensive authority for committing the financial resources of the University
- Direct access to or responsibility for controlled substances or hazardous materials
- Direct access to or responsibility for protected, personal or other sensitive data (includes auditors, information systems personnel, human resources and payroll staff, registrars, etc.)
- Administrator, Academic Administrator and Executive positions, if background check is not completed by executive search firm or other similar agency
- Other positions as defined by units that have a job-related need for additional background checks

**Sex and Violent Offender Registry Check**

Verification that the selected individual does not have undisclosed convictions of certain sex and violent crimes in every jurisdiction where he or she has resided or currently resides.

**Volunteers (working with minors)**

Unpaid individuals working with minors as defined and covered by Policy AD39 - Minors involved in University-sponsored Programs or Programs held at the University and/or Housed in University Facilities.

## BACKGROUND CHECK INQUIRIES:

Verification of credentials and other information about an employee or other individual (paid or unpaid) may include any or all of the following:

**Standard Background Check:**

- Criminal History Check
- Sex and Violent Offender Registry Check

**Additional Background Check items as required for specific positions based on job-related need:**

- Education Verification (required for all academic positions)
- Motor Vehicle Record (required for positions where it can be regularly anticipated that a responsibility of the position will be to drive a University-owned vehicle)
- Credit History Check (conducted only for sensitive/critical positions with extensive authority to commit financial resources of the University including Administrator and Executive positions; or as required by law; or due to a reasonable belief that an employee has engaged in a specific activity that constitutes a violation of the law)
- Employment Verifications
- License Verification
- Other verifications, as needed, based on job requirements

## BACKGROUND CHECK PROCESS:

A successful background check must be completed prior to the first day of work/engagement with the University in the position identified. Any exceptions will need to be approved by the Office of Human Resources' Recruitment and Compensation Division.

**Employees:**

Employees are considered to be any person whose wages are paid directly by Penn State, whether full-or part-time and regardless of whether the position is benefits-eligible. Candidates will be informed that the offer is contingent on a satisfactory background check that will be conducted by a consumer reporting agency for review by the University. The candidate will be required to complete self-disclosure and consent forms authorizing Penn State to complete the background check process.

Candidates for employment who fail to participate fully or who provide inaccurate information in a background check will be eliminated from consideration for the position. Candidates may decline to authorize a background check; in such cases, no background check will be performed, but the candidate will not be considered further.

The existence of a criminal conviction will not automatically disqualify an individual from employment or employment consideration. The University will consider the nature and gravity of the offense(s); time since conviction; completion of sentence or any other remediation; relevance to the position for which the candidate is being considered/employee is performing; and discrepancies between the background check and what the candidate/employee self-reported. When a finding adversely impacts employment eligibility, the candidate will be notified and may be withdrawn from employment consideration after Human Resources consults with the Senior Leader on the matter.

The University will provide candidates access to a copy of their background check reports upon request, regardless of outcome and without charge to the candidate. In cases where information in the background check report will result in an adverse hiring decision, the University will provide a copy of the report to the candidate without his or her request. In cases in which information in a Consumer Report, such as a background check showing criminal convictions affecting the candidate's ability to perform the specific job in question, will result in an adverse employment decision, the University will provide the candidate with all required notifications pursuant to the Fair Credit Reporting Act and applicable law(s).

Executives, Administrators, and Academic Administrators hired through an executive staffing agency or similar staffing company must complete either a Penn State background check consistent with position requirements or have confirmation of a background check of the required criteria having been completed by the staffing agency.

For employees, a break in service of six months or less does not require a new background check unless the individual returns to an assignment requiring a check(s) which was not previously performed. Individuals with a break in service of six months or less should be reminded that the self-disclosure requirement to report arrests and/or convictions within 72 hours of their occurrence is still in force. Approved employee leaves such as sabbatical leave, maternity leave, or other types of approved leaves of six months or longer will require the employee to complete a Penn State Arrest and Conviction self-disclosure form before returning to work. Other breaks in service for employees of greater than six months require a new background check to be completed.

**Unpaid Individuals:**

This includes interns, adjunct faculty or other individuals working for or engaged by the University. Depending upon the responsibilities of the position, the individual must either:

1. Follow the instructions for completion of background checks described in Penn State Information for Completing PA Publicly Available Background Checks. Complete Pennsylvania criminal history check via the Pennsylvania State Police website, Pennsylvania child abuse clearance via the Pennsylvania Department of Public Welfare website and an FBI criminal history report clearance via the Cogent Applicant Fingerprint Registration System website. All clearances must be dated within two years prior to the date of the assignment. The cost for these clearances will be the responsibility of the individual unless specifically authorized for reimbursement processing by the sponsoring organization. In addition, the individual must self-disclose any arrests or convictions as outlined in the Penn State Arrest and Conviction self-disclosure form that occur between the time of clearance and the date work begins.
2. Be sponsored by the engaging unit to have a background check(s) completed by the University based on the job requirements of the position. The background check must be satisfactorily completed prior to beginning work.

Volunteers working with minors must follow the requirements of Policy AD39 which requires that successful background checks are dated within 6 months prior to the initial date of assignment.

Successful completion of Pennsylvania criminal history check, Pennsylvania Department of Public Welfare child abuse clearance and FBI criminal history report clearance may be substituted for the Penn State background check process for unpaid individuals unless additional background checks are outlined as being required for the position.

**Third-party Employees:**

This includes consultants, contractors and temporary staffing agency employees working for or engaged by the University. Depending upon the responsibilities of the position, the individual must either:

1. Follow the instructions for completion of background checks described in Penn State Information for Completing PA Publicly Available Background Checks. Complete Pennsylvania criminal history check via the Pennsylvania State Police website, Pennsylvania child abuse clearance via the Pennsylvania Department of Public Welfare website and an FBI criminal history report clearance via the Cogent Applicant Fingerprint Registration System website. All clearances must be dated within two years prior to the date of the assignment. The cost for these clearances will be the responsibility of the individual unless specifically authorized for reimbursement processing by the sponsoring organization. In addition, the individual must self-disclose any arrests or convictions as outlined in the Penn State Arrest and Conviction self-disclosure form that occur between the time of clearance and the date work begins.
2. Be covered by a signed contractor's/vendor's agreement that confirms its employees have had background checks that meet or exceed the University's standards for the type of work being performed.
3. Be sponsored by the engaging unit to have a background check(s) completed by the University based on the job requirements of the position. The background check must be satisfactorily completed prior to beginning work.

Successful completion of Pennsylvania criminal history check, Pennsylvania Department of Public Welfare child abuse clearance and FBI criminal history report clearance may be substituted for the Penn State background check process for third-party employees unless additional background checks are outlined and communicated to the candidate and/or employee as being required for the position.

## PERIODIC UPDATES OR ADDITIONAL BACKGROUND CHECKS:

Penn State retains the right to conduct relevant background checks of current employees when it has reasonable grounds to do so, e.g., no prior check was performed, a workplace incident has occurred, upon self-disclosure of criminal activity, update of information due to designation as sensitive/critical position, or upon a change of assignment.

Further, all individuals engaged by the University (whether paid or unpaid) are required to notify the appropriate Human Resources representative of any criminal activities with which they are charged, as well as, upon final conviction of a felony or a misdemeanor within 72 hours of knowledge of the arrest or conviction. The Penn State Arrest and Conviction self-disclosure form provides the list of arrests and/or convictions that must be disclosed and this form must be used to provide the information in writing to the appropriate Human Resources representative for review. This includes any arrests or convictions that occur either between the date of disclosure for a University run background check and the date work begins, or the date of issuance of the Pennsylvania criminal history check via Pennsylvania State Police website, Pennsylvania child abuse clearance via the Pennsylvania Department of Public Welfare website and an FBI criminal history report clearance via the Cogent Applicant Fingerprint Registration System website and the date work begins. Failure to report such incidents may result in disciplinary action up to and including termination.

Information will be used only if job related and will not necessarily affect employment. Human Resources will notify the employee's department of an arrest or conviction only if it is determined that the arrest and/or conviction is pertinent to the employee's ability to carry out the duties or functions of his or her position. If reported to the employee's department, such arrests and/or convictions, depending on the facts and the employee's involvement in the events leading to arrest and/or conviction, may subject the employee to discipline, up to and including termination.

Positions where it can be regularly anticipated that a responsibility of the position will be to drive a University-owned vehicle or where an individual may be asked to transport minors, must pass a motor vehicle record check. Motor vehicle checks will be updated every three years for positions, as relevant, and it is the department's and supervisor's responsibility to initiate the process. Employees must comply with the self-disclosure requirement by notifying Human Resources of any arrests or convictions for driving while under the influence or the loss of the individual's driver's license due to traffic violations or other similar charges/convictions. This disclosure must be made within 72 hours of occurrence using the Penn State Arrest and Conviction self-disclosure form. Such convictions may subject the employee or individual to discipline, up to and including termination. Failure to report such incidents may result in disciplinary action up to and including termination.

State or federal law or regulations, professional associations, licensing entities or contracting partners may impose background screening check requirements upon certain individuals. In these cases, the affected individual and department should coordinate the need for such a check with the Office of Human Resources' Recruitment and Compensation Division. Under no circumstances should employees conduct, or seek to conduct, a background check, without first consulting with and receiving approval from Recruitment and Compensation.

## RECRUITMENT NOTICES:

All job postings (paid or unpaid) that require more verifications than the standard background check will include language identifying the need for all individuals (including current University employees) to undergo a background check appropriate to the position's responsibilities. All offers of employment to new hires of the University will be made contingent upon the results of the background check. If a current employee applies for a position that requires a non-standard background check, the offer for the new position will be contingent upon the results of the background check. All unpaid positions will be contingent upon the results of the background check or verified successful results from Pennsylvania criminal history check via Pennsylvania State Police website, Pennsylvania Department of Public Welfare child abuse clearance via the Pennsylvania Department of Public Welfare website and an FBI criminal history report clearance via the Cogent Applicant Fingerprint Registration System website. Individuals should review the information concerning completion of background checks described in Penn State Information for Completing PA Publicly Available Background Checks.

## ROLES AND RESPONSIBILITIES:

College/Campus/Unit Human Resources Responsibilities:

1. Issue all offer letters as "contingent upon successful background check".
2. Initiate the background check process via methodology proscribed by Recruitment and Compensation; communicate procedures to candidates.
3. Ensure that all individuals engaged by the University (paid or unpaid) have successfully completed a background check or provided evidence of completion of acceptable background checks (Pennsylvania criminal history check; Pennsylvania Department of Public Welfare child abuse clearance and FBI criminal history report clearance; executive search firm background clearance; police officer background check) before beginning any assignments/work responsibilities.
4. Review information provided by Recruitment and Compensation that results from the third-party vendor's background check of an individual and determine whether the information may be relevant to the hiring/engaging decision.
5. Confirm any authorization for payment for background checks for non-employees.

Recruitment and Compensation Responsibilities:

1. Secure contracts with consumer reporting agency for consumer reports including background screening services.
2. Develop procedures for oversight of the background check policy and communicate methodology, forms, and/or computer access needs to college/campus/unit Human Resources departments.
3. Coordinate with the hiring/engaging Human Resources department and the consumer reporting agency throughout the background check process.
4. Review all information resulting from the consumer reporting agency's background check of an individual and determine whether the information may be relevant to the hiring/engaging unit's decision. Forward information along with recommended guidance to the hiring/engaging unit for further review and decision.
5. If a candidate may no longer be considered for a position based on the background check results, provide written notice to the candidate including a copy of the background check report. The written notification will include a specified period of time in which the candidate may respond, which will be no less than five calendar days.
    a. If the candidate fails to respond within the specified time period, issue a second letter informing the candidate that he/she is no longer being considered for the position.
    b. If the candidate responds within the specified time period, review any appeal submitted by the candidate challenging the accuracy of information contained in the report.
6. Implement and interpret this policy and provide guidance to hiring/engaging units.

## EVALUATION OF RESULTING REPORT:

The following are among the factors that Human Resources will consider when evaluating the results of the background screening check:

- Nature and gravity of the offense(s),
- Time since conviction, completion of sentence or any other remediation,
- Relevancy to the position for which the candidate is being considered/employee is performing; and

- Discrepancies between the background check and what the candidate/employee self-reported.

The background screening check of a candidate who also is a current employee, may impact the current employee's employment, particularly absent full self-disclosure.

## CONFIDENTIALITY:

Records gathered as a result of a background screening check are part of an employee's personnel file. However, Human Resources will keep such records in files separately from the individual's general personnel file.

Records gathered as a result of a background screening check for non-employees will be maintained by the appropriate college/campus/unit Human Resources department.

The records related to the background screening check will include:

- Authorization, Consent and Release forms;
- Information collected from the check;
- Analysis and decision if criminal activity substantially relates to the position; and,
- Correspondence related to criminal background screening check

Alternatively, these records may be maintained in a secure database. Any records related to a candidate or an employee must be returned to Human Resources and will be maintained in accordance with the Penn State records retention schedule.

## RELATED DOCUMENTS:

Summary of rights under the Fair Credit Reporting Act:

www.ftc.gov/bcp/edu/pubs/consumer/credit/cre35.pdf

Penn State Arrest and Conviction self-disclosure form

Penn State Information for Completing PA Publicly Available Background Checks

## CROSS REFERENCES:

Other Policies in this Manual should also be referenced, especially the following:

AD12 - Sexual Assault, Relationship and Domestic Violence, and Stalking

AD29 - Statement on Intolerance

AD33 - A Drug-Free Workplace

AD39 - Minors involved in University-sponsored Programs or Programs held at the University and/or Housed in University Facilities

AD41 - Sexual Harassment

AD42 - Statement on Nondiscrimination

AD72 - Reporting Suspected Child Abuse

HR05 - "Regular" and "Nonregular" University Employees

HR06 - Types of Appointments

HR07 - University Appointments without Remuneration

HR08 - Establishment of a Staff or a Technical Service Position

HR11 - Affirmative Action in Employment at The Pennsylvania State University

HR13 - Recommended Procedure for Hiring New Faculty

HR14 - Forms to be Filled Out by and for Each New Regular Employee

HR34 - Employment Conditions for Staff Employees

| top of this policy | GURU policy menu | GURU policy search |
| --- | --- | --- |
| GURU home | GURU Tech Support | Penn State website |

Manufactured by Amazon.ca
Bolton, ON